CONCEPTS OF FEDERALISM

William H. Stewart

UNIVERSITY
PRESS OF
AMERICA

LANHAM • NEW YORK • LONDON

This book is a product of the Terminology of
Federalism project of the Association of Centers
for Federal Studies.

Co-published by arrangement with the Center for the
Study of Federalism, Temple University.

All University Press of America books are produced on acid-free
paper which exceeds the minimum standards set by the National
Historical Publications and Records Commission.

TABLE OF CONTENTS

	Page
Introductory Essay	1
Classifications of Concepts	13
Dictionary of Concepts	27
Bibliography	179
Name Index	223
Geographical Index	237
List of Cases	241

ACKNOWLEDGMENTS

This book could not have been produced without the cooperation of many helpful people. I am particularly appreciative of those professional librarians throughout the country who have assisted me in acquiring the materials need to give this manuscript the comprehensiveness required if it is to be of significant value to its users. My colleagues in the Department of Political Science at the University of Alabama have been continual sources of encouragement and advice, particularly Professor James D. Thomas and Professor Walter H. Bennett. Professor Daniel J. Elazar has been my major source of counsel and advice during my work on this study. However, I take full responsibility for the concepts included herein and for the accuracy of the interpretations which have been made from the sources used.

My family has been generous in sparing me from some of the usual household chores during much of the time this study has been in progress. My wife, Connie, has been gracious in being willing to listen to more talk of federal theory than she probably cared to. My son, Trey, has literally cut his teeth on these pages and it is to him that they are lovingly dedicated.

W.H.S.

The following sources have been quoted in this study with the kind permission of their publishers and/or authors:

S. Rufus Davis, The Federal Principle: A Journey Through Time in Quest of a Meaning (Berkeley: University of California Press, 1978).

Sobei Mogi, The Problem of Federalism: A Study in the History of Political Theory (2 vols.; New York: Macmillan Co., 1931).

Ivo D. Duchacek, Comparative Federalism: The Territorial Dimension of Politics (New York: Holt, Rinehart & Winston, 1970).

Parris N. Glendening and Mavis Mann Reeves, Pragmatic Federalism: An Intergovernmental View of American Government (Box 744, Pacific Palisades, Calif. 90272: Palisades Publishers, 1977).

William G. Colman, Cities, Suburbs, and States: Governing and Financing Urban America (New York: The Free Press, a Division of Macmillan Publishing Co., Inc., Copyright c 1975).

R. L. Watts, New Federations: Experiments in the Commonwealth (Oxford: Clarendon Press, 1966).

Charles D. Tarlton, "Symmetry and Asymmetry as Elements of Federalism: A Theoretical Speculation," Journal of Politics, XXVII (November, 1965), 861-74.

Bodo Dennewitz, Der Foderalismus: Sein Wesen und Seine Geschichte (Hamburg: Drei Turme Verlag, 1947).

Robert B. Hawkins, Jr. (ed.), American Federalism: A New Partnership for the Republic (San Francisco: Institute for Contemporary Studies, c 1982).

Center for the Study of Federalism, Temple University, Philadelphia (all publications).

William Riker, Federalism: Origin, Operation, Significance
(Boston: Little, Brown and Co., 1964).

Thomas M. Franck (ed.), Why Federations Fail: An Inquiry into
the Requisites for Successful Federalism (New York: New York
University Press, copyright c by New York University, 1968).

Ernst Deuerlein, Foderalismus: Die historischen und philosophischen Grundlagen des foderativen Prinzips (Munich: Paul List
Verlag, 1972).

David B. Walker, Toward a Functioning Federalism (Cambridge,
Mass.: Winthrop Publishers, 1981).

Samuel I. Shuman (comp.), The Future of Federalism (Detroit:
Wayne State University Press, 1968).

INTRODUCTORY ESSAY

The use of figurative language has been practically universal in efforts to advance knowledge of political phenomena. Although, in most research today, the emphasis is on highly abstracted and sophisticated models, metaphor continues to be, as Robert Nisbet has noted, an important "way of knowing--one of the oldest, most deeply embedded, even indispensable ways known in the history of human consciousness." (Nisbet 1976:33) Among groups of scholars, federal theorists, perhaps because of weaknesses in the empirical bases of their research, have been particularly prone to use ostensibly crude, nonmathematical, frequently metaphorical conceptualizations.

The purpose of this volume of Concepts of Federalism is to offer a convenient and reasonably comprehensive source of federalism descriptors. The principal sources relied upon fall into two general categories. Initially examined is the substantial corpus of scholarly and popular federal writings, including books, periodicals, and unpublished manuscripts written in the United States and those emanating from sources abroad. The second category of sources, utilized primarily for this introductory essay, was the general field of figurative language study. Here the writers normally were not political scientists, but rhetoricians, philosophers, metaphysicians, linguists, poets, and other literati. In reading in these sources the concern was to identify the typical functions of figurative language preparatory to assessing the suitability of such language in federal theory development.

Use of figurative language--especially metaphors--has been the object of frequent criticism, although the disparagers generally recognize the inevitability of analogical language, even as the quest for greater univocity in description continues. Martin Landau claims that "the endless parade of hyphenations," the unabating "addition of adjectives" to federalism is indefensible. Many of the adjectives, he feels, "are simply senseless." (Landau 1973:174) He pointed two decades ago to a confusing mixture of organismic and mechanical models which, he said, had the effect actually of hindering understanding of federalism. (Landau 1961:333) Deil Wright condemns what he calls the "invent-your-own federalism game" and feels that the adjectival modifier "politicizes the term." He professes disappointment that "a host of value-laden adjectives have been attached to the leading edge of a historic and significant concept and have, from whatever motives, blunted the term's meaning and thus limited its analytic utility." (Wright 1978:19) He feels principal reliance must in the future be placed not on substantially figurative adjectival federalisms but on intergovernmental relations as the "conceptual base for exploring and aggregating past and present experiences of citizens and public officials." (Ibid.)

Model as used in federalism literature has numerous
meanings. It has been referred to, for example, as an "ex-
planatory sketch," derived from the survey of a number of "kinds
or types of explanations of federal systems." (Teune in Earle
1968:216) The general view is that models should be systematic.
They should spell out as much as is feasible the relationships
which exist in the federal system being examined. Since models
attempt systematic social scientific explanation, they must be
subject to rigorous challenge. They must be susceptible to pro-
positional inventorying. The component elements must be ex-
plicated in vigorous fashion.

The representations in this volume, the adjectival
federalisms, are sometimes called shorthand phrases for a universe of complex phenomena which the architect of the protoplast
neither can nor does he or she wish to describe with the effort
and comprehensiveness of the mathematical model builder and en-
unciator. Zashin and Chapman have identified the analogy as "a
ready-made conceptual organization for something unfamiliar or
problematic." (Zashin and Chapman 1974:312) In our area of
interest this frequently involves seeing federalism as a flower,
stream, piece of flypaper or cake, gelatinous mass, kaleidoscope,
picket fence, plate of spaghetti, or some other object or system.
Figurative language ostensibly would be less useful than
mathematical models in the development of theory, if theory is
identified as "an organized and interactive body of
generalizations which is more or less widely accepted as useful
for understanding an identifiable subset of related conceptual
problems." (Galt and Smith 1976:20) But this kind of theory does
not exist as far as federalism is concerned.

Many of the models which have proliferated in federalism
writings both scholarly and popular and which are presented in
this volume have not been fully developed. Others, however, such
as integral federalism (as enunciated most clearly by Alexandre
Marc), are very comprehensive and have implications not likely to
be accepted by any but the most ardent federalist. In line with
the meaning of model presented earlier, Marc says integral
federalism "is a set, a sample set, of realistic hypotheses" and
includes "the identification of primary elements, abstract
organization of these elements, theory, decision-making, and the
transcending of the theory." (Marc in Katz and Schuster
1979:3-4) At the other extreme, some of the contemporary
notions of federalism are puns (e.g., cooptative federalism) or
plays on words possibly constructed with basically phonetic
criteria in mind (e.g., fanciful federalism). Some of the
adjectival federalisms employ alliteration for effect--repeating
the initial letter or sound--as in facade federalism, focused
federalism, flowering federalism, etc. Isophony involves re-
petition of sounds of similar words or segments of words in a
series as in effective federalism and separatist federalism.

3

(This discussion of syntactic figures is drawn from Bonsiepe in
Shibles 1972:157-58.) Adjectival federalisms also make use of
semantic figures--including antithesis--as in antagoistic
federalism, monistic federalism, concentrated federalism, and
others. Hyperbole--exaggeration--is the semantic figure con-
sciously or unconsciously employed in discussions of complete
federalism, perfect federalism, pure federalism, total federalism, and the like. Adjectival federalisms further employ irony
(antiphrasis)--as in coerced federalism, federalism by compulsion, imposed federalism, permissive federalism, and uncooperative federalism. Gradation in rhetoric involves the use
of words in an ascending order of forcefulness. This is seen in
such federalism descriptors as protofederalism, incipient
federalism, and creeping federalism--where each of the terms appearing first indicates something weaker than federalism. In
contrast, the modifier describes something more forceful than
federalism as usually defined in such fabrications as integrated
federalism, organic federalism, and personalist federalism. These
uses should not be demeaned but the author of this volume is
prepared to argue that many of the expressions presented here
have more than rhetorical utility as far as the development of
federal theory is concerned.

It is, of course, a culinary metaphor--the marble cake--
which became the most popular figurative expression used in discussions of federalism. Morton Grodzins viewed the rainbow or
marble cake as a "far more accurate image" of American federalism
than a layer cake. "As colors are mixed in the marble cake,"
Grodzins explained, "so functions are mixed in the American
federal system." (Grodzins in U.S. President, Commission on
National Goals, Goals for Americans, p. 265.) This descriptor
has become part of the standard vocabulary. Thus in 1974 David
Walker's readers readily understood what he meant when he observed that, "The recent record reveals a greater 'marbleizing'
of the intergovernmental fiscal system than ever before."
Wright found no need to adopt a new metaphor to characterize the
pre-1937 period of conflict in American intergovernmental relations when he published an overview article in the mid-1970s.
This was, he felt, the period to which the federalism metaphor
layer cake federalism best applied. Still, Wright called use of
the culinary metaphor only "a crude means of describing national,
state and local disconnectedness." Its advantage lay in its
visual effect, especially when contrasted with the marble cake
descriptor. (Wright 1974:5, 6-7)

There are obviously many other (and possibly more rewarding)
approaches to the scholarly study of federalism and thus to the
development of federal theory besides the use of figurative and
nonfigurative conceptualizations. But, practically every approach, including the heavily empirical methods, makes extensive use of metaphorical and analogical language. Thus it is
important to understand the strengths and limitations of

generally simple literal and nonliteral language as employed in academic and popular discourse.

This volume includes 497 literal as well as figurative representations of federalism. Federalisms derived wholly from the Federalist party in the United States in the eighteenth and nineteenth centuries generally have not been included. The hyphenated federalisms have been arbitrarily (and tentatively) divided into many overlapping categories which appear following this Introductory Essay. Several subnational or supranational locational federalisms are included for illustrative purposes. (For information on national models, discussed under numerous headings throughout the volume, the reader should refer to the geographical index.) Thirty-one of the 495 "federalisms" have been identified as almost wholly analogical or metaphorical. Many of the remainder are basically figurative, however.

Ten possible overlapping justifications for the use by serious students of adjectival paradigms in the development of understandings of federalism suggest themselves, based on generally approved uses in the literature and support for nonliteral language from experts outside the social sciences. While the points are stated affirmatively, the debate should really only be starting, possibly stimulated by this most comprehensive of sources on concepts of federalism. Thus the following are only conjectured advantages for the utilization of adjectival federalisms, many of which have a strongly nonliteral character:

(1) Figurative language contributes to the process of defining and redefining federalism;
(2) Naming federal phenomena increases prospects for understanding them;
(3) Adjectival federalisms aid in organizing knowledge about federalism;
(4) Adjectival federalisms miniaturize and abridge the actual dimensions of federal systems so they can be grasped as wholes and manipulated by their users;
(5) Adjectival federalisms promote popular awareness of actual or desirable patterns of intergovernmental relations;
(6) The adjectival federalism facilitates economical description and redescription;
(7) Adjectival federalisms may have a positive influence both on practitioners and theorists of federalism;
(8) Nonmathematical, frequently metaphorical, paradigms may appropriately be used to categorize "federalisms" and point out new phases in their development;
(9) Shorthand expressions have a significant amount of heuristic utility; and
(10) Adjectival federalisms aid in the generation of

hypotheses.

Again, each of these postulated merits of the uses of literal and nonliteral descriptors is open to counter-argument and, in fact, the primary intention in offering them at the beginning of this volume of Concepts of Federalism is to subject both literal and nonliteral federalism models to more intense scrutiny than they have heretofore received because so many have never been collected in a single source as has been done here.

(1) Figurative language helps give definable meaning to federalism. Franz Neumann once asked rhetorically: "Have the terms 'federalism,' 'federal government,' or 'federal state' definable meanings?" According to Neumann, "Even a most superficial study of the various kinds of federal government . . . fails to show any element common to all, except a juristic one." (Neuman in Macmahon 1955:44) Somewhat later, S. Rufus Davis argued that "federalism" simply indicated "a particular kind of jural relationship in which general and regional governments may be joined, and the formal institutional arrangements in which this relationship should be expressed." We can interpret Davis to mean that without something else beside federalism we can know

little of the precise distribution of functions between two levels of government, the range and influence of their functions, the precise set of fiscal relations created, the party system and the power structure within each party, the degree of cohesion and diversity in the community, their political skills and dispositions, their attitudes toward the formal garment, or their wealth, traditions and usages.

With federalism standing by itself the observer "can predicate neither weakness [n]or strength, radicalism nor conservatism, flexibility nor rigidity in its institutions." (Davis in Wildavsky 1967:32) Davis does not argue the case for federal additives (and they certainly do not solve all of the problems he identifies), but his professed goals would seem to require them at the present paltry stage of theory development.

The modifier, figurative or literal, thus may assist in the effort of "political theorists, students of political institutions, and constitutional lawyers . . . to make the term 'federal' more precise," (Watts 1966:10) although Landau warns that with the overparticularization of federalism by the addition of new attributes "[t]he general category is thereby lost and the object of inquiry becomes its own best description." (Landau 1973:176) Still, federalism's conceptual flexibility encourages flexibility in application. We may say that it is, as Kadushin asserted with respect to ancient Hebrew theological reasoning, "an expression of thought not hardened according to formulae but fluid and fresh as the living experience that . . . engendered it. . . . " (Kadushin 1938:22-23)

Whether because of the use of adjectival modifiers or not, the definition of federalism will continue to find new expressions and the addition of concising adjectives is part of the natural change process. Kadushin says "every change in circumstances brings with it new concretizations" of fundamental concepts. (Ibid., p. 195.) Flexibility in federalism and a variety of descriptors permits adaptation of federal institutions and processes to widely contrasting environmental settings.

Edward McWhinney has pointed out that, "Existing Western stereotypes of the federal constitutional form [are] . . . derived from advanced, industrially based societies. . . . " Consequently, they may require "considerable adjustment and modification. . . . " (McWhinney 1965:96) The adjectival expression, whether literal or figurative, may assist in this extension process as "[t]he new context (the 'frame' of the metaphor . . .) imposes extension of meaning upon the focal word"--federalism. (Black 1962:39) Ricoeur says that the model "seeks, by means of fiction"--a federal system has no literal shape as hypothesized in shape federalism--"to break down an inadequate interpretation and to lay the way for a new, more adequate interpretation." (Ricoeur 1977:240) Michael Reagan cites Grodzins's figurative marblecake image (Grodzins became more closely associated with it than McLean because of his wider audience) as "a major corrective to the older image of dual federalism," although he feels that it is now "an inadequate conception as regards the delineation of the intergovernmental relationship," since it gives inadequate emphasis to current national suasion. (M. Reagan 1972:161)

A majority of the entries in this volume are not primarily metaphorical. For example, new federalism in its many manifestations is the most common adjectival federalism. However, in defense of those federalisms which are essentially figurative we may cite Mary Hesse's support for metaphors which have the function of "correcting and replacing the original literal descriptions"--in our case perhaps conventional descriptions of federalism--"so that the literal descriptions are discarded as inadequate or even false." (Hesse 1966:174) Of course, this possible justification for the use of metaphors could just as easily be employed to oppose their use, where there is particular concern about sacrificing values inherent in traditional definitions. Another way to look at this problem is to consider federalism "as an articulation of thought and values more complicated than that which can be devised by logic," as a concept "complicated and flexible enough . . . to allow" at once for "variety" and "distinctiveness." (Kadushin 1938:v) Federalism may, therefore, be treated as "[a]n organic complex containing a large number of concepts [which] will grasp or interpret a concrete situation in more ways than will a complex with a small number of concepts. . . . " (Ibid., p. 193.) If this adaptation of Kadushin's Organic Thinking is accepted, then alarm at the apparent multiplication of both literal and figurative "federalisms" through the addition of close to five hundred modifiers may more easily be restrained.

But, assuming, as some scholars do, that federalism is inherently indefinite, the addition of the literal or figurative adjectival modifier to federalism may be said to constitute "a specific predication upon an inchoate noun." (Fernandez in Sapir and Crocker 1977:102. Fernandez has a metaphor predicating a pronoun.) "In general," Fernandez says, "the semantic movement accomplished by metaphor is from the abstract, and inchoate in the subject to the more concrete, ostensive and easily graspable in the metaphoric predicate"--the picket fence, the pinwheel, the pole. (Ibid., p. 104.) The same function is performed less colorfully by the literal federalism adjectival modifiers. Federalism's adjective schematizes what the popular or scholarly writer wishes to communicate regarding the particular federal phenomena being examined. The function of the modifier may be compared to the ingegno which, Mazzeo says, "makes order out of disorder and [substitutes] clarity where there had been only darkness and mystery." (Mazzeo 1964:57) "The primary"--federalism--"is 'seen through' the frame of the secondary." (The idea of "seeing through" was adapted from Hesse 1966:163. Hesse, of course, was not at all concerned with federalism.) Shibles says the modifier can "be regarded as a structure forcing us to see reality"--the "reality" of federal phenomena, in our case--"in a certain way. . . . " (Shibles 1971:16) The figurative or nonfigurative modifier "in its literal use . . . refer[s] to a more concrete object than its literal equivalent," federalism. (Black 1962:34) Kadushin contends that, "Because of the drive toward concretization, every organic complex creates new situations, new events informed by combinations of concepts." (Kadushin 1938:v) If we accept federalism as an organic complex, we may have here both an explanation for and a justification of the variety in federal theorizing represented in this volume.

(2) Naming federal phenomena increases prospects for understanding them. "Naming unobservables," Eugene Miller says, may be regarded as "the first step towards identifying and coming to know them." "Since the thing"--the hypothesis of the observer of federalism regarding what he or she sees or hopes to see--"has no name of its own, one is transferred to it from a familiar and accessible thing which is somehow like the unnamed thing." (Miller 1979:165) The naming function is said to be important "whenever something new is invented requiring a name or whenever it seems desirable to call attention to an undesignated aspect of something already known." (Ibid.) In the case of federalism, the easiest course has simply been to speak of a "new federalism," but this volume indicates that hundreds of more imaginative expressions frequently have been employed.

We may say with Morris Cohen that, "The universal idea"--in our case federalism--"and particular fact"--literally or figuratively labeled manifestations of federalism--"generally develop into clearness together, the particular instance helping to give body and prehensibility to the idea, and the idea making the instance clearer and more definite." (Cohen 1931:180-81 quoted in Kadushin 1938:186) Previously undescribed or inadequately described political phenomena represent situations for concepts such as federalism to "grasp or interpret." (Ibid., p. 201.)

(3) Adjectival federalisms aid in organizing knowledge about federalism. The adjective employed in connection with federalism necessarily "suppresses some details, emphasizes others," and in so doing organizes our view of the subject. There is applied to the primary subject--federalism--"a system of 'associated implications' characteristic of the subsidiary subject." The adjective "selects, emphasizes, suppresses, and organizes features of the principal subject by implying statements about it that normally apply to the subsidiary subject." (Black 1962:41, 44-45. Black is primarily concerned with metaphors.) Thus Deil Wright says the use of "feudal" with federalism--"feudal federalism"--stresses "not only the degree of autonomy that the program specialists have from policy control by political generalists, but also the separateness and independence that one program has from another." (Wright 1974:16) The modifier offers to federalism "a ready-made conceptual organization for something unfamiliar or problematic"--a specific manifestation of federalism--and suggests that "the object of concern"--the heretofore unlabeled or incorrectly labeled federalism--"is 'isometric' or parallel with or similar in relevant aspects to something else which is familiar, well-understood, and uncontroversial . . . ," that is, the modifier. (Zashin and Chapman 1974:312) In practically all instances, the word or words preceding federalism help to "establish relationships which were not previously apparent, either through creating a context of similarities and differences or by organizing one realm [federalism] through the categories of another and carrying over the relationships of the latter to the former." (Ibid., p. 317.) The first word, the referent, "call[s] to mind the ideas, both linguistic and empirical, that are commonly held to be associated with the given referent in the given language community." (Hesse 19665:160) However, the adjective is usually imprecise and unless the commonly held ideas are spelled out clearly, it may not be of much help to serious students in identifying actual patterns of political relationships.

(4) Adjectival federalisms miniaturize and abridge the actual dimensions of federal systems so they can be grasped as wholes and manipulated by their users. Somewhat like a physical model, the adjectival federalism, e.g., dialectical federalism, "simplifies drastically the true . . . phenomena and only gives

account of certain major or important aspects of it." (Suppes in
Kazmier and Vuysje 1969:169. Suppes is writing specifically with
respect to physical models.) Although the aspects emphasized are
those which the observer feels to be critical to understanding
the system being observed (at least with respect to the observer's particular object of inquiry), witnessed phenomena could
be so simplified and so many aspects of the system could be omitted, that the principal result is to entertain the reader or
listener rather than to inform. As Hesse points out, scientific
models, in contrast, "are meant to be exploited energetically and
often in extreme quantitative detail . . . they are meant to be
internally tightly knit by logical and causal interrelations."
(Hesse 1966:169)

(5) Adjectival federalisms may promote popular understanding of federalism. This has undoubtedly been the principal
function of many of the descriptors included in this volume and
is the function least open to criticism since its claims are modest ones. Particularly in communicating with a wider audience
than members of their own disciplines, "[s]ocial scientists have
often found that social phenomena are more easily understood in
terms of commonly understood physical, social, or biological
images." For the convenience of the wider audience, the modifier
"translates things which are difficult to understand into the
terms of more familiar images." (Galt and Smith 1976:26) Vincent
Ostrom sees this communicative function as extremely important.
Taking his lead from

Alexander Hamilton's question of '. . . whether
societies of men are really capable or not of
establishing good government from reflection and
choice, or . . . are forever destined to depend
for their political constitutions on accident and
force . . .'

Ostrom says "at least part of the answer" to this question "rests
upon the words used to organize the reflections of citizens, inform their choices, and guide their actions." (Ostrom 1976:32)
As the bicentennial of the most important American political
invention, modern federalism, approaches, this function takes on
even more importance.

(6) The adjectival federalism is a device of economy. It
permits the enunciation of numerous observations in relatively
brief fashion. "Traditional theory," Zashin and Chapman explain,
"was synoptic in a way that contemporary political science rarely
attempts to be." (Zashin and Chapman 1974:291) Shorthand expressions have the capacity tentatively and preliminarily to describe
vast amounts of evidence to which no other delineating terms may
readily be applied. From another perspective, however, and in
the interest of theory development, economy may not have the
highest priority. It may be necessary, at least initially, to

describe in detail the evidence discovered and be content with nothing but the most univocal terms to explicate it.

(7) Adjectival federalisms may constructively influence both practitioners and theorists of intergovernmental relations. To make the system work in the beginning, "The makers of the American federal constitution drew on the contractual and mechanistic metaphors of Hobbes, Locke, Harrington and Montesquieu." They "translated [these nonliteral expressions] into viable formulae of governmental engineering." (Eulau 1973:155)

Elazar believes that "the old theory of dual federalism was functional in its own way, not as a description of empirical reality, but as a constitutional restraint of a kind." With the demise in popularity of this adjectival expression "came an abandonment of all restraint." (Elazar 1973b:246) Ostrom says James Sundquist's Making Federalism Work (1969) anticipated "'the final burial' of the traditional doctrines of American federalism and the development of a new 'model' for making federalism work." (Ostrom 1976:26) The picket fence metaphor was viewed by Wright as a possible (though arguable) "guide to policy and administrative actions." At a minimum, it "dramatize[d] the need for powerful assertions of gubernatorial influence if state policies and programs are to be more than a hodgepodge of independent professional and functional fiefdoms." (Wright 1978:211) An expert on the use of figurative language believes that, "By entitling a difficult situation through applying what might seem an incongruous 'metaphorical name' for it"--again picket fence federalism comes to mind--"actors can resolve their problems of how to act within its context." (Sapir in Sapir and Crocker 1977:43) In Marc's view "all federal theory in effect recommends action." The adjectival paradigms "are at work right now," he feels, "influencing the behavior and the performance of public officials. . . . " (Marc 1979:12-13)

(8) Nonmathematical descriptors may be used to categorize particular manifestations of federalism and point out new developmental phases. Thus Beer invented "technocratic federalism" to illustrate the "centralizing process" he believed to be under way and "the main reasons [for it] in the new forces produced by an advanced modernity." (Beer 1973:52) McWhinney used the nonliteral expression "monistic federalism" to identify "a constitutional system characterized by increasingly centripetal tendencies in terms of effective location of policy-making. . . . " (McWhinney 1965:16-17) Livingston was said to have found his conception of socio-cultural federalism useful in that "with it he was able to arrange societies in order according to the degree to which they were really federal or unitary." (Tarlton 1965:866) Dunn employs the modifier communal to help take care of "special cases" among federal systems. He identifies socialist Yugoslavia as an instance of "communal federalism" because it is so different as to necessitate "an adapted conceptual approach

. . . . a reconceptualization which reflects Yugoslavia's special status among nominally federal systems." (Dunn 1975:136, 149)

But the adjectival federalisms presented in this volume should be regarded primarily as theoretical starting points. "Scientific explanation should not be confused," Douglas Berggren properly warns, "with the popularizer's relation of the un- familiar to what is familiar to common sense." Scientific ex- planation must at some point undertake the tedious task of "sys- tematic integration of the scientifically anomalous with the scientifically accepted. . . . " (Berggren 1963:455)

(9) Another justification for adjectival federalisms is as heuristic devices. The more useful of these expressions aid in the discovery of new regularities of behavior in federal systems. They furnish "a frame of reference from which discoveries can be made [and] contribute to the processes of discovery and re- finement." (Galt and Smith 1976:62. These writers are referring specifically to heuristic models.) Although often extremely rudimentary, nonliteral descriptors can serve the interests of science, and Hesse believes that "the heuristic function of an- alogies must be regarded as an essential part of scientific the- ories." (Hesse in Shibles 1972:175) As noted earlier, Ricoeur identifies the role of heuristic instruments as being "to break down an inadequate interpretation and to lay the way for a new, more adequate interpretation." (Ricoeur 1977:240. He is refer- ring specifically to models, as heuristic instruments.)

(10) If successful heuristically, adjectival federalisms aid in the generation of hypotheses related to observed federal phenomena. Black cautions, "Analogue models furnish plausible hypotheses, not proofs." (Black 1962:223) A limited survey of federalism literature in the mid-1970s set up theories--models--of federalism as being mostly for the purpose of enunciating propositions and findings about specific aspects of the American federal system, particularly its fiscal aspects. The primary contribution of the model builders was that they "integrated both system and unit levels-of-analysis in such a way as to generate a broad range of propositions and findings for more vigorous empirical testing." (Baker et al. 1974:39-40) Many of the expressions presented in this volume were apparently chosen so hastily that they have little utility in the generation and testing of hypotheses. However, on balance it would seem that, despite the admittedly appropriate criticisms of excessive production of hyphenated federalisms, these shorthand expressions do have legitimacy and their continued use in the development of federal theory should not be condemned outright. The need to combat what Landau nonmetaphorically identified as "hyper- factualism" two decades ago is greater than ever. The adjectival federalisms presented in the following pages do contribute to an ongoing effort "to provide some system." (Landau 1961:344)

Imaginative use of language further "enlarges the way in which
we can make sense of our experience; thereby it increases the
reality which can be intersubjectively known." (Zashin and
Chapman 1974:294)

Adaptation of metaphorical and other types of figurative and
nonfigurative language has enriched much of the popular and
scholarly writing about federalism traditionally and currently
and its continued but judicious application can make not unlimited but nonetheless valuable contributions in the arduous and
otherwise graceless process of theory development and the working
out of insightful approaches to everyday intergovernmental relations.

CLASSIFICATIONS OF CONCEPTS

ACT OR FACT OF DOING (WHAT THE VERBAL ROOT OF THE PRESENT PARTICIPLE DENOTES): bargaining federalism, community defining federalism, evolving federalism, faltering federalism, flowering federalism, frightening federalism, pact-making federalism, working federalism

ACT OR FACT OF HAVING DONE (WHAT THE VERBAL ROOT OF THE PAST PARTICIPLE DENOTES): amplified federalism, associated state federalism, balanced federalism, channeled federalism, charter-based federalism, coerced federalism, concentrated federalism, congested federalism, dictated federalism, differentiated federalism, expanded federalism, failed federalism, focused federalism, fragmented federalism, fused federalism, fused-foliated federalism, hyphenated federalism, imposed federalism, integrated federalism, interlocked federalism, intertwined federalism, limited federalism, mixed federalism, multicentered federalism, nation-centered federalism, new-modeled federalism, old-fashioned federalism, outcome-oriented federalism, process-oriented federalism, proliferated federalism, provincially-oriented federalism, purported federalism, realigned federalism, rebalanced federalism, reformed federalism, renewed federalism, restored federalism, revised federalism, self-managed federalism, shared federalism, state-centered federalism, state-oriented federalism, treaty-based federalism, unfettered federalism, urban-centered federalism

AFTER: post-colonial federalism, post-federalism, post-modern federalism, post-Second World War federalism, post-technocratic federalism

AGAIN: realigned federalism, rebalanced federalism, reborn federalism, reformed federalism, renewed federalism, responsive federalism, restored federalism, retrenchment federalism, revised federalism, revitalized federalism

AGE: classical federalism, historical federalism, old federalism, old-fashioned federalism, old-line federalism, old new federalism, old-style federalism, old urban federalism, proto- federalism, traditional federalism

14

AMONG: integral federalism, integrated federalism, intercantonal cooperative federalism, intercommunal federalism,
interdependent federalism, interlocked federalism, internal
federalism, international federalism, international law community federalism, intertwined federalism

APPROACHES TO THE STUDY OF FEDERALISM: academic federalism,
biblical federalism, community defining federalism, comparative federalism, constitutional federalism, cultural
federalism, documentary federalism, dynamic federalism, economic federalism, epistemological federalism, ethical
federalism, extra-legal federalism, federalism as fiction,
fiscal federalism, formal federalism, functional federalism,
governmental federalism, group federalism, historical
federalism, hyphenated federalism, ideological federalism,
institutional federalism, instrumental federalism, legal
federalism, lexical federalism, linguistic federalism,
literary federalism, methodological federalism, nonpolitical
federalism, nonterritorial federalism, ontological federalism, operational federalism, outcome-oriented federalism,
political federalism, private federalism, process-oriented
federalism, racial federalism, religious federalism, secular
federalism, social federalism, socio-cultural federalism,
socio-economic federalism, sociological federalism, spontaneous federalism, theological federalism, technological
federalism

ATTITUDE: adaptive federalism, antagonistic federalism,
antistate federalism, bamboozle federalism, coerced federalism, coercive federalism, comity federalism, competitive
federalism, conservative federalism, contentious federalism,
cooperative cultural federalism, cooperative educational
federalism, cooperative federalism, cooptative federalism,
creative federalism, creative-cooperative federalism, defensive federalism, destructive federalism, dictatorial
federalism, do-it-yourself federalism, flexible federalism,
frightening federalism, futilitarian federalism, gentlemanly
federalism, good federalism, healthy federalism, horizontal
cooperative federalism, ideal federalism, ill federalism,
independent federalism, intercantonal cooperative federalism, judicial cooperative federalism, kamikaze federalism,
liberal federalism, negative federalism, pacific federalism,
permissive federalism, pick and choose federalism, positive
federalism, responsive federalism, revolutionary
federalism,

romantic federalism, semi-antagonistic federalism, semi-cooperative federalism, separatist federalism, shell-game federalism, sweet and sour federalism, symbiotic federalism, uncooperative federalism, uncreative federalism, uneasy federalism, vertical cooperative federalism, welfare cooperative federalism

BALANCE: asymmetrical federalism, balanced federalism, coordinate federalism, coordinative federalism, equal federalism, polyvalent federalism, rebalanced federalism, shape federalism, symmetrical federalism, unequal federalism, upside down cake federalism

BASIS OF FEDERALISM: antivacuum federalism, bargaining federalism, biblical federalism, charter-based federalism, coerced federalism, common law federalism, compact federalism, compromise federalism, consensual federalism, consociational federalism, constitutional federalism, covenantal federalism, dictated federalism, doctrinaire federalism, documentary federalism, federalism a la carte, federalism by aggregation, federalism by compulsion, federalism by contract, federalism by decentralization, federalism by devolution, federalism via confederation, federalism without Washington, formal federalism, geographical federalism, ideal federalism, imposed federalism, international law community federalism, league federalism, legal federalism, lexical federalism, literary federalism, methodological federalism, natural federalism, pact-making federalism, piecemeal federalism, process-oriented federalism, spontaneous federalism, treaty-based federalism, treaty federalism

BELONGING OR PERTAINING TO OR CHARACTERISTIC OF: Achaean federalism, Althusian federalism, Bakunin's federalism, Bismarckian federalism, Buber's federalism, Calhounian federalism, Carter federalism, futilitarian federalism, Hamiltonian federalism, Jeffersonian federalism, Kant's federalism, Kropotkin's federalism, Leninist federalism, Madisonian federalism, Marshallian federalism, metropolitan federalism, Montesquieuean federalism, Novanglian federalism, Procustean federalism, proletarian federalism, protean federalism, Proudhon's federalism, Reagan federalism, republican federalism, utopian federalism

BEYOND NATIONAL: anti-imperial federalism, colonial
federalism, commonwealth federalism, continental federalism,
cosmopolitan federalism, empire federalism, external
federalism, global federalism, imperial federalism, international federalism, international law community federalism,
multinational federalism, pan-federalism, post-colonial
federalism, secondary federalism, supranational federalism,
transnational federalism, trilevel federalism, universal
federalism, world federalism

CLOSENESS: close federalism, congested federalism, fused
federalism, fused-foliated federalism, integrated federalism, interlocked federalism, intertwined federalism

COLONIAL: anti-imperial federalism, colonial federalism,
commonwealth federalism, empire federalism, imperial
federalism, post-colonial federalism

CONSTITUENTS: academic federalism, amphictyonic federalism,
aristocratic federalism, associated state federalism,
bureaucratic federalism, capitalistic federalism, church
federalism, city-county federalism, city federalism,
cliental federalism, club federalism, colonial federalism,
congregational federalism, consociational federalism, consumer federalism, cooperative federalism, dynastic federal-
ism, estate federalism, factional federalism, federalism of
sovereigns, feudal federalism, gentlemanly federalism,
governmental federalism, group federalism, intercommunal
federalism, international federalism, kingly federalism,
linguistic federalism, local federalism, mercantilist
federalism, metropolitan federalism, monarchic federalism,
multinational federalism, neighborhood federalism,
organizational federalism, our federalism, participatory
federalism, particularist federalism, partnership federalism, personalist federalism, polis-federalism, polyethnic
federalism, proletarian federalism, proprietary federalism,
provincially-oriented federalism, racial federalism, regional federalism, representational federalism, separatist
federalism, social federalism, socialist federalism, socio-
cultural federalism, socio-economic federalism, state-
centered federalism, state-federalism, state-oriented
federalism, states rights federalism, supranational federal-
ism, territorial federalism, trade union federalism, transnational federalism, tribal federalism, trilevel
federalism,

tripartite federalism, two-level federalism, two-tier federalism

COOPERATION: cooperative cultural federalism, cooperative educational federalism, cooperative federalism, cooptative federalism, creative-cooperative federalism, horizontal cooperative federalism, intercantonal cooperative federalism, judicial cooperative federalism, semi-cooperative federalism, uncooperative federalism, vertical cooperative federalism, welfare cooperative federalism

EXECUTIVE: administrative federalism, bureaucratic federalism, chancery federalism, executive federalism, executive-legislative federalism, managerial federalism, prefectorial federalism

FALSITY: counterfeit federalism, ersatz federalism, facade federalism, federalism as fiction, fanciful federalism, lip-service federalism, paper-federalism, pseudo-federalism, sham federalism

FROM, DOWN, AWAY: decentralist federalism, decentralized federalism, federalism by decentralization, federalism by devolution, independent federalism, interdependent federalism

GOOD: ethical federalism, good federalism, ideal federalism, more perfect federalism, perfect federalism, pure federalism, reformed federalism, religious federalism

HYPHENIC (PURE): antifederalism, confederalism, cryptofederalism, metafederalism, minifederalism, neofederalism, nonfederalism, panfederalism, postfederalism, protofederalism, pseudofederalism, quasifederalism, semi-federalism

IDEOLOGICAL: anarcho-federalism, communist federalism, conservative federalism, democratic federalism, existentialist federalism, ideological federalism, liberal federalism, socialist federalism, Whig federalism

INCIPIENCY: emergent federalism, incipient federalism, primary federalism, protofederalism

JUDICIAL: comparative judicial federalism, horizontal
judicial federalism, judicial cooperative federalism,
judicial dual federalism, judicial federalism, juridical
federalism, juridico-political federalism, juristic
federalism, new judicial federalism, vertical judicial
federalism

KIND (THEMATIC): agricultural-industrial federalism, antidysfunctional federalism, anti-imperial federalism, areal
federalism, asymmetrical federalism, biblical federalism,
categorical federalism, centrifugal federalism, centripetal
federalism, classical federalism, cliental federalism, colonial federalism, commercial federalism, communal federal-
ism, comparative judicial federalism, congregational
federalism, congressional federalism, consensual federalism,
consociational federalism, constitutional federalism, continental federalism, conventional federalism, cooperative
cultural federalism, cooperative educational federalism,
correctional federalism, covenantal federalism,
criminal-justice federalism, cultural federalism,
dialectical federalism, dictatorial federalism, dual
federalism, dysfunctional federalism, ecumenical federalism,
educational federalism, epistemological federalism, equal
federalism, essential federalism, ethical federalism,
external federalism, extra-legal federalism, factional
federalism, federal federalism, federal- legislative
federalism, feudal federalism, financial federalism, fiscal
federalism, formal federalism, functional federalism,
functional feudal federalism, fundamental federalism,
geographical federalism, global federalism, governmental
federalism, hegemonial federalism, historical federalism,
horizontal cooperative federalism, horizontal federalism,
horizontal judicial federalism, ideal federalism,
ideological federalism, imperial federalism, industrial
federalism, institutional federalism, instrumental federal-
ism, integral federalism, intercantonal cooperative federal-
ism, intercommunal federalism, internal federalism, international federalism, international law community federalism,
judicial dual federalism, juridical federalism, juridico-
political federalism, legal federalism, lexical federalism,
liberal federalism, local federalism, managerial federalism,
marginal federalism, maximal federalism, medieval-
constitutionalist federalism, medieval-corporative federal-
ism, methodological federalism, minimal federalism, multidimensional federalism, multinational federalism, municipal

federalism, mutual federalism, mutual interest federalism, national federalism, national-supremacy federalism, natural federalism, new judicial federalism, nominal federalism, nonpolitical federalism, nonterritorial federalism, occupational federalism, one-dimensional federalism, ontological federalism, operational federalism, optimal federalism, organizatonal federalism, partial federalism, patrimonial federalism, perpetual federalism, piecemeal federalism, political federalism, post-colonial federalism, practical federalism, prefectorial federalism, professional federalism, professorial federalism, racial federalism, regional federalism, representational federalism, sociocultural federalism, sociological federalism, subnational federalism, supranational federalism, symmetrical federalism, territorial federalism, theological federalism, total federalism, traditional federalism, transitional federalism, transnational federalism, universal federalism, vertical federalism, vertical cooperative federalism, vertical judicial federalism

LEGISLATIVE: congressional federalism, executive-legislative federalism, extra-parliamentary federalism, federal-legislative federalism, parliamentary federalism

LEVEL: anti-imperial federalism, antistate federalism, areal federalism, associated state federalism, city-county federalism, city federalism, colonial federalism, commonwealth federalism, communal federalism, community defining federalism, continental federalism, cosmopolitan federalism, domestic federalism, empire federalism, estate federalism, external federalism, feudal federalism, global federalism, imperial federalism, in-state federalism, intercantonal cooperative federalism, intercommunal federalism, international federalism, international law community federalism, local federalism, metropolitan federalism, multinational federalism, municipal federalism, national federalism, national-supremacy federalism, nation-centered federalism, neighborhood federalism, new judicial federalism, pan-federalism, polis-federalism, post-colonial federalism, primary federalism, provincially-oriented federalism, regional federalism, secondary federalism, small-city federalism, small-republic federalism, state-centered federalism, state-federalism, state-oriented federalism, states rights federalism, subnational federalism, supranational federalism, territorial federalism, transnational federalism, tribal federalism, trilevel federalism, two-level federalism, universal federalism, urban-centered federalism, urban federalism, world federalism

LOCAL: city-county federalism, city federalism, communal federalism, intercommunal federalism, local federalism, metropolitan federalism, municipal federalism, neighborhood federalism, new urban federalism, old urban federalism, small-city federalism, urban-centered federalism, urban federalism

METAPHOR: bamboo fence federalism, birthday cake federalism, crazy-quite federalism, facade federalism, federalism a la carte, feudal federalism, flowering federalism, flypaper federalism, fruitcake federalism, fused-foliated federalism gelatinous mass federalism, kaleidoscopic federalism, kamikaze federalism, layer cake federalism, marble cake federalism, marketplace federalism, masonry wall federalism, matrix federalism, orreretic federalism, picket fence federalism, pinwheel federalism, portfolio federalism, post-coach federalism, Procrustean federalism, shell-game federalism, spaghetti federalism, summit federalism, sweet and sour federalism, twin-stream federalism, two-tier federalism, upside down cake federalism

MODERNITY: late federalism, modern federalism, new federalism, neo-federalism, new new federalism, new-style federalism, new urban federalism, post-modern federalism

MORBIDITY: abortive federalism, congested federalism, dead federalism dysfunctional federalism, failed federalism, faltering federalism, futilitarian federalism, ill federalism, uneasy federalism, weak federalism

NATIONAL: multinational federalism, national federalism, national-supremacy federalism, nation-centered federalism, subnational federalism, supranational federalism, trans-national federalism

NEGATIVE: antagonistic federalism, antifederalism, anti-state federalism, bamboozle federalism, coerced federalism, coercive federalism, congested federalism, contentious federalism, destructive federalism, dysfunctional federal-

ism, frightening federalism, futilitarian federalism, ill
federalism, imperfect federalism, improper federalism,
impure federalism, negative federalism, semi-antagonistic
federalism, shell-game federalism, uncooperative federalism,
uncreative federalism, uneasy federalism, weak federalism

NOT: abortive federalism, anarcho-federalism, asymmetrical
federalism, imperfect federalism, improbable federalism,
improper federalism, impure federalism, independent federalism, uncooperative federalism, uncreative federalism, uneasy
federalism, unequal federalism, unfettered federalism

NUMBER: autonomous federalism, dual federalism, judicial
dual federalism, monarchic federalism, monistic federalism,
multidimensional federalism, multinational federalism, one-
dimensional federalism, pluralistic federalism, polyethnic
federalism, polyvalent federalism, premier federalism,
secondary federalism, trilevel federalism, tripartite
federalism, twin-stream federalism, two-level federalism,
two-tier federalism

OFFICE OR FUNCTION OR THE PERSONS HAVING IT: administrative
federalism, corporate federalism, federal-legislative
federalism, medieval-corporative federalism, private
federalism

OF OR PERTAINING TO: academic federalism, amphicytonic
federalism, antagonistic federalism, aristocratic federalism, authentic federalism, biblical federalism,
bureaucratic federalism, categorical federalism, classical
federalism, democratic federalism, dialectical federalism,
domestic federalism, dynamic federalism, economic federalism, ecumenical federalism, epistemological federalism,
ethical federalism, geographical federalism, genuine
federalism, historical federalism, ideological federalism,
intertwined federalism, juridical federalism, juristic
federalism, kaleidoscopic federalism, lexical federalism,
linguistic federalism, methodological federalism, monarchic
federalism, monistic federalism, monoethnic federalism, nonpolitical federalism, oligarchic federalism, ontological
federalism, organic federalism, orreretic federalism,
pacific federalism, pluralistic federalism, political
federalism, polyethnic federalism, post-technocratic
federalism, practical federalism, pragmatic federalism,

public federalism, romantic federalism, semi-antagonistic
federalism, small-republic federalism, socio-economic
federalism, sociological federalism, symbiotic federalism,
symmetrical federalism, syndical federalism, technocratic
federalism, technological federalism, theological federalism, vertical cooperative federalism, vertical federalism,
vertical judicial federalism

OF THE NATURE OF: abortive federalism, adaptive federalism,
administrative federalism, coercive federalism, collective
federalism, comparative federalism, comparative judicial
federalism, competitive federalism, comprehensive federalism, conservative federalism, cooperative cultural federalism, cooperative educational federalism, cooperative
federalism, cooptative federalism, coordinative federalism,
creative federalism, creative-cooperative federalism, defensive federalism, destructive federalism, effective
federalism, executive federalism, executive-legislative
federalism, expansive federalism, federal-legislative
federalism, horizontal cooperative federalism, intercantonal
cooperative federalism, judicial cooperative federalism,
medieval-corporative federalism, negative federalism, permissive federalism, positive federalism, responsive federal-
ism, semi-cooperative federalism, uncooperative federalism,
uncreative federalism, vertical cooperative federalism,
welfare cooperative federalism

ONE WHO DOES, MAKES A PRACTICE OF, PROFESSES: antagonistic
federalism, communist federalism, decentralist federalism,
existentialist federalism, juristic federalism, Leninist
federalism, linguistic federalism, medieval-
constitutionalist federalism, mercantilist federalism, monistic federalism, particularist federalism, personalist
federalism, pluralistic federalism, semi-antagonistic
federalism, separatist federalism, socialist federalism

OPPOSITE, AGAINST, COUNTER: antidysfunctional federalism,
antifederalism, anti-imperial federalism, antistate federalism

PARTLY: creeping federalism, federalism with a difference,
hybrid federalism, hyphenated federalism, limited federalism, little federalism, marginal federalism, minifederalism,
minimal federalism, mixed federalism, not-full federalism,
partial federalism, semi-federalism

PLACE NAME: Achaean federalism, federalism without Washington, Greek federalism, innerswiss federalism, Roman federalism, western federalism

POINT OF CONCENTRATION: centralized-militarized federalism, centrally-directed federalism, centrifugal federalism, centripetal federalism, concentrated federalism, decentralist federalism, decentralized federalism, federalism by decentralization, multicentered federalism, nation-centered federalism, urban-centered federalism

POLICIES: agricultural-industrial federalism, categorical federalism, censorship federalism, centralized-militarized federalism, cultural federalism, cooperative educational federalism, correctional federalism, criminal-justice federalism, defensive federalism, educational federalism, financial federalism, fiscal federalism, functional federalism, functional feudal federalism, income federalism, land federalism, military federalism, offshore federalism, outcome-oriented federalism, pacific federalism, regulatory federalism, service federalism, tax federalism, welfare cooperative federalism

PROCESS: antivaccuum federalism, bargaining federalism, compact federalism, compromise federalism, dictated federalism, federalism a la carte, federalism by aggregation, federalism by compulsion, federalism by contract, federalism by decentralization, federalism by devolution, federalism via confederation, imposed federalism, legal federalism, natural federalism, piecemeal federalism, process-oriented federalism, spontaneous federalism

PROPER NAME: Bakunin's federalism, Bismarckian federalism, Buber's federalism, Calhounian federalism, Carter federalism, Hamiltonian federalism, Jeffersonian federalism, Kant's federalism, Kropotkin's federalism, Leninist federalism, Madisonian federalism, Marshallian federalism, Montesquieuean federalism, Novanglian federalism, Procrustean federalism, Proudhon's federalism, protean federalism, Publius's federalism, Reagan federalism

RELIGIOUS: biblical federalism, church federalism, congregational federalism, covenantal federalism, ecumenical

federalism, ethical federalism, religious federalism, theological federalism

RULERS: academic federalism, administrative federalism,
agricultural-industrial federalism, amphictyonic federalism,
anarcho-federalism, aristocratic federalism, bourgeois
federalism, bureaucratic federalism, chancery federalism,
cliental federalism, commercial federalism, congressional
federalism, consumer federalism, corporate federalism, democratic federalism, dictatorial federalism, estate federal-
ism, executive federalism, executive-legislative federalism,
extra-parliamentary federalism, federalism of sovereigns,
federal-legislative federalism, gentlemanly federalism,
horizontal judicial federalism, judicial cooperative
federalism, judicial dual federalism, judicial federalism,
juristic federalism, kingly federalism, managerial federalism, mercantilist federalism, monarchic federalism, new
judicial federalism, occupational federalism, oligarchic
federalism, our federalism, parliamentary federalism, partnership federalism, patrimonial federalism, post-
technocratic federalism, prefectorial federalism, professional federalism, professorial federalism, proletarian
federalism, proprietary federalism, public federalism, religious federalism, representational federalism, socialist
federalism, societary federalism, syndical federalism, technocratic federalism, trade union federalism

SEPARATISM: antagonistic federalism, asymmetrical federalism, autonomous federalism, centrifugal federalism,
competitive federalism, contentious federalism, decentralist
federalism, decentralized federalism, dialectical
federalism, differentiated federalism, dual federalism,
factional federalism, federalism by decentralization, feudal
federalism, fragmented federalism, functional feudal
federalism, heterogeneous federalism,   independent
federalism, judicial dual federalism, loose federalism,
multicentered federalism, noncentralized federalism,
particularist federalism, peripheralized federalism,
pluralistic federalism, polar federalism, polyvalent
federalism, provincially-oriented federalism,
semi-antagonistc federalism, separatist federalism,
state-centered federalism, state-federalism, state-oriented
federalism, states rights federalism

SOCIAL: antistate federalism, club federalism, collective federalism, communal federalism, cultural federalism, extra-legal federalism, group federalism, intercommunal federalism, linguistic federalism, monoethnic federalism, mutual federalism, mutual interest federalism, natural federalism, neighborhood federalism, participatory federalism, personalist federalism, polyethnic federalism, public federalism, racial federalism, romantic federalism, social federalism, socialist federalism, societary federalism, socio-cultural federalism, socio-economic federalism, sociological federalism, spontaneous federalism, tribal federalism

STATE: antistate federalism, associated state federalism, estate federalism, in-state federalism, intercantonal cooperative federalism, provincially-oriented federalism, state-centered federalism, state-federalism, state-oriented federalism, states rights federalism

SUBJECT(ED) TO THE ACTION OF: balkanized federalism, centralized federalism, centralized-militarized federalism, decentralized federalism, federalism by decentralization, peripheralized federalism, professionalized federalism, revitalized federalism

TOTAL: complete federalism, comprehensive federalism, full federalism, global federalism, higher federalism, maximal federalism, optimal federalism, total federalism, universal federalism, world federalism

TRUE: authentic federalism, bona-fide federalism, essential federalism, genuine federalism, meaningful federalism, mere federalism, more perfect federalism, natural federalism, orthodox federalism, perfect federalism, proper federalism, protofederalism, pure federalism, real federalism, simple federalism, true federalism

WITH, TOGETHER, IN CONJUNCTION, JOINTLY: coerced federalism, coercive federalism, collective federalism, colonial federalism, comity federalism, commercial federalism, common law federalism, commonwealth federalism, communal federalism, community defining federalism, compact federalism, comparative federalism, comparative judicial federalism, competitive federalism, complete federalism, comprehensive

federalism, compromise federalism, concentrated federalism,
confederalism, congested federalism, congregational federal-
ism, congressional federalism, consensual federalism, conservative federalism, consociational federalism, constitutional federalism, consumer federalism, contemporary
federalism, contentious federalism, continental federalism,
contractual cooperative federalism, conventional federalism,
cooperative cultural federalism, cooperative educational
federalism, cooperative federalism, cooptative federalism,
coordinate federalism, coordinative federalism,, corporate
federalism, correctional federalism, cosmopolitan federalism, counterfeit federalism, covenantal federalism,
creative-cooperative federalism, federalism by compulsion,
federalism by contract, federalism via confederation,
horizontal cooperative federalism, intercommunal federalism,
intercantonal cooperative federalism, international law community federalism, judicial cooperative federalism,
medieval-constitutionalist federalism, medieval-corporative
federalism, post-colonial federalism, semi-cooperative
federalism, uncooperative federalism, vertical cooperative
federalism, welfare cooperative federalism

DICTIONARY OF CONCEPTS

ABORTIVE FEDERALISM   The Gordons, together with other Europeanists, speculated in a 1974 collection of essays about whether or not the Austrian Empire was actually an "abortive federation." Focusing principally on the demise of the Austro-Hungarian Empire and 70 years in retrospect, the Gordon book stresses what amounted to "attempts to create a federal empire from the Austro-Hungarian monarchy. . . . " (Gordon and Gordon 1974:viii) These attempts failed, however, and the Austrian Empire can only be looked at "as an object lesson in missed opportunities" rather than as what possibly could have developed into "a federal form of government in which each participant enjoy[ed] some scope for the realization of his aims, yet [whose] freedom was always limited by the spheres rightfully assigned to others." (Ibid., p. xi.)

ABSTENTION FEDERALISM   See the discussion of this federalism label under comity federalism.

ACADEMIC FEDERALISM   Academic federalists in Germany, during the Weimar period, were those who rejected legitimate particularist concerns, especially those of the Bavarians. Deuerlein says that this academic federalism ("akademeischen Föderalismus") was bound to fail. And, it would have to accept at least part of the responsibility for the advent of the fully unitary German state. (Deuerlein 1972:186)

ACHAEAN FEDERALISM   This term is applied to an ancient Greek association of city-states. Federal elements were comprised of: (1) common citizenship, (2) division of competence between centre and constituent units, (3) central legislature and full-time executive, (4) executive (and legislative) power to direct the poleis (constituent units) with respect to war and peace, (5) autonomy of poleis in areas other than war and peace, (6) equal representation of the poleis in the central assembly, and (7) lasting character of the treaty which established the Achaean league. Davis, who identifies these purported elements of Achaean federalism, doubts that all of them actually were operational. (Davis 1978:27)

ADAPTIVE FEDERALISM   This is a new conceptual mode of federal-provincial policymaking identified by Todres in Canada in the 1970s, specifically in an examination of the development and implementation of the Ontario Tax Credit System. "The adaptive mode," Todres explains, is "characterized by a change in the policymaking process and the nature of substantive fiscal policy enacted" as the result of "both provincial and federal policy initiative[s], bilateral or multilateral negotiation[s], policy-oriented and technical discussions, participation by both political executives and officials, [and] different patterns of relations as between each of the provinces and Canada." (Todres 1977, from the abstract)

ADMINISTRATIVE FEDERALISM   This expression is used to characterize operations of a federal system from the administrative perspective. Examples: (1) "Administrative federalism . . . refers [in the United States] to programs carried on cooperatively among government agencies of different jurisdictional scope." (Henry 1975:282) (2) In Austria, "every significant new policy . . . is initiated by the Centre, but the detailed application of most policies is left to Regions. . . . One could call such a system . . . administrative federalism, emphasizing the purpose of preserving any area of autonomy at all. . . . " (Sawer 1969:218)   (3) "A federal system whose constitution permits an easy regrouping of existing units or creation of new ones, especially without the consent of units concerned, has been sometimes referred to as administrative federalism. . . . " (Duchacek 1970:240)

AGRICULTURAL-INDUSTRIAL FEDERALISM   Mogi says Pierre-Joseph Proudhon "projected the creation of an agricultural-industrial federation as the ideal means of preventing the misery resulting from the existing economic structure of society." (Mogi 1931b:1114) Numerous references to and labels for the thought of Proudhon appear in this volume. All are indicated in the name index.

ALTHUSIAN FEDERALISM   This is a label for the political thought of medieval philosopher Johannes Althusius (1557-1638). Hueglin says Althusius constructs his society, consisting of the commonwealth and a network of public and private associations, "as a federal building, which gives existential priority to the private associations as its fundaments, without which the encompassing universal association at the top could not exist." (Hueglin 1979:20) Hueglin acknowledges that "Althusius' federalism . . . bears little resemblance to the classic example of American federalism [but] . . . [i]t seems . . . unfair to restrict the discussion of the federal elements in Althusius . . . to the one and only case of American federalism." (Ibid., p. 40.)

AMPHICTYONIC FEDERALISM   (1) Amphictyonies in ancient Greece were "associations for worship in connection with the cult of some god: for example, the Delphic amphictyony." (Davis 1978:13) The amphictyony thus represented a kind of federal association.   (2) Kant identified, on a broader scale, "a 'lawful international constitution' as one 'where every state, even the smallest, may expect its security and its right not from its own powers . . . but alone from this great union of nations (foedus Amphictyonum), from a united power and from decisions according to the will of them all. . . . '" (Quoting Kant, Riley 1979:5)

AMPLIFIED FEDERALISM   This term, along with expanded federalism, is employed by Martin in his discussion of "the new, three-level federal system" which prevails in the United States

at present. In a 1965 book he was concerned to identify "consequences [which] have followed in the wake of the amplified
federalism." (Martin 1965:171) "There is," he says, "no longer
need for any city to suffer for want of knowledge, imagination,
or perspective with relation to any of the federal-local programs" and "[t]his nationalization. . . of resources," he contends, "may be as important a consequence of the amplified
federalism as any." (Ibid., p. 173.) The notion of an amplified
federalism was picked up in a Swiss journal a decade after its
original use by Martin. (See Frenkel 1975:727.)

ANARCHO-FEDERALISM   (1) According to a French source, an-
archist federalism, as set forth by Proudhon, was a reaction to
state centralism emanating from the French Revolution. (Dictionnaire Encyclopedique Quillet, 1969 ed.) (2) Martin Buber is
pointed to by Susser because of "his anarcho-federalist outlook."
(Susser 1979:104) The theologian's "anarcho-federalism" is, Susser feels, "the projection of the pre-industrial 'natural' ordering of society . . . into a dynamic and promethian vision of
freely associating, naturally federated social units. . . . "
(Ibid., p. 105.) Comprising Buber's anarcho-federal society are
"a cooperative communal law . . . authority as an outgrowth of .
. . natural social functions and associations . . . and . . .
[the] federation of . . . autonomous communities into voluntarily
large cooperative unions dealing with society wide issues."
(Ibid., pp. 105-06.) Buber "regards the ultimate significance of
human cooperative behavior in the messianic terms of 'the Kingdom
of God.'" (Ibid., p. 106.)

ANTAGONISTIC FEDERALISM   The antagonistic conception of
American intergovernmental relations holds that "the national
government is essentially imperialistic and absorbs all the power
with which it comes into contact." Thus, "Proponents of the antagonism theory [assert] that under all conditions the States
must constantly be on their guard to ward off encroachment and
interference from Washington." (View reported in Dvorin and Misner 1968:67)   "[T]he national government [inevitably] subverts
the best interests of American citizens in the exercise of their
traditional freedoms," according to this model. (Ibid.) Grodzins
observed in 1960 that the federal government would likely stimulate further improvements in the quality of state administration
as suburban and rural interests which dominated many state
governments sought to discourage exclusionary federal-local relationships. "Antagonistic, rather than amiable cooperation may
be the consequence," Grodzins noted. "But it is a cooperation
that can be turned to politically effective measures for a desirable upgrading of state institutions." (Grodzins in U.S. President, Commission on National Goals, Goals for Americans, p.
280.)

ANTIDYSFUNCTIONAL FEDERALISM   A criticism of the American
federal system of the 1980s, viewed as highly dysfunctional.

Walker identifies himself as part of a group which "warn[s] that an excessive preoccupation with [heavy federal outlays and deficits] in no way addresses the malady of an overloaded system." (Walker 1981c:246) "[T]he key question these antidysfunctional federalists pose" is whether "the emerging countervailing forces of constraint [will] be powerful enough to go beyond the basics of budgets to rebuilding the system itself. . . . " (Ibid.)

ANTIFEDERALISM   This term has had several usages, among them the following: (1)   It denotes opposition to the ratification of the U.S. Constitution. The fight to get the Constitution ratified frequently is viewed as a struggle between Federalists, proponents, and Antifederalists, opponents. Scholars often point out that the Antifederalists were the truer federalists according to then current notions of federalism. (2) In contemporary U.S. politics, Wright identifies antifederalists as a specific set of actors.   These antifederalists are administrators who, when surveyed, expressed the belief that "all three forms of federal aid [categorical grants, block grants, revenue sharing] should be cut back or who wanted GRS [general revenue sharing] and categorical aid reduced." (Wright 1978:269)   (3) Antifederalism also refers to indigenous opposition to federalizing movements in areas newly liberated from colonial rule. "Many of the present generation of African leaders," Franck observed in the late 1960s, "cut their teeth on the politics of antifederalism." (Franck 1968:28)

ANTI-IMPERIAL FEDERALISM   This expression is used by Mogi in a nineteenth-century context. He identifies Goldwin Smith and John Morley as, in the mid-1890s, "the champions of . . . antiimperial federalism." Their expositions, he contends, were "unquestionably a blow to the federalists" within the British Empire. (Mogi 1931a:243)

ANTISTATE FEDERALISM   This term is associated with such nineteenth-century theorists as Pierre-Joseph Proudhon and Michael Bakunin. Twentieth century expressions of antistate theory are seen in the writings of the Yugoslav theorist, Jovan Djordjevic.   Schechter comments: "Drawing on Proudhon's antiStatist federative model, Djordjevic proposes that . . . federalism must change from its 'traditional' form (as an association among co-equal territorial, i.e., political communities) to a new 'polyvalent' form" made up of both territorial and nonterritorial entities. (Schechter 1975:12)

ANTIVACUUM FEDERALISM   In the American context this is "Federal action in an area of national importance, where state action is permissible, but where the state deliberately does not undertake the necessary action." Under what Shuman terms antivacuum federalism the federal government has acted in such areas as pure food and drug legislation and automobile safety standards because the states did not. (Shuman 1968:12)

APPARENT FEDERALISM   Chacon argues that, in the case of
Brazil, federalism has been only apparent ("federalismo
aparente"), whether one is considering the federalism of the Emperor Peter II in the nineteenth century or the federalism of
subsequent republican regimes.   In a 1976 essay ("Federalismo
Aparente e Unitarismo Permanente no Brasil"), Chacon evaluates
the claims to federalism and finds that a more genuine unitarism
has characterized Brazil since independence.   He believes, however, that Brazil is capable of being transformed into a real
federation. (Chacon 1976:107ff.)

AREAL FEDERALISM   According to Henry, "Areal federalism, in
its most 'ideal type' form, refers to the authority relations
among governmental jurisdictions." Thus "the [U.S.] Constitution
establishes the state government as the jurisdictional area
[emphasis added] for the education of the citizenry, while it
specifies that the national government has the sole authority for
printing money." (Henry 1975:281)   Most of the federalisms presented in this volume are basically areal or territorial.

ARISTOCRATIC FEDERALISM   Examples of ancient aristocratic
federations cited by Montesquieu include the hegemonial "rule of
the Athenians and Spartans over their 'leagues' of client and dependent cities." (Riley 1978:81-82 citing the thinking of Montesquieu)   To Montesquieu, aristocratic federalism was defective
since it meant that "a few or one decide[d] for allegedly autonomous cities. . . . " (Riley acknowledges his indebtedness to
Diamond for his interpretations of Montesquieu.)

ASSOCIATED STATE FEDERALISM   This form of union "involves
small states with some necessary relationship to a larger state,
often a former colonial power." (Elazar 1979a:24)   This association provides the smaller unit with internal autonomy and self-
government, but also "the benefits which come from association
with a greater power, without being incorporated within it."
Elazar cites the Netherlands with Curacao and the United States
with Puerto Rico as "particularly good examples of associated
state federalism." (Ibid.)

ASYMMETRICAL FEDERALISM   "The ideal asymmetrical federal
system" Tarlton posits as "one composed of political units
corresponding to differences of interest, character, and makeup
that exist within the whole society." Thus "the diversities in
the larger society find political expression through local
governments possessed of varying degrees of autonomy and power."
(Tarlton in Kasperson and Minghi 1969:95)   "[E]ach component unit
[in the asymmetrical federalism has] about it a unique feature or
set of features which . . . separate in important ways, its
interests from those of any other state or the system considered
as a whole." Therefore, "Clear lines of division [are] necessary
and jealously guarded. . . . " (Ibid.)   About the only thing the
components are agreed on is that the federal system itself ought
to continue to exist.   In the setting beyond the traditional

nation-state, Duchacek notes that "the French Community was plagued by . . . problems that are perhaps inevitable in all asymmetrical federal associations, especially those that combine a highly developed nation with weak and underdeveloped ones." (Duchacek 1970:132) Stevens has become most closely associated with asymmetrical federalism recently. (See Stevens 1977.)

AUSTERITY FEDERALISM   A negative interpretration of Reagan new federalism.   (Its use was first reported in Matheson 1982:506.) This expression stresses the belief that the primary but underlying aim of new federalism was to reduce the level of federal outlays to state and local governments, not to augment the power position of these governments in the American federal system.

AUTHENTIC FEDERALISM   (1) Synonym for true federalism. (2) More substantively the concept is used in a discussion of the ideas of theologian Martin Buber (1878-1965). For Buber genuine federalism involves spirited men relating to each other inform- ally, spontaneously, and essentially.   In Buber's system, the "only men who are capable of truly saying Thou to one another [are those who] can truly say we with one another." Communities can participate effectively in the large associations of com- munities in which Buber believed ony if there exists in the con- stituent units a true sense of community among individuals. (Buber 1964:175-76)   Susser 1979 provides an exposition of the elements composing Buber's federalism. He identifies it as the "authentic 'federalism of the interhuman.'"

AUTONOMOUS FEDERALISM   A short time after discussing the Paris Commune in print, Marx attempt to change the socialist International, which from the start had been a group of autonomous federations, into a centralized association of workers parties. (Lehning 1972:472)

BAKUNIN'S FEDERALISM   "Bakunin's federalism," King ex- plains, "builds from the bottom up, from commune to nation and beyond, with each freely contracting association arising from that beneath it." (King 1982:41) Pyziur concludes that the "main task" Bakunin charged federalism with was "so parcelling out political power that the result would be the total annihilation of the state and of all political domination and power." (Pyziur 1955 cited in ibid., p. 42.)

BALANCED FEDERALISM   This expression is frequently used. (1) One occurrence was in the title of a publication issued by the American business group, the Committee for Economic De- velopment, in 1967: A Fiscal Program for a Balanced Federalism. (See Elazar et al. 1969:194-98.)   Anderson points out that,"Scholars, statesmen, and publicists used to speak of . . . a hypothetical or actual balance of powers and functions between

the national and state governments." A balanced American
federalism "was supposed to have been established by the people
through the Constitution and to be a desirable as well as a permanent and unchanging arrangement." (Anderson in ibid., p. 57.)
(2) Saladin argues that a federally structured system is always
in the condition of an unstable balance. "A federal system is
never final; federalism doesn't condense itself to a 'system'; it
is an idea, 'a political sentiment,' 'a habit of mind,' a principle which must be rethought in every new historical constellation
and--in structure and ways of operating--has to be shaped anew."
(Saladin 1978:407; citations omitted. Tr. Petra Schuler)

    BAMBOO FENCE FEDERALISM   This conceptualization represents
a moderating of picket fence federalism in the United States.
Walker reports that federal aid administrators in the mid-1970s
had a "lesser commitment to standpat positions . . . greater
flexibility in confronting broad managerial and interlocal issues
. . . much more moderate professional concerns regarding state
and local counterpart personnel. . . . " (Walker 1977:17)   In
place of the picket fence stands one composed of "softer
materials . . . [with an] elaborate horizontal wiring system, and
. . . greater capacity to bend to prevailing winds.   Whether
'bamboo fence' federalism accurately captures the vertical
functionalism, continuing professionalism, greater flexibility,
and realism of these contemporary administrators," Walker admits,
"depends in part on one's taste in metaphors." (Ibid.   See also
Walker 1981:128.)

    BAMBOOZLE FEDERALISM   A caustic adaptation of bamboo fence
federalism.   Elazar believed that American federalism in the late
1970s had "been through [its] own form of the Johnstown flood . .
. we have gone from 'bamboo federalism' to 'bamboozle' federalism.'" (Elazar in Katz and Schuster 1979:73)   Bamboozle is a verb
meaning to hoax, deceive, or cheat.

    BARGAINING FEDERALISM   This concept is most closely as-
sociated with Riker.   It "entails a voluntary grouping [on the
basis of negotiation] of existing sovereignties and identities
into a new collective one while preserving the main features of
the previous diversity." (Interpretation by Duchacek 1970:240)
Pentland identifies Riker's "bargaining" model as one of a number
of "dynamic, sociological approaches [which] have been put forward" and which present a "challenge . . . [to] classic concepts
and analytical tools of federalist theory." (Pentland 1973:160)

    BIBLICAL FEDERALISM   Elazar asserts that "[t]he Biblical
grand design for human kind" can be viewed as federal from at
least three perspectives:

    (1) It is based upon a network of covenants
    beginning with those between God and man, which

weave the web of human, especially political
relationships in a federal way--that is through
compact, association and consent. . . . (2) The
classical Biblical commonwealth was a fully articulated federation of tribes instituted and reaffirmed
by covenant to function under a common constitution
and laws. . . . (3) The Biblical vision for the 'end
of days'--the messianic era--not only sees a restoration of Israel's tribal system but what is, for all
intents and purposes, a world confederation or league
of nations, each preserving its own integrity while
accepting a common Divine covenant and constitutional
order. (Elazar 1979b:3)

BIRTHDAY CAKE FEDERALISM   The preferred culinary metaphor
for the American federal system, for Wildavsky, is not a marble,
layer, or fruitcake.   Instead, it is "a more individualistic
cake, favoring a diversity of governments and a variety of programs."   (Wildavsky in Hawkins 1982:182-83)   "[B]irthdays,"
Wildavsky notes, "come at different times and are celebrated in
different ways"; this is "what federalism [is] supposed to be
about--diversity, variety, and not a little competition." (Ibid.,
p. 183.)   "When the fruitcake gives way to the birthday cake designed for individual expression," Wildavsky contends, "when
citizen choice characterizes federalism, the taste will differ
state by state--which is as it should be if we want government to
adjust to individual taste rather than for people to adjust to
their government." (Ibid., pp. 185-86.)

BISMARCKIAN FEDERALISM   The German Empire dating from 1871,
in Dennewitz's view, showed Otto von Bismarck's preference for an
unequal union which is best termed a hegemonial federal state.
Bismarck was particularly concerned to preserve the dynastic
interests of the Prussian monarchy. (Dennewitz 1947:74) Deuerlein
contends that the Weimar Constitution represented a more united,
broad-based spirit which was contradictory to Bismarckian
federalism ("Bismarkischen Föderalismus," Deuerlein 1972:174)
But, ironically, the states had to give up so many of their
rights to the central government that it was hardly justifiable
even to refer to them as states any more.

BONA FIDE FEDERALISM   This is one of many expressions which
respond positively to claims that a particular system is federal.
Thus Dunner identifies the United States as a bona fide federal
system and adds that, "Other bona fide federal governments are
usually considered to be Canada, Australia, and Switzerland."
(Dunner 1964:181)

BOURGEOIS FEDERALISM   This is a frequent Communist designation for western manifestations of federalism.   It occurs,
for example, in the title of a book by Levin and Vajl published

in 1978: Sovremennyj burzuazoyi federalizm. As would be expected, "Soviet scholars of federalism find substantial differences between the Soviet variety of federalism and bourgeois
federal systems." (Sugg in Yarbrough et al. 1972:111)

BUBER'S FEDERALISM   The personalist and existentialist
model of federalism identified with theologian Martin Buber
(1878-1965). To get at "the core of Buber's federalism," Susser
feels that we must understand that, for Buber, federalism, "like
dialogue . . . is based on respect for ones own integrity and
interests as well as concern and responsibility (but not
necessarily agreement with) the larger world of which this unit
is a part. In a very significant sense, federalism[,] as Buber
understands it, is the principle of dialogue writ large and
socialized." (All Susser 1979:104)

BUREAUCRATIC FEDERALISM   For Walker bureaucratic federalism
is synonymous with picket fence federalism.   Both expressions
should highlight "a cluster of concepts that emerged from opinion
surveys [of federal aid administrators] that combined to suggest
a certain view of the [American federal] system." (Walker
1981c:102)   Four themes are said most to characterize
bureaucratic federalism:

--Functionalism, or the administrator's preoccupation with protecting and promoting the purposes of
individual grant programs . . . --Professionalism,
or a deep faith in the merit-system principle and
to the ethical and technical standards of the spe-
cialized group to which they belonged . . . --
Standpattism, or the vigorous defense of traditional
practices and program principles . . . Indifference,
or the seemingly 'cavalier' dismissal of serious
questions of broader intergovernmental, managerial,
and fiscal significance . . . (Ibid., p. 125.)

A 1975 poll of federal aid administrators demonstrated that these
four bureaucratic "behavioral norms were [still] present . . .
[but] they were much less striking and strident . . . " (Ibid.,
p. 126.) In a suggestive paper in the mid-1970s, Garson traced
the evolution of "Federalism: From [a] Religious to [a]
Bureaucratic Ideal." (See Garson 1975.)

CALHOUNIAN FEDERALISM   This is a personalized expression
for the federal theory of John C. Calhoun. It conveys a great
deal about separatism and sociocultural autonomy even in the
twentieth century and outside the United States. Thus McWhinney's readers could easily understand his meaning when he pointed
out that, "[T]he Quebec position seems almost Calhounian in its
insistence on regional self-determination even at the expense of
ultimate national interest." (McWhinney 1965:17. McWhinney's
footnotes not included.) The Calhounian approach to federalism

McWhinney refers to more frequently as dualist. Calhoun is, of course, most noted for his principle of "the government of the concurrent majority" which, he believed, "exclude[d] the possibility of oppression, by giving to each interest, or portion, or order . . . the means of protecting itself, by its negative, against all measures calculated to advance the peculiar interests of others at its expense." (Calhoun quoted in Jacobson 1932:449) Because of the brilliance and intensity of his constitutional analysis, Calhoun is regarded as more than simply a southern apologist for slavery.

CARTER FEDERALISM   President Jimmy Carter did not seriously attempt to put his imprint on American federalism in the comprehensive manner of his predecessor Richard Nixon or his immediate successor Ronald Reagan. Nevertheless, the expression "Carter Brand of Federalism" was used by Stone in an intergovernmental policy and program management teaching package shortly after Jimmy Carter was inaugurated as President. According to this writer, "the President [apparently] stressed cooperation between the federal government and the states in dealing with unemployment, inflation, energy, welfare, and problems of cities." (Stone 1977) Light, writing in 1978, argued that Carter gave a good deal of lip service to the notion that state and local governments would have important roles in determining the ultimate success of his national energy plan, but his intergovernmental rhetoric and his operating procedures not infrequently diverged markedly. (Light 1978:21-22)   Carter pledged to subnational officials while campaigning that he would work with them "to bring about a restoration of a true system of federalism." (Quoted in Stanfield 1978:40)   Yet, as President, Carter referred to "state and local sectors [as simply] the delivery mechanisms for most of the actual services the federal government provides." (Ibid.)   As Stanfield interprets Carter, what he had in mind when he spoke of restoring a true system of federalism was lessening red tape and regulations while increasing consultations, areas which had frustrated him as Governor of Georgia--not altering the constitutional balance   between national and state governments or curbing the growing tripartite dimensions of the American federal system." (Ibid., p. 47.)   Due to the severe federal financial constraints which began to be felt most strongly during the Carter Administration, the federal government now had fewer resources with which, particularly through narrowly focused project grants, to aid and, hence, direct state and local governments.   For this reason a new era in American intergovernmental relations actually may have begun late in the Carter years, despite the absence of any pronouncement to this effect by the President himself.   In his vision for the future of the United States generally and for its federal system of government in particular, President Carter was much more restrained than his immediate Democratic predecessor, Lyndon Johnson.

CATEGORICAL FEDERALISM   An aspect of cooperative federalism which indicates the long-standing emphasis on narrow, functional grants-in-aid to states and localities, an emphasis which supposedly had the effect of sharply limiting subnational discretion in the use of funds received from federal sources. Nixon's "New Federalism, consisting [in contrast] of decentralization, bloc grants, revenue sharing, and income components . . . was launched at . . . [a] time when the pendulum had just begun to swing away from categorical federalism." (Colman 1975:330)

CENSORSHIP FEDERALISM   Without further discussion, Frenkel identifies censorship federalism ("Zensurföderalismus") as one of many federalisms frequently bandied about in the Swiss daily press. (Frenkel 1975:726) When used in official contexts, censorship generally refers to programs and policies restricting radio and television broadcasts and performances and displays or works of literature, books, plays, etc.

CENTRALIZED FEDERALISM   This descriptive adjectival federalism, which has as its aim the location of power in the federal system under examination, is frequently employed and only a small sample of references will be presented here. Centralist and centralizing federalism (indicating movement) also are used. (1) The notion of movement conveyed by "centralizing federalism" is used in Scheiber's historical discussion. He identifies the years 1860-1933 in the United States as the period of "centralizing federalism" since, "[g]radually[,] the power shifted" and "the central government gradually preempted functions and policy-making powers formerly lodged in the lower levels of government." (Scheiber in Smallwood 1967:26-27)   (2) For Wright centralized federalism is synonymous with nominal federalism; that is, in this system subnational units "are governing entities in name only." (Wright 1978:25)   (3) Riker uses centralized federalism as one of his principal variants. His "scheme for measuring the difference between [centralized federalism and peripheralized federalism] leads him to 'the assertion that the proximate cause of variations in the degree of centralization (or peripheralization) in the constitutional structure of federalism is the variation in degree of party centralization." (Riker 1963:129 cited in Kuic in Yarbrough et al. 1972:13)   (4) The expression "centralist" is used by Black in his discussion of "ways in which the Canadian political elites have viewed their federal arrangements over the years." (Black 1975 cited in Leach 1977:127)

CENTRALIZED-MILITARIZED FEDERALISM   The nineteenth century German writer Constantin Franz strongly attacked the North German Union. He said the Constitution of the Union was hegemonial and centralized-militarized and worthy of no higher designation than pseudo-federative. (Deuerlein 1972:158)

CENTRALLY-DIRECTED FEDERALISM   This label is given by Hall and associates to an American federalism in which "National legislators generally distrust the states' willingness and/or ability to exercise sufficient control over problems" and "States often retain some responsibility for implementation of public policies, but are effectively shut out of policy formulation functions." (Hall et al. 1978:193-94. Footnotes of these authors are omitted.)   Criteria for a centrally-directed federalism are drawn by these writers from policy studies by Charles O. Jones and Harvey Lieber in the area of federal air and water policies. When this model prevails "a sharing of power [is] directed, if not dictated, by the federal government." (Ibid., p. 193.)

CENTRIFUGAL FEDERALISM   A federal system properly characterized as centrifugal is one in which diversity is stronger than unity and separatist tendencies are stronger than centralist tendencies.   In an African context, Franck comments that when one leader, Buganda, "fastened on centrifugal federalism," another, Obote, "fastened on Pan-African federalism, and the two, though having little else in common, were at least both agreeably contrary to the [middle-range] regional federal solution to which Kenya and Tanganyika thought every one was committed in principle."   (Franck 1968:32)   While centripetal federalism has, in recent years, generally been seen as stronger within most federal polities than centrifugal federalism, Duchacek notes that "even long-established nations . . . suffer from the pull of centrifugal lingual or ethnic forces." (Duchacek 1970:293)   Diversity of religion would be another centrifugal force.   Sharma and Choudhry posit that "the tendency that creates or may create a federation is not only aggregative but disruptive in its nature according as the centripetal or centrifugal forces are stronger." (Sharma and Choudhry 1967:13)

CENTRIPETAL FEDERALISM   Interaction between unifying and diversifying factors in a political system which has predominantly centralizing tendencies.   McWhinney writes: "[T]he federal system of the United States . . . has been characterized, in the long range, by continually centripetal tendencies, tendencies . . . that reached their height during the revolutionary New Deal era of planning and during World War II." (McWhinney 1965:16) In the late 1960s, Desmond observed: "One of the great currents in American life today is rapid centralization-- centripetal federalism. . . . " (Desmond in Shuman 1968:89)

CHANCERY FEDERALISM   Deuerlein uses this expression to denote increasing tendencies toward centralized ministry direction of cultural and economic affairs in West Germany. ("Kanzleiföderalismus," Deuerlein 1972:274)   In general, the Christian Democratic Union (CDU) tended to oppose chancery federalism, the Social Democratic Party (SPD) to be more sympathetic with the need for centralized coordination both within the Federal Republic and between the Republic and Europe at large. (Ibid., pp. 274-75.)

CHANNELED FEDERALISM   This expression is used by Wright to characterize intergovernmental relations in the United States during the years 1945-60.   He selected a hydraulic metaphor because "[t]he flow of influence combined with the concentrated or focused flow of funds" bring the picture of water taps to mind. (Wright 1978:9)

CHARTER-BASED FEDERALISM   This is a synonym for constitutional federalism.   Chapter I of McWhinney and Pescatore's 1973 study is entitled, in part, "'Classical' (Constitutional Charter-Based) Conceptions of Federalism. . . . " (1973:1)

CHURCH FEDERALISM   Bayang has examined contemporary local church federalism in New England.   He found federalism most common among the United Church of Christ, Methodist, Baptist, and Unitarian-Universalist denominations.   Particularly during economically depressed times, churches in hard-hit communities have been encouraged to federate as a money saving measure. (Bayang 1974.   These points were derived from the abstract.)

CITY-COUNTY FEDERALISM   "Federation," explained in the American local government context, "means an existing county being converted into a general-purpose metropolitan body by the transfer of power to a county from units within the county." ("City-County Consolidations, Separations, and Federations," 1970:12)

CITY FEDERALISM   This type of federalism is evidenced "[w]here governmental power over an urban area is divided between the principal city and its boroughs or municipalities. . . . " London, Toronto, and Miami are cited by Dunner as instances of federated cities. (Dunner 1964:182)

CIVIL FEDERALISM   Civil federalism deals with the relationship between the U.S. Supreme Court and state courts as regards the issuance of injunctions in civil cases.   Koury discussed what he termed "the civil federalism issue" in a 1979 law review effort. (See Koury 1979:659-712.)   In civil comity cases the Burger Court has generally declined to enjoin noncriminal prosecutions in state courts, but also proceedings related to the execution of criminal statutes.   Such deference is closely associated with "our federalism."   It arouses the most controversy in civil rights litigation.

CLASSICAL FEDERALISM   This expression has three principal categories of uses: (1) It is a synonym for premodern federalism. From the Greek perspective, Diamond writes, "Classical or pre-modern federalism was not conceived as an essential aspect of government; it had nothing to do with the nature of the polis or the polity, but was only something that polities did to protect themselves or to participate in certain religious activities." (Diamond 1973:132) (2) Federalism as developed and understood by the framers of the American Constitution and their immediate descendants has become classical federalism. Wilson says, "Classical federalism was a growth out of state, and previous national, experience; it was a reflection of the experience in government during the years of the Revolution and in the short years immediately following." (Wilson 1949:113) (3) Classical federalism is also traditional, political federalism.

CLIENTAL FEDERALISM   Systems of consumer and beneficiary support in the United States for intergovernmental grant programs.   The term's originator, Martin, observed that: "Many important federal-state programs generate consumer interest and support at both levels; and, when these consumers organize on a national basis to support a total program, as they frequently do, it is not far-fetched to speak of a cliental federalism." (Martin in Bailey 1965:172)

CLOSE FEDERALISM   Adjectival expression applied to federal Nigeria and indicating the operation of a central government which is stronger than the state governments.   Hicks writes that, "The Mid-West delegates [to a Nigerian constitutional assembly] . . . wished to maintain a close federation with a strong centre and a larger number of states."   Close federalism was at times less favored by other regions which stressed territorial integrity and simply the performance of common services, an approach that was "effectively confederate rather than federal." (All Hicks 1978:134)

CLUB FEDERALISM   "[G]roups like Women's Club Federations and the League of Women Voters . . . the various Civic Clubs (Rotary, Kiwanis, etc.) extending throughout the nation, have become instruments of forming opinion in the United States that have the greatest political significance, in spite of their nonpolitical character." (Elliott 1928:434)   Elliott contends that, "The whole structure of modern society is associational [federal], even where its political methods tend to run to 'mass democracy.' . . . " (Ibid., pp. 434-35.)

COERCED FEDERALISM   Elazar pointed in the early 1960s to "[r]adical states'-righters [who detested] what they call[ed] 'coerced federalism,'" that is, federalism involving "cooperation between the two levels [national and state] of government in the implementation of new programs" in the United States in areas which, according to these state autonomists, had "previously [been] the sole responsibility of the states. . ."

(Elazar 1962:23) "Coerced federalism" meant "an inevitable sharing of the same functions, with arrangements for joint financing and, generally, some type of federal supervision. . . . " (Ibid.) Far from being harmless, in the view of the states'-righters, this essentially involuntary type of federalism signaled "the destruction of the true constitutional system. . . . " (Ibid.)

COERCIVE FEDERALISM   What has been termed coercive federalism obtained in Australia in the World War II era and for a long time afterwards. Cranston says "the Uniform Tax Case [South Australia v. Commonwealth (1942) 65 C.L.R. 373] enabled the Australian federal government to dominate the States." (Cranston 1979:121)   "Coercive federalism," he points out, "was characterized by bitter disputes over finance, and by the growing use of . . . specific purpose grants which enabled the Australian government to influence State government spending." (Ibid.) It is generally "defined as a system which seeks to concentrate decision-making powers in the hands of the national government." (Ibid., p. 128.)

COLLECTIVE FEDERALISM   Federalisms tend to develop from a condition of being egocentric-particularistic to the state of collectivity ("kollective-föderalistischen"), according to Dennewitz. (Dennewitz 1947:43)   That is, the federal union solidifies but diversity is not lost completely.

COLONIAL FEDERALISM   One usage of this expression was for the proposed system of representation for colonies in a new British imperial federal parliament. Mogi notes that, "At the conference on colonial question[s] on July 20, 1871 . . . [F. P.] Labilliere read a paper on Imperial and Colonial Federalism in which he advocated the direct choice of members of the [proposed] imperial parliament by the people, not by the provincial governments of the different parts of the empire, and insisted that the number of this legislative body should be large enough to choose and form the federal cabinet from it." (Mogi 1931a:237)

COMITY FEDERALISM   "The Burger Court's vision of federalism," Rosenfeld says, "offers states an opportunity to earn a reputation for justice among advocates of minority rights and civil liberties which was largely given up for lost during the last decade of the Warren Court."   "As it effects state courts," he notes, "this federalism has various labels--comity, abstention, and exhaustion of state remedies." (Rosenfeld in Dailey 1979:113, his footnotes omitted)   Each brand of judicial federalism "hold[s] that federal courts should refuse to adjudicate constitutional claims against state laws and state officials" when federal incursions would amount to interference with the privilege and obligation of state officials to enforce their own laws in their own tribunals. (Ibid.)

COMMERCIAL FEDERALISM   "Federation, Commercial" is a subject in Palgrave's Dictionary of Political Economy. (Higgs
1963:45-48. This is a reissue of a very old volume.) Basically,
the expression referred, "as applied to the British empire, [to]
aims at establishing closer and more favourable trade relations
between the colonies and the mother land. . . . " (Ibid., p. 45.)
A principal motive for commercial federalism in the British
imperial context was "[t]he persistent advance of protective systems abroad [which] . . . turned attention to commercial federation as a means of maintaining industrial prosperity." (Ibid.)
Thus "[t]he attitude of foreign nations on trade questions
[would] probably go far to determine the strength of the forces
which [would] make for or against commercial federation." (Ibid.,
p. 48.)

COMMON LAW FEDERALISM   A general federal common law does
not exist in the United States. The Supreme Court so affirmed in
1938 in Erie Railroad Co. v. Tompkins (304 U.S. 64).   As
Bartholomew interprets the case the federal courts have no power
to develop a general common law. There exist only the respective
bodies of common law as developed within the individual states.
"The authority and only authority is the state, and . . . the
voice adopted by the state as its own should utter the last
word." (Bartholomew 1965:89) Recently Rosenfeld took note dis-
approvingly of "Burger Court efforts to remand [Civil Rights (or
Ku Klux Klan) Act of 1871] section 1983 cases to state courts
under common law federalism." (Rosenfeld in Dailey 1979:118)   In
Younger v. Harris (401 U.S. 37 (1971)) the Supreme Court re-
validated the common law principle which discourages federal
injunctions against state criminal prosecutions which are in progress.

COMMONWEALTH FEDERALISM   (1) The "conception of a federal
commonwealth of free (i.e., contractual) societies was being
urged in the 1760's on both sides of the Atlantic by conciliatory
statesmen who hoped that the economic strife between motherland
[England] and [the American] colonies could be subordinated to a
scheme of constitutional reform, but, as the world knows, what
proved to be an impractical scheme for imperial commonwealth
quickly became a working basis for colonial co-operation and then
for a federal union of states." (Schneider 1963:73) (2) For one
attempted application of commonwealth federalism to Malaya in the
modern period see Simandjuntak 1969:290-91.

COMMUNAL FEDERALISM   Applied to Yugoslavia and defined as
"a system in which leaders and groups in local communities share
a greater relative influence over what occurs in society as a
whole than leaders occupying positions in provincial, republic,
or federal organs." (Dunn 1975:130)

COMMUNIST FEDERALISM   According to Gitelman, "In the
Marxist-Leninist perception, federalism is a necessary evil, held
over from the capitalist stage of development.   Therefore,

"Socialist or Communist federalism is seen as a transitional stage on the way to the disappearance of the state altogether--one designed to accommodate the realities of national identity." (Gitelman in Elazar 1979a:168-69)

COMMUNITY-DEFINING FEDERALISM   States, Hart believes, must concern themselves with defining new, more inclusive local and metropolitan communities to promote a more rational allocation of financial resources, better representation, and stronger accountability of governments to the publics they are supposed to serve.   This ongoing definitional process is community-defining federalism. (Hart 1965:147-56)   Probably the primary stimulus for the new community-defining federalism was the increased importance of federal grants during the Johnson Adaministration and the need to make better use of them.

COMPACT FEDERALISM   (1) From the perspective of the American compact federalism of 1787 and its subsequent development, Shaw observes that, "The deep forces of our political life were working toward their own conclusions while the lawyers were debating the nature of the federal compact." (Shaw 1907:26)   It was more common in previous centuries to speak of the American Constitution as a compact than it is today.   (See Standard Encyclopedia, 1860:12.)   (2) In the context of ancient Rome, Schechter observes that "[t]he later experience of republican Rome illustrates [the] application of federal pacts as an empire-building instrument to neutralize those people too powerful or too valuable to subjugate. . . . " (Schechter 1975:5)   In contrast, "the later Hellenistic polis on the decline provides [an] illustration of the use of federal pacts to form powerful leagues (which, after the fifth century, came to be referred to as Koinon or 'community' based on common interest) as a defense against [emphasis omitted] imperial domination. . . . " (Ibid.)

COMPARATIVE FEDERALISM   The study of more than one federal system.   Most succinctly, comparative federalism can be defined as the "'federalism' of other countries." (Leach 1973:20)   (1) Nelson contends that de Tocqueville "may well be one of the first of the students of comparative federalism as an empirical discipline.   His predecessors never went out into the field." (Nelson 1975:25)   (2) Schechter, introducing a volume of essays on federalism, said his authors were not attempting "to lay claim on some hitherto unexplored 'field' of research but rather to remind students of comparative federalism and comparative local politics of some of the essential connections between their fields of study." (Schechter 1975:3)

COMPARATIVE JUDICIAL FEDERALISM   Porter and Tarr use this concept as a tool with which to analyze "the role which the [American] state [supreme] court plays in state governance, and, by extension in American federalism more generally." (Porter and Tarr 1982, from the abstract)

COMPETITIVE FEDERALISM   (1) Corwin observes that the "relationship which on the whole prevailed with the [Supreme] court
[during the period of dual federalism] was a competitive conception." (Corwin 1941:98)   That is, "the National Government and
the states [were looked at] as rival governments bent on mutual
frustration."   It was "the supreme duty of the Court to maintain
the two centers of government in theoretical possession of their
accustomed powers, however incapable either might be in fact of
exercising them." (Ibid., p. 99.)   (2) Long after Corwin wrote,
Wright used "competitive" to characterize the period in American
federalism beginning in 1965. (Wright 1974:5)   Not particularly
anxious about competitive federalism, Wildavsky feels that "the
genius of American federalism is competition . . . Its key terms
are separation and division." (Wildavsky n.d.:74-75)   What must
be done, in his view, is to "create competition for citizen
favor"; if this is done "it may confidently be predicted . . .
that . . . federalism . . . will be said to have a fine future."
(Ibid., p. 75.)   (3) In another federal system, that of West
Germany, Cerny, like Corwin primarily concerned with judicial
outputs, says that the West German Federal Constitutional Court
has "apparently prefer[red] to avoid the concept of a competitive
federalism." (Cerny in Earle 1968:164)

COMPLETE FEDERALISM   (1) The anonymous author of a book entitled The Republic of Republics: A Retrospect of Our Century
of Federal Liberty (1878) identified the American federal system
which went into effect in 1789, distinguished from the Articles
of Confederation, as a "complete federal system." (Anon.
1878:149-50)   (2) As Carney interprets Althusius, the full
(plena) union is a complete federal system; the not-full (non-
plena) union is an incomplete union.   According to Friedrich,
this distinction between the complete and the partial association
"resembles that later made between the Bundesstaat and
Staatenbund . . . because it turns upon whether the confederates
retain their sovereign rights . . . or not." (Friedrich in Carney
1964:x)

COMPREHENSIVE FEDERALISM   All-inclusive, biblically-
oriented federal systems.   Elazar argues that "grand designs
growing out of federal principles . . . like the Biblical grand
design . . . are comprehensive. They mean to provide a basis for
organizing all aspects of the polity and its social order in the
manner of Scriptural law and teachings. . . . [E]very aspect of
the polity is to be informed by federal principles and
arrangements in the manner of the network of Biblical covenants."
(Elazar 1979b:3)

COMPROMISE FEDERALISM   "Some federal states," de Blij
notes, "have been established as a result of the willingness of
the participating peoples to give up some of their individual
advantages in the interests of a greater state." (De Blij

1967:455)   Federal India, for example, "has required a great deal of compromise and adjustment on the part of many people. . . . Nigeria constitutes another compromise federation." (Ibid., pp. 455, 457.)

CONCENTRATED FEDERALISM   The period in the development of American intergovernmental relations designated by Wright as concentrated (along with other descriptors) is 1945-60.   Concentrated federalism would represent "the specific, functional, highly focused nature of intergovernmental interaction that evolved and dominated the Truman-Eisenhower years." (Wright 1974:7)

CONFEDERALISM   Riley notes that "much effort has been devoted to drawing fairly precise distinctions between federalism, confederalism, decentralization, devolution, corporatism, and pluralism." (Riley 1976:38)   In fact, this is impossible.   In Switzerland federalism and confederalism have the same meaning. Confederation designates, in French, the Swiss Union established in 1874; Bund, or federation, is the preferred term in the German-speaking cantons.

Confederation and associated words go back further than federation.   Confederacy and confederate were in use as nouns as early as the fourteenth century.   Confederation, to denote an association of states less closely aligned than is the norm in modern federations, came into use in the seventeenth century. (Cranston and Lakoff 1969:52)   Elazar says that constitutions previous to the American Constitution of 1787 typically provided for associations of states which were what nowadays would be called confederal associations. (Elazar 1981c:58)   The American Articles of Confederation (1781-89) is the prime late eighteenth-century example of confederalism.

Freeman observed that federal governments could be divided into two classes.   The first was the class of confederacies, the second was supreme federal governments.   In confederacies "the Federal Power represents only the Governments of the several members of the Union; its immediate action is confined to those Governments; its powers consist simply in issuing requisitions to the State Governments. . . . " (Freeman 1893:8-9)   In contrast, in supreme federal governments, "the Federal Power . . . [is] a Government, which, in the [confederal] class, it can hardly be called."   The supreme federal government "will act . . . directly on every citizen. . . . It will be a Government co-ordinate with the State Governments, sovereign in its own sphere, as they are sovereign in their sphere." (Ibid.)   In Freeman's view, the Articles of Confederation had characteristics pertaining to both of these classes.   Only the central authority could conduct foreign relations, but, internally, the central authority could operate only on state governments, not on citizens directly.   The German term for "the less strictly organized union or league" is Staatenbund. (Taylor 1911:114) Justice Story said that another distinction between confederalism and American federalism dating from 1787 was that in the former each compactor to the unifying articles was "the supreme judge of his own rights and duties" and could withdraw participation in the confederal association as warranted. In contrast, the modern federation "is a permanent form of government, where the powers, once given, are irrevocable, and cannot be resumed or withdrawn at pleasure. . . . " (Joseph Story quoted in Wright 1929:493) According to Cerny, in the early part of the nineteenth century the state-centered league of 39 German states which was the product of the 1815 Congress of Vienna provided another classic example of the confederal system of government; that is, a Staatenbund rather than a Bundesstaat, or modern federal state. (Cerny in Earle 1968:143)

Beer uses confederal in a contemporary American administrative context when he observes that "the confederal model," as a theory of organization, "offers the solution of dividing the bureaucratic forces and dispersing control over their incentives among several levels of government linked by the contract." But he warns against confederalism as a "solution."   "The American experience with functional federalism amply attests . . . that such a classic confederal tactic is weak and even dangerous in the face of the tendency of professionals to work together across intergovernmental boundaries for policy aims of their own." (Beer in Oates 1977:33, quoted in ACIR 1981c:15)

A modern interpretation of confederalism from the perspective of movements for comprehensive European integration has been made by Jean-Jacques Servan-Scheiber. He believes that "[t]he confederal system for producing integration implies that decisions must be made by unanimous vote and that a secretariat would be entrusted with the task of working out compromises between the divergent national interests." (View reported in Nelson 1975:58)   Confederalism, in Scheiber's view, would be unsatisfactory so far as undertaking cooperative industrial projects was concerned.

CONGESTED FEDERALISM   Lawson and Stenberg note that, "After years of concern and complaints about a 'congested' federal system, a significant and more than likely sustained effort [by the Reagan Administration] is underway to relieve congestion." (Lawson and Stenberg 1982:41)

CONGREGATIONAL FEDERALISM   Calvin saw "the need of federating the self-contained congregations in a universal church." (Friedrich in Carney 1964:ix)

CONGRESSIONAL FEDERALISM   This label was given by Walker to the contemporary pattern of American intergovernmental relations as shaped principally by Congress in the 1970s. Congressional federalism was a refinement of cooperative federalism. The content of congressional federalism is derived from the mix of congressional policies, the essential aspects of which are characterized by Walker as "incremental, confrontational, strongly categorical (as well as anti-block grant and anti-general revenue sharing), heavily conditional and politically cooptive." (Walker 1981c:108) These attributes, "[i]n combination . . . have tended to place Congress at the center of the system and to make it the major molder of the present pattern of intergovernmental relations." (Ibid., p. 112.)

CONSENSUAL FEDERALISM   This is Friedrich's label for Althusius's federalism, the "extension of government by consensual federation" through a continually expanding network of public and private groups. This extension by consensus suggests "the basic solution to ever-widening political cooperation." (Friedrich in Carney 1964:x,xi)

CONSOCIATIONAL FEDERALISM   For Esterbauer, consociational federalism is identical with nonterritorial federalism. (Esterbauer 1978:594.   He is drawing primarily from Elazar and Sharkansky 1978:17ff.)   Esterbauer feels that consociational federalism should be considered as a model for the future association of Palestine and Israel.   They would be associated but without the connotation that one territory was being ruled conjointly.   Israel "is a formally centralized state de facto, [but] on a consociational basis[,] with a minimal expression of political matters territorially." (Elazar 1977a:26)   This conforms with the dictionary defintion of consociate; that is, "to come into friendly association," to be united, without the implication of territoriality.   Consociates are simply partners or companions. (American Heritage Dictionary, 1971 ed.)

CONSTITUTIONAL FEDERALISM   (1) An ACIR report asserts that the American "concept of constitutionalism above all else involves a system of regularized constraints on both the governors and the governed and in the American context a basic constraint is the effective application of the federal principle." (ACIR, 1981d:148-49)   Constitutional federalism also encompasses "informal 'rules of the game' to which all political participants adhere . . . reciprocally responsible relationships between government[s] and the electorate, and . . . a citizenry that is as mindful of its responsibilities as of its rights (whether individual or collective, whether majority or minority). . . . " (Ibid., p. 149.) Thus federalism becomes synonymous with the American system, however identified.   (2) Deuerlein says that the constitutional federalism ("verfassungsrechtliche Foderalismus") of postwar West Germany was shaped by the catastrophic experiences of the years 1933-45, the ideas of the new political party coalitions, the interests of the lander, and the conditions of the occupational authorities.   This extremely heterogeneous set of forces made constitutional federalism in Germany unstable from the start. (Deuerlein 1972:285)   (3) A less substantial synonym of constitutional federalism is formal federalism.

CONSUMER FEDERALISM   Consumers are organized into federations for the advancement of their perceived interests. Hence, we may speak of consumer federalism. In the United States, an important interest group is the Consumer Federation of America which is active in the legislative process. Seabury observed in 1950 that "consumers [were] organizing themselves in federated societies." (Seabury 1950:141)   Consumers are more organized in the 1980s than in the 1950s. However, the current consumer movement is much more national than federal in character.

CONTEMPORARY FEDERALISM   (1) Hitchner and Harbold employ the expression contemporary federalism to point out the obsolescence of dual federalism.   "Contemporary federalism is . . . a 'new federalism,'" they argue, because "we no longer have national and local problems that may be adequately handled by two distinct and independent governments, acting separately.   (2) American federalism of the present day, whether viewed positively or negatively.   A study by the Senate's subcommittee on intergovernmental relations, on the basis of a survey of federal aid officials, observed that "the Federal grant and other aid devices are, and will continue to be, the most prominent and positive features of contemporary federalism." (Quoted in Wright 1978:308)   According to Beam, "Contemporary federalism is in serious disarray.   Like the economy, and like the political system generally, intergovernmental relationships have lost their pragmatic virtue: in many respects, they no longer work." (Beam 1980:6)   Contemporary federalism has no substantive content.   (3) The expression appears as the title of a 1963 book by Pierre Duclos, Le federalisme contemporain.

CONTENTIOUS FEDERALISM   This term is used by Kearney and Garey in their examination of what they feel is the resurgence of the states as political actors in the American system of federalism.   Their particular emphasis is radioactive waste management. So strident are the relationships between the federal government and the states in this area that contentious federalism rather than cooperative federalism may become the norm in the future. These authors' use of this negative adjective carries no unique meaning.   It conveys the same message as many other federalisms in this volume with opposing prefixes. (See Kearney and Garey 1982:15.)

CONTINENTAL FEDERALISM   This is a descriptive term for groupings of nation-states based on continental location. Brugmans identified a federalist strategy for a "world, confronted with problems of peace and security, development and global solidarity, [which] could only deal with them through larger structures such as continental federations." (Brugmans in Yarbrough et al. 1972:87)

CONVENTIONAL FEDERALISM   This term refers to whatever is regarded as the historically or contemporaneously accepted model of federalism. (1) Michael Reagan contends that, "Conventional federalism is a static notion." (M. Reagan 1972:3) This seems not to be the case, however, since what is conventional has undergone continuous evolutionary if not revolutionary change. (2) Beginning in the FDR era in the United States, cooperative federalism was conventional federalism. Gilbert and Smith observed in the late 1960s that "conventional federalism" was "a form of decentralization and social pluralism combined with central finance." (Gilbert and Smith in Stedman 1968:141) This is likely continue to be the case regardless of how much conventions change.

COOPERATIVE CULTURAL FEDERALISM   This concept is closely associated with cooperative educational federalism defined immediately below. Roth feels that it is in cooperative cultural federalism ("kooperative Kulturföderalismus") that the best safeguard will be found for western liberal values. Cooperative educational federalism among the German lander may be the best defense against the socialist cultural revolution. (Roth 1976:16)

COOPERATIVE EDUCATIONAL FEDERALISM   More cooperation in school matters among the German lander is urged by Roth. This is designated cooperative educational federalism. ("kooperativen Bildungsföderalismus," Roth 1973:3) Instead, the theme in recent years has been a pronounced cultural particularism. For Roth, cooperative cultural federalism is perhaps the most effective weapon against state socialist educational authoritarianism.

COOPERATIVE FEDERALISM   This is probably the most important of all the definitional federalisms presented in this volume. To allow space for treatment of less familiar images, only a relatively few sources on cooperative federalism are presented in the text. Others may be located in the bibliography. Many of the conceptions of federalism presented throughout the book, however, are basically offshoots of cooperative federalism. Walker feels, for example, that the creative federalism of Johnson and the new federalism of Nixon are essentially "subspecies of the generic cooperative federal concept." (Walker 1981c:101. Walker footnotes omitted)
    In 1937 Dimock was attempting to get his readers to understand that, in the United States, "Levels of government do not divide into watertight compartments . . . federal, state, and local governments co-operate, their jurisdictions dovetail." (Dimock 1937:54-55) Beer attributes the coining cf the expression cooperative federalism to Jane Perry Clark (1938). The "practice [of inducing the states to carry out national policy by means of federal grants] was so greatly increased [in the New Deal days] that it amounted virtually to a new phase of federalism." "Appropriately," Beer continues, "a new term, 'cooperative federalism' was invented [by Clark] to characterize

this new phase." (Beer 1973:74) Corwin defined "the cooperative conception of the federal relationship" as one in which "the states and the National Government are mutually complementary parts of a single governmental mechanism all of whose powers are intended to realize, according to their applicability to the problem in hand, the purposes of good government the world over." "This is the conception," Corwin explained, "on which the New Deal rests." (Corwin 1941:98.   Italics are omitted.)   Corwin admitted that a "great objection to cooperative federalism . . . [was] that cooperative federalism spells aggrandizement of national power."   This Corwin did not deny: "Resting as it does primarily on the superior fiscal resources of the National Government, Cooperative Federalism has been, to date [1941], a short expression for a constantly increasing concentration of power at Washington." (Ibid., pp. 101-02.)

Walker sees cooperative federalism in the United States as achieving its "high point of maturation and acceptance" in the decade of the fifties. (Walker 1981c:65) To explain the increasing interrelatedness of American governments it was in this general period that Grodzins popularized the marble cake metaphor to make clear to Americans generally the cooperative character of public activities.   More definitely, Grodzins identified seven premises of cooperative federalism:

1. "The American federal system is principally characterized by a federal-state-local sharing of responsibilities for virtually all functions."
2. "Our history and politics in large part account for this sharing."
3. "Dividing functions between the federal government, on the one hand, and the states and localities, on the other," is not achievable "without drastically reducing the importance of the latter."
4. "No 'strengthening' of state governments will materially reduce the present functions of the federal government, nor will it have any marked effect on the rate of acquisition of new federal functions."
5. Noncentralization [an expression coined by Daniel J. Elazar] is still genuine in the United States. It is "the result of independent centers of power and . . . operates through the chaos of American political processes and political institutions."
6. "Federal, state and local officials are not adversaries. They are colleagues."
7. "The American system is best conceived as one government serving one people." (These premises were identified as such in Walker 1981c:66.   The quoted material is from Grodzins in Goldwin 1964:21-22.)

Grodzins's posthumously published work, The American System, has been identified as "the bible of cooperative federalism." (Glendening and Reeves 1977:119) Dvorin and Misner point out that, with cooperative federalism, "Vexatious questions of legal jurisdiction give way to emphasis upon the most effective way of solving urgent social, economic, and political problems." Debating respective spheres of competency is regarded as a "sterile and irrelevant" exercise. (Dvorin and Misner 1968:68) "The cooperation theory assumes," they believe, "that there is no need for confrontation and conflict . . . antagonism and competition between the national and state governments are not part of the vocabulary of this theory." (Ibid.)

Walker believes that although the period 1960-80 "witnessed the utlimate realization of many of the tenets of cooperative federalism," their achievement (ironically) "produced the collapse of the concept as an accurate descriptive theory of intergovernmental relations," although "not as an ideal prescription of what these relations should be." (Walker 1981c:100, 101) This collapse is explained by the apparent impossibility of full cooperation in massively increased areas of public activity. Whereas before the 1960s most municipal activities and approximatly half of state functions were not covered by federal grant programs, afterwards most local and state programs were within the purview of federal aid. (See ACIR, 1981d:2.)

A recurring debate among students of American federalism is about whether cooperative federalism is a new, twentieth-century phenomenon, or whether it is older than that. (For the latter view see Scheiber in Smallwood 1967. More immediately see the entry for dual federalism.) The view that cooperative federalism, even though it long went unlabeled, is as old as the republic has been most widely disseminated by Grodzins and Daniel J. Elazar. In The American Partnership, Elazar asserts that

> federalism in the United States, as practiced,
> has traditionally been cooperative . . .dual
> federalism as demarcation of responsibilities
> has never worked in practice. . . . Governmental
> activities in the nineteenth century, as in
> the twentieth, were shared by the federal and
> state governments in collaboration despite
> formal pronouncements to the contrary. (Elazar
> 1962:24)

It is Elazar's thesis that

> the American federal system has been fundamentally
> a co-operative partnership of federal, state, and
> local governments since the early days of the
> Republic. Within a dualistic structural pattern,

> the governments of the United States have
> developed a broadly institutionalized system of
> collaboration, based on the implicit premise that
> virtually all functions of government must be
> shared by virtually all governments . . .
> (Ibid., p. 297.)

The ACIR feels that cooperative federalism is theoretically suspect. Writing for the Commission, Conlan takes the position that cooperative federalism is logically inferior to dual federalism. It "creates theoretical ambiguities, such as blurring the distinction between federalism and decentralization." (ACIR, 1981c:4) Another Commission publication asserts that cooperative federalism has the negative function of "avoiding any clear-cut delineation of the proper federal role, of avoiding responsibility, and of superficially realizing the status quo." (ACIR, 1981d:6) The result may be cooperation, but antagonistic cooperation. (See Grodzins in U.S. President, Commission on National Goals, Goals for Americans, p. 280.) Sawer criticizes cooperative federalism from another tack. An Australian observer, Sawer found it surprising that "no systematic, continuous cooperation occur[red] at the highest levels of national policy in general. . . . " (Sawer 1969:72) The President met only occasionally with state governors and "even conferences of lower-level administrators tend[ed] to involve [just] restricted groups of Regions at a time, and to be connected with specific cooperative agreements. . . . " (Ibid.)

Whatever its theoretical or practical defects, cooperative federalism is still very much a part of the lexicon of students and practitioners of American federalism. Thus, in 1982, Senator David Durenberger, a Minnesota Republican, was predicting, in effect, further life for cooperative federalism. This was because "the evolution in the political and fiscal structure of state and local government has not kept pace with the revolution in the economic structure of our society." (Durenberger 1982:25-26) Further, "the agencies of state and local government were not staffed by the technicians who could integrate a high-speed, complex society with the necessary capital facilities" to meet citizen needs. (Ibid.)

See Bloch 1979 for a discussion of cooperative federalism in welfare policy in recent years. (See also entry for welfare cooperative federalism.) Breen 1979 uses the expression cooperative federalism to describe intergovernmental cooperation in the World War I period. Maier 1976 employs cooperative federalism in the context of international trade.

Cooperative federalism (comparative). As the most popular modifier of federalism, cooperative federalism has been widely used to characterize patterns of intergovernmental collaboration in other political systems.

In the Canadian context, in 1976 Dyck analyzed the Canadian Assistance Plan as "the ultimate in cooperative federalism." (Dyck 1976:587-602)   Earlier, in the 1960s, Leger took note of "what is now commonly understood as 'cooperative federalism.'" In a critical vein, he asserted that cooperative federalism referred "almost exclusively to matters within the jurisdiction of the provinces."   It was, therefore, only "the new face of centralization." (Leger 1963 quoted and paraphrased in Meekison 1968:284-85)   Gallant said, however, that the time in which he was writing, the mid-1960s, was, for Canada, an "age of 'cooperative federalism.'" (Quoted in ibid., p. 287.)

In West Germany the Trager Commission put forward the notion of Gemeinschaftsaufgaben as a type of cooperative federalism. (Referred to in Cerny in Earle 1968:177)

COOPTATIVE FEDERALISM (or COOPTIVE FEDERALISM)   A play on words, satirizing cooperative federalism in the United States. Walker asserts that, "Cooperative federalism and its many derivatives, in fact, have become cooptive federalism, and the public interest groups have paramount responsibility to help reverse this destructive course." (ACIR, 1981d:110)   Cooptative federalism means that all governments and most important interest groups are folded into the national system.   In the mid-1970s, Baker and associates said that cooptative federalism meant that "states as collectives [would] act or perform activities which they would not otherwise have done in the absence of [a] grant-in-aid." (Baker et al. 1974:3)

COORDINATE FEDERALISM   Apparently very close to dual federalism.   (1) Wheare labels coordinate federalism the situation in which "both levels of government operate independently within the field set for them by the Constitution." (View of Wheare 1946 and subsequent editions as summarized by Hicks 1978:vii)   (2) Black 1975 feels that, "The coordinate concept . . . underpins the constitutional status quo [and] is the most conspicuous concept of federalism" in Canada. (Black 1975 noted in Leach 1977:128)   (3) Cranston says that, in Australia, "A system of co-ordinate federalism operated for the first quarter of the [twentieth] century, where the Australian and State governments were co-ordinate and independent in their respective spheres." (Cranston 1979:121.   His footnotes omitted)

COORDINATIVE FEDERALISM   Without explanation for the grammatical distinction, Cranston identifies separate coordinate and coordinative phases of Australian federalism. Coordinate federalism prevailed in the first-quarter of the twentieth century and represented national-state separatism. However, coordinative federalism "represents the attempt from 1975 [onward] by Australian [central] governments to introduce co-operative planning, to reduce conditions attached to [specific purpose] grants and to introduce tax sharing arrangements." (Cranston

1979:121)   Cranston believes coordinative federalism probably
should be viewed as a later form of cooperative federalism.   And,
it should comprehend "policy and functional co-ordination by Australian and State governments." (Ibid., p. 137.)

CORPORATE FEDERALISM   (1) A recent use of corporate
federalism occurs in the United States where, it has been asserted, government organization follows the model of the modern
corporation.   In a very influential essay, Ways argued that, "The
art of modern management consists largely in discovering what to
centralize and what to decentralize and in constructing the channels through which information and decisions generated at many
levels flow." (Ways 1966 quoted in Elazar et al. 1969:623)   This
approach works, Ways feels, both in business and government.
Elazar is not impressed with the corporate model's alleged
applicability to the American federal system.   In this approach,
as he views it, "centralized decision-making authority is partially devolved to units lower down in the hierarchy [e.g., subnational governments] so long as they conform to the overall
policies set unilaterally at the top." (Elazar 1973b:257)   "This
new kind of decentralization" Elazar saw most clearly in Nixonian
new federalism.   (2) In the comparative sphere corporate federalism generally refers to a federal system in which special constitutional recognition is given to the different ethnic groups
living in the country.   Thus "the federalism chosen for Cyprus
was what might be called 'corporate federalism,'--a scheme once
proposed for the solution of the nationality problems of the
Hapsburg Empire and afterward adopted in Estonia," in which
offices and powers are apportioned among major ethnic groups.
(Friedrich 1968:124)   In corporate federalism "[t]he federal
character of the . . . society is . . . achieved and maintained .
. . by fundamental guarantees of rights or freedoms to particularist ethnic-cultural groups. . . . " (McWhinney 1966:17)

CORRECTIONAL FEDERALISM   This expression is the title of an
article discussing the tangled Canadian system of punishment for
crime. (Jaffary 1967:362-76)   Because responsibility has not been
clear, effective action in response to contemporary needs in corrections has been slow in coming.   To provide a modern correctional system, Jaffary recommends a cooperatively federal-
provincial program similar to that used in other functional areas
(education, welfare, urban planning, etc.).   Even at this point
Jaffary suspected that Quebec would elect not to participate in a
new program of correctional federalism and doubted that anything
could be done to compel its involvement.

COSMOPOLITAN FEDERALISM   Approach to federalism associated
with Immanuel Kant (1724-1804).   Riley says, "legal justice [is]
guaranteed, at the end of political time, by a 'cosmopolitan'
federalism [which] . . . is instrumental to morality in two ways,
one of them stronger than the other: in a slightly weaker sense,
it simply creates conditions for the exercise of a good will; in

a somewhat stronger sense, it (legally) enforces what 'ought' to be (e.g., no murder) even where 'good will' is absent and only legal 'incentives' are present." (Riley 1979b:51)

COUNTERFEIT FEDERALISM   One of many characterizations of false federalism, particularly a federalism not socially grounded. Kuic contends that, "To understand federalism fully, we must . . . recognize federal political culture as an independent variable, for without it there is only counterfeit federalism." (Kuic in Katz and Schuster 1979:9) Without the "spirit of federalism" (Maurice Vile's expression) any federalism is counterfeit federalism.

COVENANTAL FEDERALISM   Elazar uses the expression covenantal federalism in a discussion of the evolution of American federalism. The covenantal prefix stresses, for Elazar, the fact that American federalism is more than intergovernmental relations, more than a constitutional distribution of powers. It is, instead, "the animating and informing principle of the American political system flowing from a covenantal approach to human relationships." (Elazar 1982:2) Because of the comprehensive use of covenants for so many purposes during this period, Elazar believes that "[i]t was within the five generations of American colonial history that the basis was laid for a covenantal federalism." (Ibid., p. 3.) The inspiration for a "network of covenants beginning with those between God and man" is the biblical system of compacts divine and human (Elazar 1979b:3)

CRAZY-QUILT FEDERALISM   Davis said he saw in the mid-1970s in the United States a "'crazy-quilt' pattern of intergovernmental relations. . . . " (Davis 1978:121) A crazy-quilt is "a patchwork quilt made in fantastic patterns or without any plan." (Oxford Universal Dictionary, 1955 ed.)

CREATIVE-COOPERATIVE FEDERALISM   Hybrid of creative federalism and cooperative federalism. Creative-cooperative federalism is defined as a situation in which "states participate very actively in expenditures on programs that have national impact, as was the case in the United States between 1961-1969. . . . " (Raymond 1978:216)

CREATIVE FEDERALISM   The germ of creative federalism generally is credited to Nelson Rockefeller, in the course of a series of lectures at Harvard University in 1961. Governor Rockefeller said that federalism was an "adaptable and creative form of self-government." (Rockefeller 1962:3) Federalism was characterized by not one but a plurality of "center[s] of sovereign power, energy, and creativity." (Ibid., p. 6.) Problems would be solved through the "free play of individual initiative, private enterprise, social institutions, political organizations, and voluntary associations." (Ibid.)   "By

providing several sources of political strength and creativity,"
Rockefeller noted, "a federal system invites inventive
leadership--on all levels--to work toward genuine solutions to
the problems of a diverse and complex society." (Ibid., p. 9.)
    Lyndon Johnson is usually identified as the principal author
of creative federalism. The first reference apparently came in a
speech at the University of Michigan in the spring of 1964. (He
amplified his thoughts on federalism in the book My Hope for
America, Johnson 1964.) His Great Society, the President declared in his Ann Arbor address, "rest[ed] on abundance and
liberty for all." This society "demand[ed] an end to poverty and
racial injustice. . . . " (President, Public Papers, 1963-64)
But, "The solutions to these problems [did] not rest [simply] on
a massive program in Washington." "Nor," the President continued, could the nation "rely on the strained resources of local
authority." Instead, solutions necessitated that the American
people "create new concepts of cooperation, a creative
federalism, between the National Capitol and the leaders of local
communities." (All ibid.)
    For Shuman, creative federalism means "federal action in
areas which have generally been regarded as within the prerogative of the states, but where the states have not acted."
(Shuman 1968:12) Illustrations of creative federalism in operation are cited as Great Society legislation, antipoverty programs, and Warren Court rulings on educational opportunity and
the administration of criminal justice.
    For Judge J. Skelly Wright, the keystone of Johnsonian crea-
tive federalism was "its orientation around problem-solving. . .
. If it opts for delegation of responsibility to local political
organizations, it does so not through any philosophic antipathy
to the federal establishment but because it appreciates that decentralization is often, though not always, the shrewdest
administrative maneuver." (Wright in Shuman 1968:77) Deil Wright
observed that, in fact, the political and policy assumptions of
creative federalism approached unitarism. (Wright 1974:11)
    Creative federalism is "an extension of cooperative federal-
ism in that it emphasizes cooperation." However, Leach notes, it
is "differ[ent] in its recognition of local and private centers
of power as well as national and state centers, and in its concern for the development of cooperation not only between the
national and state governments but between them and local
governments and private organizations as well." (Leach 1970:15)
    Ways, in his influential 1966 article, said that creative
federalism represented "a major turn from the politics of issues
to the politics of problems. . . . " (Ways 1966:121) "'Creative
federalism,'" as Ways viewed it, "include[d] a deliberate policy
of encouraging the growth of institutions that [would] be
independent of and, in part, [even] antagonistic to the federal
government power." (Ibid., p. 222.) Walker sees creative
federalism as differing from cooperative federalism "in its range
of new grant programs, in its diversity of participating state
and especially local units and nonprofit agencies, in its

expanding federal outlays, and in its urban and city emphasis."
(Walker 1981c:104)
Creative federalism in practice saw approximately 70 direct
federal-local grant programs in operation by 1968. More than 200
additional major grant programs in all were authorized during the
Johnson Presidency. While principal reliance was placed on narrow categorical grants, some experimentation was begun with block
grants (Partnership for Health) and regional federalism programs
(Appalachia). When Johnson took office federal aid amounted to
$10.1 billion, when he left, to $20.3 billion. (Ibid., pp. 102,
104, 175.)
In Lowi's view, "creative federalism [is] not federalism."
This is said to be so because, "Federalism divides sovereignty
between duly constituted levels of government." In contrast,
creative federalism involves "a parceling of powers between the
central government and all structures of powers, governments and
non-government governments." (All Lowi 1969:82) Lowi opposed
creative federalism because he believed governments should take
the lead in providing solutions to public problems. He does not
feel that "governmental groups" should be treated as just another
type of group participating in problem-solving coalitions, as was
the case in the antipoverty programs of the 1960s. Special
treatment is necessary because "governmental groups" may employ
coercion and coercion is essential if unwilling forces are to be
made to yield control over the resources which they are employing
for their own selfish benefit. As Henry interprets Lowi, creative federalism was "overly decentralized" and contributed to "a
'crisis of public authority' [which was] antithetical to the
national interest. . . . " (Henry 1975:281, citing ibid.) However, most critics have attacked creative federalism for being
overly centralized rather than for the reverse. In Elazar's
view, creative federalism "fueled the engine of . . . 'concentrated cooperation'" in "a 'Great Society' [which presumed to]
set out the direction . . . toward improving the quality of life
for all by the sheer process of enlargement." (Schechter 1981:135
reporting the view of Elazar) Through the use of "sound management practice, including PPBS (planning-programming-budget-
systems]," there would be supplied "the steering mechanism of
'concentrated cooperation' so that . . . 'through the tools of
management the full promise of a finer life [could] be brought to
every American at the lowest possible cost.'" (Ibid. The last
words in this quotation are those of President Johnson.)
Creative federalism also has been employed in a comparative
context. Deuerlein, a West German commentator, identifies creative federalism as an ambiguous term which attempts to remove the
obstacles set by traditional federalism which makes it difficult
for a society to develop as it should. (Deuerlein 1972:293)
Trager identifies federation attempts in East Africa,
Rhodesia/Nyasaland, the West Indies, and Malaysia as "four experiments in creative federalism, each occurring at the end of
the same imperial connections." (Trager in Franck 1968:ix)

CREEPING FEDERALISM   This expression was used by an anonymous audience participant during a series of lectures held
under the auspices of the U.S. Department of Agriculture during
the Lyndon Johnson administration.   It may be a caricature of
creative federalism. (See Nicoll 1967:24.)   According to the
questioner, "Grants-in-aid persuade the States to go along with .
. . Federal program[s] . . . [and] this [is] more or less a form
of creeping federalism."   Federalism is employed here synonymously with national dominance.   In his formal remarks in this
series, Mayor Jerome Cavanaugh of Detroit picked up the phrase.
In his view, "The monster [so-called], creeping federalism, which
has sparked the oratory of States rights politicians for years,
[was] beginning to look considerably different."   Creative
federalism was offering "new programs [in which] the emphasis is
on meeting local problems instead of meeting the strictures of
the Federal Government." (Ibid., p. 84.)

CRIMINAL-JUSTICE FEDERALISM   Like land federalism and other
policy-based federalisms identified in this volume, criminal-
justice federalism refers to federal policies in the United
States in a particular functional area.   Federal criminal law and
federal law enforcement efforts traditionally have been nowhere
near as important as state and local efforts.   However, in the
1960s, particularly with the passage of the Omnibus Crime Control
and Safe Streets Act of 1968, there was a major shift in the
federal posture. Thus there was a need, such as that responded to
by Feeley and associates, "to gather information about the operations, functions, and problems of the Safe Streets Act and the
criminal-justice federalism that it fostered." (Feeley et al. in
Gardiner 1977:204-23 at p. 206.)

CRYPTO-FEDERALISM   Literally, this would mean "hidden"
federalism.   In this usage, it seems to denote hypocrisy.   To the
ACIR, crypto-federalism in the United States stands for a
pathological condition which "confuses roles, convolutes responsibility, and recoils from facing administrative, programmatic, and regulatory realities."   (ACIR, 1981d:150)
"Crypto-federalists" are those who lack sympathy with constitutional federalism and are unconcerned that "practically all
of domestic American government is now caught up in the intergovernmental labyrinth." (Ibid.)

CULTURAL FEDERALISM   (1) Several scholars have pointed to
the existence of a cultural federalism in the United States and
elsewhere, contemporaneously and historically.   Elazar has argued
convincingly that many of the differences among the states in the
American federal union--for example, their responses to grant
programs--"appear to be stimulated by differences in political
culture among the states." (Elazar 1966:84)   "The national
political culture," he believes, is "a synthesis of three major
political subcultures"--individualistic, moralistic, and

traditionalistic--"which jointly inhabit the country." (Ibid., p. 86.) Culture and federalism are thus joined through:

(1) the set of perceptions of what politics is and what can be expected from government, held by both the general public and the politicians;
(2) the kinds of people who become active in govern- ment and politics, as holders of elective offices, members of the bureaucracy, and active political workers; and
(3) the actual way in which the art of government is practiced by citizens, politicians, and public officials in the light of their [culturally influenced] perceptions. (Ibid., pp. 84-85.)

(2) Nichols writes of a "multitude of attitudes within [the] cultural federalism descernible [sic] during the ante-bellum [pre-Civil War] days" in the United States, attitudes which "were particularly dangerous in their conflict-breeding potentialities." (Nichols 1963:183)   (3) Wauwe recommended for Belgium the creation of "regional cultural organizations." This would bring cultural federalism because the regional organizations would have significant powers in the areas of fi- nance and education. (Wauwe 1971:21)

DEAD FEDERALISM   Davis asks, "What precisely is the status of the 'sharing hypothesis' as a theory of federalism? Does the 'federalism of sharing,' like 'cooperative federalism,' simply betoken an adjustment in our vocabulary to pacify the 'ghost' of a dead federalism . . . or is the federal spirit of [the United States in] 1787 still alive and well, though clothed in other dress?" (Davis 1978:185)

DECENTRALIST FEDERALISM   This was Diamond's characteriza- tion of the American federal system in the 1970s. "American federalism," Diamond argued, "is not, strictly speaking, a federal system, but is rather a national system that is pro- foundly (and valuably) tilted toward decentralization by its unique admixture of elements of authentic federalism. If then it is to be considered a federal system at all, we may term it decentralist-federalism . . . a federalism the end, and hence the nature, of which is no longer properly federal, but rather the end of which is to generate new modes of decentralization." (Diamond 1973:135-36)   In essence decentralist federalism is "decentralization constitutionalized by means of vestigal authentic federalism. . . . " (Ibid., p. 137.)

DECENTRALIZED FEDERALISM   This is one of "several forms of federalism [as classified] according to the degree and scope to which sovereign powers are shared by the central government and the units of the federation." (Raymond 1978:216)   (1) Raymond

identifies Canada as a case of "decentralized federalism . . .
[in part because] the units of the federation enjoy far greater
autonomy than is the case in the United States. . . . " (Ibid.)
(2) Zeh suggests, in the case of West Germany, that the need for
a decentralized federalism for internal political and administrative reasons may now exceed in importance the original
motivations for unity based on foreign policy and economic considerations. (Zeh 1977:488) (3) Sharma and Choudhry point to the
popular assumptions that "a confederation is a decentralized
federation, while a federation is a centralised federation."
(Sharma and Choudhry 1967:12. They question these assumptions.)

DEFENSIVE FEDERALISM   This characterization is indicative
of the most ancient motivation for the formation of federal systems.   But even many centuries after the federations of the ancient Greeks, Calvin was advocating "the federation of [small]
republics for defence and other common concerns."   "This idea,"
according to Friedrich, "becomes a persistent strand, culminating
in the theories of Montesquieu, Rousseau, and Kant." (Friedrich
in Carney 1964:viii-ix)   This "defensive federalism was re-
inforced," Friedrich explains, particularly of Calvin, "by the
protective role of guardians of a constitutional order, such as
the ephors of ancient Sparta. . . . "   For Calvin, "The spiritual
as well as a body survival called for a federal union. . . . "
(Ibid., p. ix.)

DEMOCRATIC FEDERALISM   Merrian and Merriam seem to view the
"American governmental system" and "democratic federalism" as
synonymous. (See Merriam and Merriam 1954:131.)   Elazar asserts
that the "ideal of federal democracy [was] the theory upon which
the union was founded" in 1787.   "Federal democracy," he believes,

> is the creation of the American founders.   It
> emphasizes recognition of human and social di-
> versity as the basic principle of popular
> government, with its corollary of respect for
> minorities and rule through coalitions.   It
> fosters representative institutions as the
> means for popular decision-making, with their
> emphasis on debate and deliberation.   And it
> is built upon the constitutional diffusion of
> power as the basis for democratic political
> organization to safeguard the rights of indi-
> viduals and groups. (Elazar 1973b:246-47)

With this legacy, "Federal democracy is [rightly regarded as] the
authentic American contribution to democratic thought and republican government." (Elazar 1976:12)
But Riker believes that federalism and democracy should not
be so closely associated.   Thus he identifies the Soviet Union as
federal but not democratic. (View cited in Ranney 1966:536)

Rosenfarb also argues that, "There is no necessary connection between democracy and federalism or between a unitary state and dictatorship." (Rosenfarb 1948:199)   Watts uses the democratic adjective as a means of classifying federations into two categories. Thus he says that "among the new federations we may distinguish between democratic and oligarchic." (Watts 1966:138)

DESTRUCTIVE FEDERALISM   This was the late journalist and magazine editor David Lawrence's antithetical characterization of the Johnsonian creative federalism of the 1960s in the United States.   In his conservative view, instead of exercising a constructive, creative role the federal government had "taken charge and, in the role of disciplinarian, ha[d] begun to exercise punitive powers. The States and cities and counties must toe the mark . . . or . . . be denied federal funds. . . . " (Lawrence 1966:108) Federal grants were, for Lawrence, "not just forms of generous assistance but bludgeons and weapons intended to secure conformity by coercion. This means that 'creative federalism,' instead of becoming a co-operative federalism, could in the long run turn out to be a destructive federalism." (Ibid.)

DIALECTICAL FEDERALISM   (1) This is a special model of judicial federalism, accepting conflict and indeterminancy as givens, which supports as a positive good arguments about rights among judges, lawyers, and other court actors.   "This model obtains," Cover and Aleinikoff explain,

> whenever jurisdictional rules link state and federal
> tribunals and create areas of overlap in which neither
> system can claim total sovereignty. Conflicts will
> arise where values identified by the Supreme Court
> are interpreted by the two court systems. Where the
> Supreme Court refuses to impose a solution, an open-
> ended dialogue can ensue. The 'dialectical federalism'
> that emerges becomes the driving force for the articu-
> lation of rights. (Cover and Aleinikoff 1977:1048)

Fay v. Noia (372 U.S. 391 (1963)) is notable for its contemplation of a dialectical process of criminal law reform.   (2) Federalism generally, when viewed in an historical context, Saladin says, represents a compromise between competing views and is, therefore, essentially a dialectical principle. (Saladin 1978:408)   (3) Heraud traces dialectical federalism to Proudhon. He indicates that its philosophical opposite is integral federalism. Dialectical federalism is essentially a form of historical rationalism. (Heraud 1976:27)

DICTATED FEDERALISM   This expression of Dennewitz ("oktroyierte Föderalismus") would have the same meaning as imposed federalism as defined below. Dictated federalism is federalism forced on unwilling political units.   Federalism should represent a situation in which participants join together voluntarily to pursue common objectives. Dennewitz does not regard the dictated federalism as a real federalism. He cites as an example of a dictated federalism the second Rhine Union which Napoleon established in 1806. (Dennewitz 1947:24, 51, 52)

DICTATORIAL FEDERALISM   The linking of the political concepts of dictatorship and federalism indicates that a political system can be both. Thus the Soviet Union is cited as an example of a federation which is dictatorial rather than democratic (e.g., United States) due to the type of "executive-legislative-judicial relationships and the role of the people" in the U.S.S.R. (Dunner 1964:182-83)   Riker also believes that "federal government . . . is not the same thing as democratic government . . . nations like the Soviet Union . . . demonstrate that it is possible to combine one-party dictatorships with scrupulous maintenance of the forms of federalism." (View of Riker is attributed in Ranney 1966:536)   Dictatorial federalism as practiced in the U.S.S.R. does "allow considerable linguistic and cultural autonomy in the Republics," even if "all other matters are highly centralized." (Ibid.)

DIFFERENTIATED FEDERALISM   Zeh contrasts what he terms differentiated federalism ("Differenzierungsföderalismus") with unitary federalism ("Vereinigungsfoderalismus", Zeh 1977:475)   His preference is for the former. Federalism should not be viewed as a process of increasing standardization, but as a process of differentiation, by which the various elements of the federation are enabled, with central help where needed, to achieve certain objectives which the central government acting alone could never accomplish.

DIRECT FEDERALISM   Refers to "national-city relationships [in the United States] that bypass state governments . . . " (M. Reagan 1972:160) Colman writes: "The Kennedy administration was pointed in its intention to deal directly and extensively with the cities--some called it 'direct federalism.'" (Colman 1975:321) Direct federalism is said to be new: "Any direct relations between the national government and local units that developed before the present century were minor. 'Direct federalism,' or direct national-local relations with no intervening government, was the exception to the normal pattern of inter-relationships." (Glendening and Reeves 1977:169)

DOCTRINAIRE FEDERALISM   In the period of the German Empire (post-1871) Deuerlein says that true federalists were a very small group. Their ideas found expression in certain magazines and newspapers of limited circulation. And, their federalism was doctrinaire ("doktrinaren Foderalismus").   They were unable to provide the leadership needed to secure popular acceptance for a broader, actually workable federalism. (Deuerlein 1972:163)

DOCUMENTARY FEDERALISM   A federalism which is so because there is a written constitution which explicitly or implicitly declares the system to be federal. According to Stevenson, there were, in the early 1970s, "in the documentary sense fifteen federal states, ranging in size from the U.S.S.R. (8,647,172 square miles) to Switzerland (15,491 square miles). That is, in each of these states there is a documentary constitution whose terms allocate some powers to the central government and some others to subordinate governments." (Stevenson 1973:235) Documentary federalism does not evaluate the truth or falsity of the constitutional federal claims.

DO-IT-YOURSELF FEDERALISM   This expression was coined by Shannon.   In his (and Calkins's) opinion, "students of American fiscal federalism may well point to 1981 as the beginning of the 'do-it-yourself' era of intergovernmental relations." (Calkins and Shannon 1982:29)   Due to "major and sustained constraints on federal fiscal resources," there is much less "federal ability to aid and direct state and local governments." (Ibid.)

DOMESTIC FEDERALISM   Federalism within a nation-state. In contrast, Kant's federalism is cited as non-domestic in emphasis. "One might think," Riley writes, "that any 'federalist' would want to break down 'indivisble' sovereignty by creating federal structures both beyond and within the national-state plane, and be a partisan of both 'domestic' and international federalism . . . but Kant's federalism moves mainly in one direction--beyond the national state. . . . " (Riley 1979b:43)

DUAL FEDERALISM   To Corwin is attributed the first use of the expression dual federalism.   It was dual federalism, he explained, with which

> the great mass of the American people . . . in 1789 or
> even three quarters of a century later [identified].
> Their experience was local, their immediate interest
> local, and through Jefferson and Madison this
> localistic outlook found expression in a . . . version
> of the Constitution . . . which treated it as resulting
> primarily from a compact among the states and . . .
> required that its interpretation be directed to the
> . . . maintenance of that greatest of constitutional
> contrivances, dual federalism. (Corwin 1934:47-48
> quoted in Elazar 1962:12)

Dual federalism was, for Corwin,

> a conception of the federal relationship which
> regard[ed] the National Government and the states as
> rival governments bent on mutual frustration, and on a
> conception of the judicial role which [made] it the
> supreme duty of the [Supreme] Court to maintain the two
> centers of government in theoretical possession of
> their accustomed powers, however incapable either might
> be in fact of exercising them. (Corwin 1941:99)

The following, Corwin said closer to the end of his professional career, were the postulates of dual federalism:

1. The national government is one of enumerated powers only; 2. Also, the purposes which it may constitution-ally promote are few; 3. Within their respective spheres the two centers of government are "sovereigns" and hence "equal"; 4. The relation of the two centers with each other is one of tension rather than collabo-ration. (Corwin 1950:4 quoted in Mason in Earle 1968: 23)

As Kelly and Harbison understand dual federalism it

asserted that the Tenth Amendment had altered the nature of the American constitutional system, to abolish the unconditional supremacy of federal powers. . . . [Henceforth,] the reserved powers of the states were [to be regarded as] inviolable, and [they] could not be impaired or limited by the assertion of federal authority even under the powers specifically delegated to Congress under Article I, Section 8, of the Constitution. . . . Nor could federal powers be reconstrued merely because new national problems, not originally foreseen by the constitutional fathers, had made their appearance. (Kelly and Harbison 1970:693-94)

In 1859, in Abelman v. Booth (21 Howard 506), the Supreme Court asserted that, "The powers of the general government, and of the state, although both exist and are exercised within the same territorial limits, are yet separate and distinct sovereignties, acting separate and independent of each other, within their respective spheres." (Quoted in ACIR, 1981c:3) Seventeen years later, in the 1876 case of U.S. v. Cruikshank (92 U.S. 542), the Court observed that the American political system featured

a government of the United States and a government of each of the several states. Each one of these governments is distinct from the others. . . . The powers which one possesses, the other does not. They are established for different purposes, and have separate jurisdictions.

The British statesman and scholar James Bryce reflected dual federalist thinking when he noted that "[t]he problem which all federalized nations have to solve is how . . . to keep the cen-trifugal and centripetal forces in equilibrium, so that neither the planet states shall fly off into space nor the sun of the Central government draw them into its consuming flames." (Bryce 1914:348 quoted in Mayfield 1925:89-90) Conlan, writing for ACIR, believes that, "In strictest terms, dual federalism

constituted an ideal form." That is, "The courts used the
concept as an analytical device for interpreting the
Constitution. Scholars used it for examining governmental forms,
to evaluate their degree of federalism." (ACIR, 1981c:3)
  As noted in the entry for cooperative federalism, a debate
has gone on for many years among scholars as to which conception,
dual or cooperative, is most appropriate for interpreting American political history prior to the New Deal. According to
Walker's reading, "some of the cooperative but far more of the
dual federal theory can find support in the [Constitutional] Convention debates and in the Constitution." (Walker 1981c:42)
Further, the years 1789-1860, for Walker, "for the most part, reflected an adherence to . . . dual-federal themes--constitu-
tionally, politically, and operationally." (Ibid., p. 47.) Even
farther on, in fact to 1930, "despite dramatic social, economic,
and governmental changes . . . the dominant theory and practice
of federalism . . . still warrant the dual-federalism
designation," Walker believes. (Ibid., p. 54.)   Vile also feels
dual federalism is the best descriptor for American federalism
until the 1930s and the beginning of a multitude of new social
programs. (Vile 1961:159f.)
  By 1940, dual federalism had apparently been scrapped for
good. "In most of the significant areas of national policy,"
Christenson remarks, "the restraint upon Washington was [now] its
sense of self-restraint." "Federalism," he argues, when "seen as
separate schemes of federal and state power, each protected from
encroachment by the other, had suffered such a drastic transformation as to be scarcely recognizable from earlier textbook
descriptions." (Christenson 1973:118)
  Corwin identified five reasons for the demise of dual
federalism:

  1. "We have fought two world wars. . . .
  2. "We have passed through an economic crisis which was
  described by [Franklin D. Roosevelt] as 'a crisis greater
  than war.' . . . "
  3. Isolationism has had to be abandoned.
  4. Cold War has replaced actual fighting in the field.
  5. "[T]he most wide-spread and powerfully organized
  political interest in the country, that of organized
  labor, has come to accept unreservedly a new and
  revolutionary conception of the role of government.
  (Corwin 1950:1)

  Dual federalism (comparative).   The expression dual (or
dualistic) federalism also has been used in other federal systems.   Thus McWhinney observed that "French-Canadian juristics
might . . . wish to add a [new] mode of classification to meet
the special case, as they see it, of Quebec's contemporary role
in the Canadian federal system--Dualistic federalism." (McWhinney
1965:17. His footnote omitted)   But Black believes that the

dualistic theory is "more than a defense mechanism on the part of Quebec." (View reported in Leach 1977:128)

Dual federalism was seen as an inadequate model for post-World War II European unification efforts. Instead of the "dualistic notion of the federal state," Pentland suggested that "the 'cooperative federalism' model, with its less rigid conception of the division of powers, might . . . prove highly appropriate for Europe." (Pentland 1973:176)

DYNAMIC FEDERALISM   (1) "Although the [U.S.] Constitution confers powers on the national government, reserves powers to the states, and to some degree restricts both," the concept of dynamic federalism holds that

> such power definition is not the sole source for
> determining the proper [American] federal-state
> relation at any given time. There are some problems
> which are of such a nature and dimension that they
> cannot be handled by the states. These should be
> dealt with by the national government and by it
> only, state action being 'preempted.' (Freeman 1972:
> 639 citing the view of Bennett 1964 and others)

Dynamic federalism is thus not a static but "a developing concept of when the needs of society can best or only be met by federal intervention." (Freeman 1972:648)   (2) Zeh characterizes West German federalism as a constant dynamic union process which cannot develop in an unlimited manner in one direction; it must halt at a certain point and go in another direction. (Zeh 1977:487)

DYNASTIC FEDERALISM   In a dynastic federalism the character of the union is shaped by the dynastic struggles which led up to its creation. Dennewitz identifies a dynastic federation as one in which there is either a weak or a firm union among two or more dynasties. The key problems for this federal system are dynastic interests, dynastic borderlines, and dynastic ambitions. It is generally the case that these matters are more important to the dynastic powers than the needs of the people they are supposed to be trying to protect. (Dennewitz 1947:32-33) Dennewitz observes that the German union of 1871 developed out of dynastic-federalistic demands. But he says that the dynastic interests of Prussia prevented the development of a well-balanced federation. Nowadays, dynastic interests rarely would be the force behind the formation of western federations.

DYSFUNCTIONAL FEDERALISM   A recent indictment of the American federal system asserts that, "dysfunctionality has been substituted for functionality, and rigidities for flexibility" in American intergovernmental relations. (ACIR, 1981d:7)   "Contemporary intergovernmental relations," according to the ACIR, "have become more pervasive, more intrusive, more unmanageable, more ineffective, more costly, and, above all, more unaccountable." (Ibid., p. 68.) The chief sign of dysfunctional federalism is said to be an increasingly strong "tendency to 'intergovernmentalize' seemingly everything that becomes a public issue. . . . " (Ibid., p. 101.) Walker, long associated with ACIR, contends that dysfunctional federalism stands in place of the older dual and cooperative models. (Walker 1981c:68)

ECONOMIC FEDERALISM (1) From a partisan perspective, Grimes writes about "Federalist economics." (Grimes 1960:175) Economic federalism included a system of national banks and tariffs to encourage the development of infant industries. It also expanded the privileges of private property through special charters and monopolies. In contrast, "Jacksonian democracy called for free competition as the true economic expression of an equal-rights system." (Ibid.) (2) Miller believes that "the recipient of economic power--the large corporate enterprise or factory community--[is] probably the most important of the groups in American society." These entities Miller identifies as "the functional units of economic federalism and the basic units of a system of private government . . . [T]he factory community operates as the recipient of delegated power to carry out important societal functions. It is the economic counterpart--and superior . . . of the unit of political federalism, the forty-eight [now 50] state governments." (Miller 1958:634, 637, quoted in Wright 1978:26) (2) The concept of economic federalism frequently is employed to capture the ideas of Proudhon, "who advocated a form of economic organization based on groups of producers, the members being bound by signed contracts and the groups being linked, also by contract, to form a pyramidal structure which would organize and control the whole economic life of the state, and so make political organization unnecessary." (Cranston and Lakoff 1969:53) (3) The economic federalism of the syndicalists, who were strongly indebted to Proudhon, had the labor union as "the basic unit of society, with workers in each trade in charge of production through their un- ions. All property would be owned by society as a whole, and the unions (local and national) would simply manage it with society's consent." Further, "In each locality the unions, representing the various trades, would be grouped in the bourse--something like a central trades council in an American city, but with additional responsibilities for local governmental administration." (Rodee et al. 1967:176) (4) Gooch predicted in the France of 1931 that, "[s]ome day groups of each kind [would] federate throughout the country and from the combination of Economic Regionalism and economic federalism the unity of a national economy will be born." (Gooch 1931:112) (5) The most recent European expression of this kind of thinking has come from Marc who calls for "a federal economic system [which] represents a matrix of autonomous units, ranging from work groups to entire industries," which make "free and fair exchanges in the market" and are "sustained as part of a larger social system deliberately and carefully organized for liberty and justice." (Marc 1979:125)

ECUMENICAL FEDERALISM   "Churches," Duchacek points out, "often represent a combination of territorial and ecumenical 'federalism.'" (Duchacek 1970:190) While parishes, the essential territorial units, may be joined in "higher regional, national, and international federations . . . in addition, different denominational Protestant groupings are federated in a World Council of Churches," providing a semblance of "unity combined with both territorial and creed diversity." (Ibid.)

EDUCATIONAL FEDERALISM Without elaboration, Frenkel points to educational federalism ("Erziehungsföderalismsus") among other federalisms often discussed in the Swiss newspapers. (Frenkel 1975:726)

EFFECTIVE FEDERALISM   (1) Teune uses effective federalism to distinguish between genuine and spurious federal systems. (Teune in Earle 1968:214-15) However, Teune feels that "even a very simple distinction between federal forms such as 'effective' or 'formal' results in so few cases that it is difficult to generalize." (Ibid., p. 215.) Rosenbaum, Spanier, and Burris in the early 1970s counted eight nations (Australia, Brazil, Cameroon, Canada, West Germany, Switzerland, Uganda, and the United States) which had anything like a "significant [division] of powers between a national government and local governments that [gave] to local governments any important measure of political independence or autonomy. . . . " (These were the only effective federalisms. (Rosenbaum et al. 1971:318) (2) This expression can mean that a federation legally is operative as between the member units. Thus while the Indian subcontinent was still under British rule and post-independence political arrangements were being discussed, one plan proposed a federated India which, when acceded to by half of the states, "would be regarded as justifying the inauguration of a Federation (that was what Government [the British Government] meant by 'effective federation')." (Gangulee 1936:137) (3) Finally, effective federalism can express primarily a value judgment. For Deuerlein, an effective federalism ("effektiven Föderalismus") represents a significant distribution of power and prevents its misuse. In contrast, a centralized federalism allows a dangerous concentration of power. (Deuerlein 1972:289)

EMERGENT FEDERALISM This term may have originated with the publication of the book edited by Macmahon in 1955, Federalism Mature and Emergent. The volume identified numerous manifestations of federalism in the United States and abroad, including federalism in the political, economic, and social realms. Elazar also feels that an important way of organizing knolwedge about federal systems is to distinguish between "mature and emergent federal systems, including the use of federalism as a means of promoting political integration." (Elazar 1972:4-5. See also pp. 23-25 in this source.)

EMPIRE FEDERALISM   Using this term Martin traces the debate concerning the federal character of the British Empire in the period 1820-70. He deliberately uses empire instead of imperial federalism because he believes the term imperial federation "has come to acquire too precise a meaning, that of a representative council of the Empire with executive powers." (Martin 1973:65) Empire federalism, for Martin, along with imperial parliamentary union, designated "a family of ideas about close imperial unity," the most frequent of which was to let colonies select representatives to sit in Parliament, even while keeping their colonial legislative bodies.   The other two forms of empire federalism,   besides   the   parliamentary,   were   the extra-parliamentary (agents, boards, conferences) and the super-parliamentary (imperial federation, as defined by Martin). (Ibid., p. 66.)

EPISTEMOLOGICAL FEDERALISM   Epistemology is "the study . . . of the nature and grounds of knowledge, esp. with reference to its limits and validity." (Webster's New Collegiate Dictionary, 1979 ed.)   Marc laments that "the struggle against the blind forces of domination . . . and [the] sadistic quest for power has no end."   But, the "epistemological . . . federalism . . . pursued by [the integral federalism] school . . . reveals the same isomorphic pattern that is embodied in American political federalism."   This is true because, "Autonomy is its base and participation its fulfillemnt." (Marc 1979:129-30)

EQUAL FEDERALISM   (1) Davis identifies foedus aequum as one of two types of the Roman alliance agreement, along with foedus iniquum.   In the first type, "[B]oth parties [are] on an equal footing." (Davis 1978:9.   Davis draws principally from Sherwin-White's contribution to the Oxford Classical Dictionary, 1949 and 1970 eds.)   The foedus aequum may be an alliance of an offensive or defensive nature. (Davis 1978:46)   (2) Bodin separated unions founded on treaties into two categories, foedera aequa, equal federalisms, and foedera iniqua, unequal federalisms.   As Mogi reads Bodin, "Equal federation meant federation of powers marked by a diversity of form[s] of government, strength, riches, etc., this being not more than a mere association of friends."   "[T]he one is nothing superiour unto the other in the treatie," Bodin wrote, "and that the one hath nothing above the other for their prerogative of honor, albeit that the one must do or give more or lesse than the other for the aid that the one oweth unto the other." (All Mogi 1931a, quoting Bodin)

ERSATZ FEDERALISM   Ersatz is defined as "a substitute; especially an inferior imitation." (American Heritage Dictionary, 1971 ed.)   Mayton says that the U.S. Supreme Court deference to state courts in the matter of enjoining their proceedings amounts to ersatz federalism.   It does not apply to "a state's efforts to vindicate its own programs and policies in its own courts," but, instead, such deference is limited "to the more benign areas of the state litigation between private parties where the plaintiff seeks to enforce a right contrary to federal regulatory legislation." (Mayton 1978:330. His footnotes omitted)

ESSENTIAL FEDERALISM   "[F]ederalism," King argues, "may represent an argument for centralization[;] . . . it [may also] represent an argument for decentralization. . . . There is no 'essential' federalism which any more excludes the one development than the other." (King 1982:39)

ESTATE FEDERALISM   Federal movements were prominent among the estates of the Holy Roman Empire, particularly in the fourteenth century.   Estate federations ("landstandische Foderationen"), Dennewitz explains, were established in opposition to the power of the princes.   The princes also established federal associations, their aim being to check the power of the emperor.   The Swabian city federation dating from 1376 is cited as an example of a federation of estates. (Dennewitz 1947:58-59)

ETHICAL FEDERALISM   This normative concept of federalism states that "each individual, group or state shall mind its own business, to the extent at least that each should not interfere with the rights or interests of others."   Further, according to Seabury, "each individual, group or state . . . must leave each free to exercise toward others those sympathetic or benevolent faculties which are appropriate to the relation which all sustain toward one another." (Seabury 1950:140)

EVOLVING FEDERALISM   This expression is used to denote growth and change in intergovernmental relations.   (1) Thus Glendening and Reeves entitle one of the chapters in their book on American federalism, "National-State Relations: Evolving Federalism." (Glendening and Reeves 1977:257-84) Hitchner and Harbold find "[m]ost interesting . . . in the evolution of federalism . . . the development of co-operative action by the central and local governments." (Hitchner and Harbold 1965:189) Other writers are concerned about the nature and growth of the intergovernmental system in other areas. Berle, for example, observes that, "Dynamic forces in American economics have engendered, and are compelling, intense evolution of the federal system in a vast area of life [economic affairs] formerly considered outside the range of the central government, if not outside the scope of government at all." (Berle in Macmahon 1955:73) (2) Other federal systems, of course, are also evolving. Pierre-Elliott Trudeau found in 1968 that Canadian federalism was "evolving in the direction of much greater decentralization." (Trudeau 1968:37-38)

EXECUTIVE FEDERALISM   Although in the United States legislation passed by the central government may be expected to be implemented by central bureaucracies, Germann explains that in Western European federations the norm is to entrust to the regional governments the carrying out of federal programs. (Germann 1976:223) Of course, in the United States much central legislation, particularly legislation involving grant programs, is implemented by subnational governments.   Germann says that in Switzerland executive federalism, the name for the European practice, is particularly strong. Cantons have much discretion in implementing centrally passed legislation.   However, because the cantons differ markedly in their administrative capabilities, executive federalism sometimes results in uneven program quality.

EXECUTIVE-LEGISLATIVE FEDERALISM   "The bulk of the legislative power [is left] to the federal center," Duchacek explains, "while . . . administrative and judicial powers [are transferred] largely to the states, with the exception of foreign affairs, defense, and the mail." (Duchacek 1970:270) This is obviously close to executive federalism as defined immediately above.   The longer expression was used in the title of an article by Merkl in 1959. (Merkl 1959:732-41) McLaughlin and Hart noted many years earlier that, in imperial Germany, "in certain instances, the central government act[ed] mediately through the states, forcing its action utlimately by what is known as an execution." (McLaughlin and Hart I, 1914:718)

EXISTENTIALIST FEDERALISM   Existentialism is popularly defined as the philosophy that "human existence [is] not exhaustively describable or understandable in scientific terms." Also it "stresses the freedom and responsibility of the individual." (Webster's New Collegiate Dictionary, 1977 ed.) Marc includes a discussion of "les existentialismes" in his 1961 work Dialectique de Dechainement: Fondements philosophiques du federalisme.   See the name index for other references to the federal thought of Alexandre Marc.

EXPANDED FEDERALISM   Federalism in the United States has come "to be expanded to include the cities as a third partner," along with the federal government and the states.   Thus Martin writes of "identifiable consequences of the expanded federalism, some [of which] are direct and intended, others [being] incidental and proximate." (Martin 1965:171) Basically, Martin believed, "the expanded federalism reflects recognition of the need to match public problems with public resources." (Ibid., p. 172.) The expression expanded federalism has been picked up by at least one scholar outside the United States.   See Frenkel 1975:727.

EXTERNAL FEDERALISM   This expression ("federalisme externe") is used in a French source to designate the federation of entire societies rather than subunits of a single society.

Each society gives up a portion of its sovereignty to a common power. Alexander the Great is cited as an early practitioner of external federalism. (Grand Larousse Encyclopedique, 1961 ed.)

EXTRA-LEGAL FEDERALISM   This expression refers to relations among nongovernmental groups which bear a strong resemblance to relations among public entities.   Berle identifies in the United States "a powerful and growing group of industries which have not come under continuous governmental control, perhaps because through wisdom or good fortune neither the community nor the industry feels need of   relief, but which nevertheless have achieved (in effect) an extra-legal federal system." (Berle in Macmahon 1955:71) He cites specifically copper and steel as two industries the operating corporations in which exhibit extra-legal federalism. Extra-legal federalism, like legal federalism, shows regulated entry, planning, and extensive inter-unit relations.

EXTRA-PARLIAMENTARY FEDERALISM   This expression identifies Britishers in the nineteenth century who favored imperial federalism but opposed colonial representation in Parliament. Martin identifies Charles Tupper as "an extra-parliamentary federalist [who was] opposed to more formal schemes" for solidifying the colonial-Mother Country relationship. (Martin 1973:90)

EXTREME FEDERALISM   Federalism carried to the outer limits of decentralization. Deuerlein feels that the threat of extreme centralism is greater than that of extreme federalism ("extremen Föderalismus").   To prove his point he contrasts the Germany of 1871-1945 with the history of the Holy Roman Empire.   In the extreme federalism, with all its problems, at least the abuse of power is, because of its wide distribution, rendered more difficult. (Deuerlein 1972:289)

FACADE FEDERALISM   Friedrich believed in the late 1960s that the phase "reached in the evolution of Yugoslav federalism [could now] be [described as] one of 'real' as contrasted with facade federalism." (Friedrich 1968:167)   Indicating a belief "that a federal constitutional system needs a judicial umpire to resolve conflicts of jurisdiction and invasions of rights and freedoms," the Yugoslav constitutional commission's decision to try out judicial review signaled that federalism in Yugoslavia might be more than a facade. (Ibid.)

FACTIONAL FEDERALISM   Helliwell employs this expression in his paper on "The Distribution of Energy Revenues within Canada." (Helliwell 1980)   Factional federalism is encouraged in Canada because of the uneven distribution of energy resources, Alberta, for example, having the prospect of collecting in energy taxes ten times the amounts likely to be realized by governments outside this one province. Maldistribution of energy resources encourages intergovernmental disputes.

FAILED FEDERALISM   This term identifies experiments in federalism which were unsuccessful. Elazar has prepared a table of failed federations. (Elazar 1972:Table 5) The expression is useful because it suggests another approach to the development of federal theory, "the success-failure approach to the study of nation-states" of Deutsch and associates. (Citation of Deutsch 1969 [reprint] occurs in Teune in Earle 1968:216) Franck and his colleagues are also concerned with instances of failed federalism in their examinations of East Africa, Rhodesia and Nyasaland, Malawi, and the West Indies. (Franck 1968)

FALTERING FEDERALISM   This laconic adjective was applied to the troubled Canadian Confederation in 1977. Federalism in Canada was faltering, Lithwick and Winer believed, because "the central actors in our federal system . . . have used the existing system to aggrandize their respective powers. . . . " (Lithwick and Winer 1977:44) On the one hand, "The federal government has been intent on extending its powers . . . [b]y denigrating the importance of provinces as communities." On the other, "The province of Quebec has been intent on extending its own powers . . . [to] where it could define itself as different than the other provinces." (Ibid., p. 45.)

FANCIFUL FEDERALISM   This harsh characterization of contemporary patterns of American intergovernmental relations was provided by ACIR. So distressing are current conditions that the Commission "recommend[ed] that the President . . . convene at the earliest convenient time an assembly of key federal, state, and local officials, as well as lead spokesmen for the public-at-large, to confront the symptoms of and to come up with some solutions to the dysfunctional features of the system." (ACIR, 1981d:150)   "Such a convocation," the ACIR contended, "would dramatize that the era of fanciful federalism is clearly over and that the nation has need for more than incremental politics-as-usual approaches to the domestic difficulties that will face us in the 1980s." Basic symptoms of fanciful federalism are congestion, lack of discipline, and faulty perspectives of governmental missions. (Ibid., p. 111.)

FEDERAL FEDERALISM   This expression is perhaps the most nonsensical. Deuerlein contrasts centralized federalism, which represents the abuse of power in a federally organized but centrally dominated state, and federal federalism, which is characterized not simply by federal structures but also by federal attitudes which find continuous practical expression. (Deuerlein 1972:211)

FEDERALISM A LA CARTE   (1) For Livingston, federalism a la carte "recalls the nonterritorial notions of federalism developed in the work of Althusius, Proudhon, Laski, and others." (Livingston 1956:2)   (2) This characterization is applied to functional arrangements among members of the European Community. In these situations federalism "attaches to a particular function exercised by the [supra-national] organization and is used to denote, as to that function, a hierarchical relationship between the Communities and their members." (Hay 1966:90)   Armand and Drancourt invoke federalism a la carte when they urge Europeans to "proceed, without awaiting any hypothetical unification, to a series of agreements which will link groups of informed collectivities to accomplish the tasks set by evolution." (Armand and Drancourt 1968:195, quoted in Pentland 1973:69-70) McWhinney and Pescatore describe federalism a la carte when they point to the determination of Europeanists "to be pragmatic and empirical and thoroughly problem-oriented in all their operations." (McWhinney and Pescatore 1973:1)   In other words, "the building of a new, integrated Europe was conceived, in the early 1950s, as having its reality in the step-by-step establishment of particular, concrete institutions having a high degree of functional specialization and over-all operational utility." (Ibid., p. 2.)

FEDERALISM AS FICTION   This expression indicates that the federal system so designated is not federal.   (1) Shaw contends that, in accordance with eighteenth century understandings of federalism, the American Union of 1787 actually made the preexisting compact of states under the Articles of Confederation "a mere legal theory--a piece of fiction comparable with that in accordance with which the king of England is still the source of all authority and power." (Shaw 1907:27) (2) In the late 1930s, Dimock argued that "federalism creates a fiction. The assumption is that authority is parceled out among the several levels of government"; in fact, "a functional analysis shows that the most important powers are usually shared by two, three, and sometimes four different hierarchies of government." (Dimock 1937:54) Dimock's argument closely matches the marblecake theory enunciated later.

FEDERALISM BY AGGREGATION   In this conceptualization, the units comprising a federation already had an active existence prior to formation of the new union. Hicks cites Australia as "essentially a federation by aggregation" since "the different colonies becoming states had launched out on a variety of activities even before federation was discussed." (Hicks 1978:145)   In this type of federalism, "[i]nitially . . . the Federal Government [is] relatively weak" and "[t]he States [are] givers of power, not receivers. The Constitution conform[s] . . . to the classic image of a federation with each level of government supreme and independent within its own sphere. . . . " (Ibid. Hicks is referring only to Australia.)   Kantor believes that "the successful federal countries of the world became federal through the fusion of previously existing organized self-governing units." (Kantor in Earle 1968:200)   Of course, federal systems might "evolve by a complex process of both aggregation and devolution." (Watts 1966:115) India, Pakistan, Nigeria, and, before them, Canada, have been identified as "federations [which] were the product of both devolution and aggregation." (Ibid., p. 116.)

FEDERALISM BY COMPULSION   The reference is to "unions ordained by external Powers . . . [and] unions made by conquest . . . [T]hey can all be put together in a single class under the title of unions effected by compulsion." (Hammond 1903:454-55) Hammond commented that "unions of dissimilar communities . . . are afterwards dissolved . . . unions of similar communities . . . are permanent." (Ibid., p. 454.)

FEDERALISM BY CONTRACT   (1) Price says that beginning particularly with World War II "the government contract brought private corporations within the scope of a . . . type of federalism . . . founded on the government contract rather than the grant-in-aid." (Price in Altshuler 1968:246) The extension of the system of federalism by contract following World War II in the United States "brought private scientific institutions-- universities as well as business corporations--into a connection with the federal government" which Price characterizes as "intimate" and "active." It seemed to Price as if federalism by contract might transform government-business relations "much as the grant-in-aid system transformed federal-state relations. . . . " (Ibid.) As the grant programs eroded the legitimacy of claims to states rights so would federalism by contract put a damper on the sanctity of private enterprise. This new type of federalism meant, perhaps ironically, that "the fusion of economic and political power" was "accompanied by a considerable diffusion of central authority," thereby obliterating "the notion that the future growth in the functions and expenditures of government . . . necessarily take[s] the form of a vast bureaucracy. . . . " (All ibid., pp. 246-47.) (2) Grawert calls attention to an increasing use of contracts between the central government and the land governments in the Federal Republic of Germany, particularly in the area of community services. (Grawert 1967:159) Contractual intergovernmental cooperation (which may be the source of considerable tension) has become more important than more traditional and more legalistic forms of interaction.

FEDERALISM BY DECENTRALIZATION   See federalism by devolution immediately below.

FEDERALISM BY DEVOLUTION   This expression, like federalism by decentralization, denotes "a process of constitutional 'devolution' from a formally unitary colonial administration. . . . " (Watts 1966:116) "In India and Pakistan," for example, "the achievement of provincial autonomy in 1935 was the culmination of a long history of increasing decentralization within British India." (Ibid. These political systems also show strong evidence of federalism by aggregation.) In Nigeria, "the constitutions of 1946, 1951, and 1954 progressively devolved authority to the regions until in 1954 they became fully autonomous." (Ibid. A serious qualification must be borne in mind. Aggregative processes also were very strong.) Watts feels that federalism by devolution "accounts for the relatively strong central powers assigned by the federal constitutions of Nigeria." (Ibid., p. 117.) Welch also points to Nigeria as an example of a country in which "the Constitution initiated the process of federalism by devolution"; that is, "a single country, ruled in theory as a unit, was subdivided." (Welch 1966:160)

FEDERALISM OF SOVEREIGNS   The political association designated by this expression would be one in which the components have retained, not surrendered, their sovereignty.   If applied to the United States, particularly in discussions of the Articles of Confederation period, it would mean that there was in effect a Staatenbund, that is, a "federation of sovereigns," not a Bundesstaat, a "sovereign 'union-state.'" (This discussion is adapted from Schneider 1963:160-61.)   John C. Hurd denied that the United States was ever a federation of sovereigns.   Even "prior to the adoption of the Constitution . . . the several states were [not] sovereign"; instead, "there was even then 'a single possessor of the entire sum of sovereign powers . . . in the person of thirteen states manifesting the will and force to hold such power as one national State within all the territory known as that of the United States.'" (Hurd 1890 quoted in ibid.)

FEDERALISM VIA CONFEDERATION   An "eclectic, indirect strateg[y] of integration," specifically in the European context. (Pentland 1973:176)   Before a full-scale supra-national union would come a confederation with weaker central authorities.   To the more enthusiastic Europeanists, however, "'federation via confederation' . . . [was] really just [a] sophisticated [form] of escapism or procrastination." (Ibid.)

FEDERALISM WITH A DIFFERENCE   This expression is adapted from an article entitled "Federation with a Difference" published in Canada late in 1978. (Logan 1978)   The author, Robert K. Logan, said that the terms of the Canadian federation almost certainly would be changed.   Personally, he favored a new division of federal and provincial powers and "a new federalism [which takes] . . . into account in a more realistic way, the role of urban centres which did not exist when the BNA [British North America Act] was drafted." (Ibid., p. 23.)   "Federalism with a difference" was a middle option between the Quebec-preferred sovereignty-association and Canamerican (Canadian-American) union supported by some western Canadians.

FEDERALISM WITHOUT WASHINGTON   In a 1949 task force study prepared by Morton Grodzins for the Council of State Governments, which was under contract with the Hoover Commission, the "increasing effort among the States, acting on their own, to coordinate common activities" was identified as "federalism without Washington." (U.S. Senate 1949:43) Grodzins pointed to these efforts as generally "successful alternatives to National-State administration" which "signif[ied] an increasing appreciation of the flexibility of State-to-State relations in the Federal structure." (Ibid.) Particularly important were interstate compacts, uniform laws, reciprocal legislation, and administrative collaboration. In American Federalism: A View from the States, Elazar discussed "the growing routinization of interstate relationships that are not routed through Washington and which acts as a counterbalance to federal activity." These patterns of routinized interstate relationships he treated under the heading, "Federalism without Washington." (Elazar 1966:158ff.) A section entitled "federalism without Washington" which discusses interstate compacts appears in Elazar et al. 1969:388-414.

FEDERAL-LEGISLATIVE FEDERALISM   In West Germany, "[b]ecause the federal government has not established its own field agencies, the Lander administer the rules, initiated by the federal cabinet and enacted by the federal parliament, with their own local agencies, personnel, and funds." (Duchacek 1970:271) The more familiar term for this system is executive-legislative federalism. For Duchacek this system has merit because it "entails minimum inteference in the long-established structures and practices" of the Lander.

FEUDAL FEDERALISM   (1) In the United States feudal federalism has been used in a figurative sense. Wright likes the metaphor feudal federalism because it emphasizes "not only the degree of autonomy that . . . program specialists have from policy control by political generalists, but also the separateness and independence that one program has from another." Feudal federalism captures the "lack of horizontal linkages [which] prompts interprogram, interprofessional and interagency competition." (Wright 1974:15)   (2) When this expression is applied retrospectively to the Middle Ages it would refer to decentralized political systems in which counts and dukes on their separate fiefs exercised the principal political powers and central authorities were very weak. (3) When applied to political systems of modern times feudal federalism refers to undemocratic expressions of territorial pluralism. Elazar cites Latin American federalism as "the primary modern manifestation of feudalistic federalism with jefes and caudillos replacing counts and dukes." (Elazar 1972:17) (3) Most recently the label feudal federation has been applied to the "definitely feudal rather than democratic . . . federation of the United Arab Emirates." (Hicks 1978:14)

FINANCIAL FEDERALISM   See the more heavily used term
fiscal federalism below. Martin chooses financial federalism to
refer to "the labyrinth of arrangements by which federal-state
activities are financed" in the United States. (Martin in Bailey
1965:171) Leach also refers to the "'federalism' of finances."
(Leach 1973:18-19)

FISCAL FEDERALISM   "In essence," Henry says, "fiscal
federalism . . . is the granting of funds by one government to
another; the uses to which such funds are put may be specified by
the grantor, or the money may be given in the form of grants with
no strings attached, allowing the recipient to use the funds in
any way desired." (Henry 1975:282. All special emphases omitted)
Fiscal federalism or related expressions have long been in use.
Thus, as distantly as 1892, a book was published with the title,
The Fiscal Federation of the Empire (Medley). This entry cannot
treat in depth all of the instruments of fiscal federalism. The
effort here will be principally to identify the contexts in which
the expression fiscal federalism has been employed. The
bibliography suggests sources for further reading in fiscal
federalism.
     Break observes that fiscal federalism began in the United
States when the new federal government under the Constitution assumed the old state Revolutionary War debts. He believes that
"[t]he debt assumption bargain . . . was the first bold step
taken toward the exercise of federalism within a community of
states far more accustomed to the bachelor condition of semi-
autonomous confederation than to the married one of federal union." (Break, n.d.:12)
     The foremost fiscal resource of the federal government dur-
ing the nineteenth century was the public domain. It, therefore,
"serve[d] as the principal instrument of fiscal federalism"; that
is, "land grants . . . perform[ed] the same function in the
nineteenth century that money grants were to do in the
twentieth." (Ibid., p. 4.)
     In the period from 1914 to 1917 three important national
grant programs were established in the areas of vocational education, agricultural extension, and highways.
     In the New Deal, James notes, "a large number of new and
very significant grant-in-aid programs . . . expanded the scope
and intensity of intergovernmental relationships . . . [and
bound] together national, state and local administrative agencies
within functional categories on a continuing basis . . . " (James
1975:2-3) Lerner believes that, "With the Great Depression the
breakdown of local finances led to a system of direct Federal aid
to local units which transformed the whole power gridiron."
(Lerner 1957:402)
     Beginning in 1964 there was "a decade of innovation easily
comparable and arguably more important than . . . previous periods . . . more than 240 new categorical grant programs . . . the
extensive innovations in extending participation involving

citizen participation requirements, community corporations and
public-private sharing . . . new strategies for categorical grant
coordination represented by the Demonstration [model] Cities . .
. and Partnership for Health [block grant] Act[s]. . . . " (James
1975:2-3)
    Elazar identified numerous instruments of fiscal federalism
in a 1966 publication, including the following: (1) grants-in-
aid, (2) shared revenues, (3) direct payments to individuals, (4)
payments to states and localities for discharging federal responsibilities, and (5) grants and contracts awarded on similar
terms to public and private applicants. (Elazar 1966:68-72)
    Sneed pointed in the mid-1970s to four features of the
categorical system for "allocating federal funds to meet local
needs," which, he noted, "have frequently been mentioned as
impediments to efficient resources allocation":

    [1] the increasing number of more narrowly focused
    programs . . . [2] The increasing complexity of the
    funding system . . . [3] The growth of functional
    bureaucracies that are relatively independent of
    locally elected officials . . . [4] The development of
    community based agencies [which,] although a source of
    change in local systems--has made local policy making
    and planning more difficult and has diffused accounta-
    bility for program administration. (Sneed in Sneed and
    Waldhorn 1975:1-2)

    Corwin stated that cooperative federalism "rest[ed] on the
superior fiscal resources of the National Government." (Corwin
1941:102)   As DeGrove views the 1960s and 1970s he sees "[t]he
dominant theme of fiscal federalism [as] . . . increasing federal
response," grounded in this apparently growing fiscal superiority, "to state and local needs."   Most recently, however,
federal grants as a percentage of state and local expenditures
have been declining.   The high point came in 1978 when federal
grants amounted to 26.7 percent of state and local expenditures.
It is important to note that this high point occurred before the
advent of Reagan new federalism.   As DeGrove interprets his data,
they "show that the Reagan administration initiatives [did] not
reverse trends in the general direction of fiscal federalism."
(All DeGrove 1982:76)   Calkins and Shannon suggested early in
1982 that future years might well "be marked by major and sustained constraints on federal fiscal resources with a consequent
reduction in federal ability to aid and direct state and local
governments." (Calkins and Shannon 1982:99)
    For some modern scholars, fiscal federalism is synonymous
with rational choice theory.   Their emphasis is almost solely on
public economic or fiscal affairs.   (For a contrary interpretation see ACIR, 1981c:23, n. 80.)
    Fiscal federalism is also utilized in discussions of other
federal systems.   Thus Hicks notes that "tax sharing is the
keynote of German fiscal federalism," although a number of
specific grants are also employed. (Hicks 1978:192)

General treatments of fiscal federalism listed in the bibliography include Oates 1972, Musgrave 1965 and 1969, Hellerstein 1968, ACIR 1975, Mueller 1971, and Break 1980. Warner 1975 examines fiscal federalism in the specific field of health care.

FLEXIBLE FEDERALISM   This alliterative eye-catcher was used in the subtitle of a 1979 book on Canadian federalism, Canada: Flexible Federalism or Fractured Nation? (Rawlyk et al. 1979) In the nineteenth century, "The Fathers of [the Canadian] Confederation [had] faced a major hurdle in forging a new nation in British North America; how to overcome the forces of disunion and create one nation out of several different colonies." (Ibid., p. xii.) Now, the major dilemma was how to deal with the question of regionalism and to provide for a "flexible federalism" while maintaining national unity.

FLOWERING FEDERALISM   This expression is hesitantly put forward by Wright in an "attempt to capture the elaborate, complex, and intricate features" of intergovernmental relations as practiced in the United States in which Lyndon B. Johnson was President, particularly the mid-1960s. (Wright 1974:11)

FLYPAPER FEDERALISM   The growth of federal restraints on American state and city recipients of federal grants is labeled flypaper federalism by David Walker, Assistant Director of ACIR. He explains that states and localities welcome federal money but "before you are through, you are in the middle of all sorts of side effects. There are more and more things you get stuck to." (Quoted in Peirce and Hamilton 1981:1637)

FOCUSED FEDERALISM   Another alliterative device of Wright. Its meaning is identical with channeled federalism. Its approximate climax period was 1945-60, during which time the principal problems perceived were programmatic and capital project-oriented and the chief norms of IGR participants were professionalism, objectivity, neutrality, and functionalism.   The main IGR mechanisms during the period of focused federalism (more generally referred to by Wright as concentrated federalism) were categorical grants and service standards. (Wright 1974:5)

FORMAL FEDERALISM   This expression usually refers to the constitutional arrangements which identify a particular political system as assertedly federal.   The United States is usually labeled an actual as well as a formal federalism. But Michael Reagan argues that "the one practical administrative consequence of formal federalism" in the United States is "the inability of federal officials to fire recalcitrant state or local employees." (M. Reagan 1972:148)   Most scholars probably would see more consequences of formal federalism, and even Reagan admits that "formal federalism . . . indirectly maintain[s] a base for local political strength . . . since political parties revolve around offices, and states provide offices to be filled by election rather than by national government appointments. . . . " (Ibid., p. 158.) The Soviet Union is frequently identified as only a formal federal system. (Teune in Earle 1968:214-15)

FRAGMENTED FEDERALISM   (1) This expression has been used as a synonym for picket fence federalism. (Wright 1974:11)   (2) It has also been applied to interlocal relations, particularly in metropolitan areas in the United States. (See Glendening and Reeves, Chapter 9, "Interlocal Relations: Fragmented Federalism," pp. 285-309.)   Fragmented federalism accurately captures the reality that "the local system of government is the most fragmented part of the federal system." (Ibid., p. 291.)

FREE FEDERALISM   (1) Refers to the ancient Greek context of federalism.   The expression pertains to a union of previously independent states which retain most of their independence.   It is the opposite of the situation in which one member of a federation exercises hegemony over "client and dependent cities" in the union.   Riley cites Montesquieu's approval of this form of federalism. (Riley 1979b:81-82)   (2) On a broader scale, Kant was supportive of a "world organization . . . worked out in terms of sovereignty, in terms of a free federation of corporate bodies voluntarily obeying international law. . . . " (Riley 1979a:9)

FRIGHTENING FEDERALISM   This alliterative expression was made when President Reagan gave the major enunciation of his new federalism initiative in his 1982 state of the Union speech.   New York Demoratic Congressman Mario Biaggi asserted that the United States had gone "from the New Deal to the Great Society and [was] now [at the stage of] Frightening Federalism." (Birmingham News, January 27, 1982, p. 8A.)

FRUITCAKE FEDERALISM   One of the successors to the layer and marblecakes.   Wildavsky's description of current American intergovernmental relations is a "'mishmash' which [he] calls 'fruitcake federalism' [because it is] bogged down in governmental plums and puddings. . . . " (Wildavsky n.d.:10) Wildavsky prefers the fruitcake metaphor because of "the symbolic sense of being bogged down, congealed, suffocated, sodden and shapeless." (Ibid., p. 51.)

FULL FEDERALISM   A federal system in which member states have limited their sovereignty and in which the central government is capable through its agencies of performing multiple functions.   (1) Full federalism is contrasted with limited federalism in the case of Europe where, in the post-World War II period, "sovereign powers . . . [were] transferred in part[.] [T]he [new] Communities [were] limited federations to the extent of their sovereign powers." (Hay 1966:89)   (2) Friedrich sees in Althusius a "distinction between the full and the not-full confederation [which] resembles that later made between the Bundesstaat and Staatenbund, between the federal and confederal union." (Friedrich in Carney 1964:x) The distinction "turns upon whether the confederates retain their sovereign rights, their jura majestatis, or not." (Ibid.)

FUNCTIONAL FEDERALISM Functional federalism could relate to the methodology used to study federalism. Thus, in the American context, Dimock says that "a functional analysis shows that the most important powers are usually shared by two, three, and sometimes four different hierarchies of government." (Dimock 1937:54)

Anderson used the expression "functional federalism" in 1946 in a discussion of the evolution of cooperative functional relationships between national and subnational governments. (See Anderson 1946:1-16.) From the perspective of the mid-1940s Anderson cited the decade 1933-43 as the peak period for cooperative national, state, and local action: "To relieve distress and unemployment and to promote new measures for the general welfare, national, state, and local governments worked together as never before." (Ibid., p. 14.)

For Rosenfarb functional federalism meant the combination of "centralized direction" and "local participation." What was needed, in his view, was a drastic revision of the American federal system to permit a "proper rationalization of administration in terms of centralized planning, direction, and supervision, with a certain measure of decentralized autonomy in execution," since this could only "be accomplished . . . when the central authority has control over the circumference of power." (Rosenfarb 1948:199-200)

Michael Reagan identifies as an illustration of "a kind of functional federalism" the "alliances developed between functional professionals working in . . . local CAPS [community action programs in the Johnson War on Poverty] and in OEO [Office of Economic Opportunity] headquarters--alliances that constituted . . . a conscious alternative to the predominantly status quo orientation of the regular government structures under the control of local elites." (M. Reagan 1972:70)

Walker asserted in 1981 that "a new functional theory [of federalism was] needed to provide the conceptual means of narrowing the gap between intergovernmental practices and principles." This new theory of functional federalism

> would focus on the functions of government, their
> funding, the functionality of the system, the sharing
> of some . . . servicing obligations, parity of the
> partners, the need for strong territorial repre-
> sentation in Washington, and the significance of
> constraining legislative and party procedures and
> processes. . . . At the same time, it would empha-
> size that there are necessarily limits to sharing,
> to the extent of intergovernmental penetration,
> to ignoring structural and constitutional
> issues. . . . (Walker 1981c:260)

From a comparative perspective, Young says that "Federalism is a form of government of which the 'federating' function is to develop a central governmental authority and administration in cases where the absence of one or more of these factors rules out a real national government" while "the federalizing function . . . is to distribute governmental authority and decentralize administration. . . . " (Young 1941:13-14)

Cooperative and functional federalism were viewed as synonymous by Raymond: "Cooperative or functional federalism," he wrote, were "forms of federalism [in which] the central government shares power extensively with the units of the federation as well as with the local governments (e.g., the Federal Republic of Germany). . . . " (Raymond 1978:216)

Zylstra believes that, "Functional federalism is the heart of [Harold] Laski's political pluralism." Laski developed his notion of functional federalism "in terms of the relation between the state and the economic 'groups' of society." (Zylstra 1968:77) It culminated in "a federalism in which the powers represented are not [primarily] areas but functions." (Ibid., p. 79.)

Nongovernmental groups are functional federations. Thus Duchacek notes that, "[F]unctional federations are often so grouped as to represent extensions of political parties into different personal fields." The French labor group Confederation generale du travail, a functional federation, traditionally has been linked to the Communist party. (Duchacek 1970:189-90)

FUNCTIONAL FEUDAL FEDERALISM   A figurative expression which points to the fact that conditional grants in the United States "have a functional focus . . . [and] engender a powerful programmatic emphasis among the specialists in any field receiving grants." (Wright 1978:145)

FUSED FEDERALISM   A metaphor used by Wright to picture federalism in the United States during the Johnson Administration. "The ties between national-state and state-local sectors [were] broad and weld[ed] [that is, fused] the segments into closedly linked systems." (Wright 1974:11) But, Wright believes, there may have been only the "superficial appearance of fusion." (Ibid.) Or, it may have been an accurate descriptor for some areas but inaccurate for others, so diverse were the intergovernmental fiscal and other links.

FUSED-FOLIATED FEDERALISM   Wright's combination of his fused and flowering metaphors for describing American federalism in the Lyndon Johnson era (1960s). Wright comments that President Johnson's Great Society ideas indicated his preference for "centralized objective-setting." (Wright 1974:11) "Fused" points to the welding of intergovernmental participants "into a closely linked system," "foliated" to the "elaborate, complex, and intricate features of IGR that developed in this phase." (Ibid.)

FUTILITARIAN FEDERALISM   An alliterative reference to the allegedly unsatisfactory character of current American inter-governmental relations. Walker argues that "citizens everywhere find themselves in [a quandary] as a result of the dysfunctional, if not futilitarian, form of federalism that now prevails." (Walker 1981:100)   "Futilitarian" is defined generally as "the view that human endeavor is futile," i.e., to no avail. (American Heritage Dictionary, 1971 ed.)

GARRISON FEDERALISM   This is apparently a label for such federal forms as existed during the Hitler period in Germany. It denotes extreme militarism in which the dominant operatives were soldiers with spit-polish shines on their jack-boots. (See Deuerlein 1972:9.)

GELATINOUS MASS FEDERALISM   As David Walker observed "a major expansion of eligibles (for federal funds)" in the late 1970s in the United States he was prompted to describe "the federal system as a 'gelatinous mass . . . oozing, slithering, squishing [in the] ways in which the jurisdictions are apparently interrelated [but] do not interrelate . . . in any coherent fashion whatsoever.'" Much of the blame for gelatinous mass federalism could be placed on "congressmen 'playing neighborhood councilmen' . . . [who] add programs and specificity to make for a messier gelatinous mass.'" ("Fiscal Restraint or Fiscal Paralysis," 1979:346)   In this situation in which governmental jurisdictions are steadily more indistinct, "functions float between levels of government [and] even government managers lose track of who's in charge in any area." (Peirce 1980:7 quoting Walker)

GENTLEMANLY FEDERALISM   Gentlemanly Federalist is a Parrington characterization of surviving adherents of the Federalist party in the United States. "Gentlemanly Federalists" were identified by their "lingering prejudices in favor of rank," strains both of Arminianism and the older Calvinism, and hostility "to all democratic Jacobinism." (Parrington II, 1927:366-67)   The "gentlemanly Federalists [were representative] . . . of a stately old order . . . [which was set against] a somewhat bumptious new. . . . " (Ibid., p. 367.)

GENUINE FEDERALISM   (1) Actually federal, not spurious. Porter says John Stuart Mill recognized as a "genuine federal state" that entity in which "the federal state . . . [has] power to act directly on individual citizens as in the United States and Switzerland. . . . " (Porter 1977:111,113)   (2) In 1951, Wheare identified only the United States, Canada, Switzerland, and Australia as genuine federal states. (Cited in Davis 1978:218)   Contrasting genuine federalism with modern rational choice theory, Timothy Conlan asserts:

[G]enuine federalism may be inimical to rational

choice theory. The fixed jurisdictional boundaries and rigid constitutionalism inherent to
[genuine] federalism are inconsistent with the
precepts of rational choice theory [which] . . .
[require] the easy creation of new jurisdictions
and the simple alteration or elimination of
established ones in response to constantly changing conditions of economic development
externalities and individual preferences.
(ACIR, 1981c:13)

GEOGRAPHICAL FEDERALISM   Federalism conceived of as a
"geographical or territorial representation of interests." (Vile
1961:36-37, quoted in Hay 1966:90-91. Vile says that in the United States federalism generally has not been conceived of in a
purely geographic sense.) According to Schmandt and Steinbicker,
federalism is "a form of geographic pluralism which embodies the
idea that the values cherished by local areas must be preserved
and guarded by giving them recognition in the political structure." (Schmandt and Steinbicker 1954:327) Pranger comments that
"federalism operates to encourage and to compound ambition by
proliferating forms of government. This is to be accomplished by
geographical federalism, in the multiplication of governments at
several levels. . . . " (Pranger 1973:107)

GLOBAL FEDERALISM   The late Justice William O. Douglas of
the U.S. Supreme Court wrote in 1968 of a global federalism which
would   transcend   the   bitter   struggles   which   persistently
characterize international relations. Douglas believed that, if
the right people are placed in global leadership positions, the
international can be as tranquil as the national political arena
usually is.   Human beings, Douglas was convinced, are generally
alike in their deep respect for law, which would be, under global
federalism, the principal governing force. (Douglas 1968; ideas
summarized from Forsyth 1970:766)

GOOD FEDERALISM   This is the title of a simulation game developed by Govea and Wolohojian and published as The Good
Federalism Game: Participant's Manual for a Simulation of Intergovernmental Relations. The game is recommended as "an opportunity to observe the process of government at three different
levels" and experience "elements of both conflict and cooperation
among the various authorities, as well as within each authority."
(Govea and Wolohojian 1975:1)

GOVERNMENTAL FEDERALISM   Type of federalism involving only
relations between public entities.   "When people think of
Federalism," Diamond noted, "they think of enumerated powers in
the Constitution or [a] mechanical division of authority between
the central government and the states." (Quoted in Davis
1978:200. Diamond believed that American federalism is "a much
richer textual thing than that.")

GRAND FEDERALISM   An example of grand federalization ("grande federalisation") would be a federation of European nations. In contrast, national federation (as proposed recently for Belgium) would be a smaller-scale federalism. (Wauwe 1971:115)

GREEK FEDERALISM   The eras in which federalism flourished in Greece are identified as (1) after the time of Thucydides (471-400 B.C.) and (2) after the flourishing of Polybius (approximately 203-121 B.C.).   In other than these times "the independent city-commonwealth was the dominant political idea." (Taylor 1911:110) "The less brilliant period of Hellenic freedom occupied by the history of Greek federalism" was perhaps most notable for the operation of the Achaean League. (Ibid.)

GROUP FEDERALISM   According to Friedrich, John C. Calhoun's Disquisition on Government was built "on the idea of a kind of group federalism expressed in his notion of concurrent majorities,   meaning that a community's will can only be ascertained by taking into account the majorities in each of its major constituent groups." (Friedrich 1968:21)

HAMILTONIAN FEDERALISM   Federalist ideas associated with Alexander Hamilton (1755-1804), particularly the notion of a strong central government. Corwin observes that

> by the Hamiltonian theory, the national government, although a government of enumerated powers, is within the range of powers a truly sovereign government, and so is under no constitutional compulsion, either in the selection of means whereby to make its powers effective or in the selection of objects to be attained by their exercise, to take account of the coexistence of the states or to concern itself to preserve any particular relationship of power between itself and the states. (Corwin 1934:47-48 in Elazar 1962:11)

In its original form, "Hamiltonian Federalism was commercial . . . [and] Jeffersonian democracy was agrarian." (Anderson 1961:268) Parrington says that in his early career Calhoun was for all intents and purposes "a Hamiltonian Federalist" since he "was a thoroughgoing nationalist of the school of loose construction" and "advocated a protective tariff. . . . " (Parrington II, 1927:67) In the development of his theory of the concurrent majority, however, "instead of rejecting [the principle of democracy] . . . as an unworkable hypothesis, as the Hamiltonian Federalists had done, . . . [he] proposed to establish it on a sound and permanent basis." (Ibid., p. 73.) Leach feels that Hamiltonian federalism has never been fully accepted in the United States.   However, "Prolonged failure of . . . [states and cities] to perform . . . could rapidly sour the traditional affection Americans feel for them [these subnational units and thus open the door at last to the Hamiltonian model." (Leach in Yarbrough et al. 1972:78) (2) Hamiltonian federalism has also been important in modern European political thought.   Italian European unificationists in the post-World War II period, particularly Altiero Spinelli and Mario Albertini, were Hamiltonian federalists.   They believed that, "while the content of . . a European [federal] state must, of course, be democratic, the federalist idea should be applied to the organization of Europe itself and ha[d] nothing to do with . . . communes. . . . " The "'Hamiltonian' . . . federalists . . . were not interested in the problems of a 'European society' and reject[ed] 'integral federalism.'"   "For them," Greilsammer continues, "all that mattered was that the European federal state be established as soon as possible." (All Greilsammer in Elazar 1979a:116)

HEALTHY FEDERALISM   Federalism which is functioning well ("Gesunden Föderalismus," Deuerlein 1972:9)

HEGEMONIAL FEDERALISM   Dennewitz admits that the term hegemonial federalism contradicts itself since federalism, in his view, represents the desire for freedom in a voluntary union. Hegemony, in contrast, indicates that a few are dominating many. Nevertheless, he sees instances of hegemonial federations and calls the attention of students of federalism to them. (Dennewitz 1947:48ff.)   For example, the North German Union and the Empire of Bismarck both show that a constitutionally based inequality of constituent units formed the basis of a hegemonial federal state. Prussia was possessed with the idea of hegemonial federalism, according to Dennewitz.

HETEROGENEOUS FEDERALISM   An association of nations, e.g. a European federation or a world federation, would exemplify a heterogeneous federation ("heterogene Föderation").   A nation-state organized on federal principles probably would be relatively homogeneous. (Deuerlein 1972:322)

HIGHER FEDERALISM   Signifier of a more advanced form of federalism now prevalent in the United States.   "[F]or some," Davis notes, "federalism in America is dead.   For some, it is dying.   For some, a new-style federalism (creative, cooperative, higher, national), has arisen in the place of the old style (dual federalism), and for some, only the death of the 'old' is certain while the character of the 'new' is still as vague and uncertain as its future." (Davis 1978:182)   Further on, Davis says that the higher federalist is "one who lays the Constitution aside to project a society of 'higher federalism' where there is no demarcation, no separation, only a fluid, multi-faceted partnership of all with all, all organizations of state with all the associations of society." (Ibid., p. 200.)

HISTORICAL FEDERALISM   Federalism considered from the time dimension. (1) Glendening and Reeves point out that in the American system, "the historical models [of federalism] are periodically resurrected and reexamined during periods of systemic crisis. During the aftermath of the Brown v. Board of Education decision, many apologists for the South focused on Calhoun's model for federalism." (Glendening and Reeves 1977:318) (2) A general use of the expression historical federalism occurs with Marc who writes: "The philosophical approach advocated by integral federalism [see this term] lends to historical federalism a special capacity to develop much faster than ever before. . . . " (Marc 1979:122)

HOMOGENEOUS FEDERALISM   A nation-state structured according to federal principles is more likely to be a homogeneous federation ("homogene Föderation") than an association of nations, e.g. a European or a world federation. (Deuerlein 1972:322)

HORIZONTAL COOPERATIVE FEDERALISM   This is Siegrist's characterization for cooperation among the states in the American federal system. (Siegrist 1976:27) He notes the faith of some that its full adoption in Switzerland would bring great benefits.

HORIZONTAL FEDERALISM   (1) In the United States horizontal federalism refers to "[t]he relationships among the states of the Union either imposed by the Constitution or undertaken voluntarily." (Plano and Greenberg 1972:38) The Constitution calls on each state to give "full faith and credit to the public acts, records, and judicial proceedings of other states, grant the citizens of each state the privileges and immunities of their own state, and return fugitives from justice." (This summary appears in ibid.) Although they are under no compulsion to do so, states may also make interstate compacts (subject to congressional approval), pass standardized laws, and meet regularly in forums of discussion and common action.   (2) In other than American settings, horizontal federalism has different meanings. According to Porter, in West Germany "a horizontal division of powers exists between the Bund and the Laender." This means that "[l]egislative powers at the national level are extensive while national administrative powers are limited.   Conversely, administrative responsibilities are far more important at the Laender level than are than are legislative powers.   Land execution of Bund law is the rule." (All Porter 1977:107) "Horizontal" in the governmental lexicon can also refer to the separation of powers at a single governmental level. (See particularly Carey in Earle 1968:43.) (4) McWhinney identifies a proposal in South Africa "to develop a classical-type federal society, operating horizontally through territorial dispersal of the constituent racial groups and communities" in the 1950s. (McWhinney 1966:41)   McWhinney's research demonstrates that, "The successful examples of multi-racial societies are

invariably examples of . . . 'horizontal' federalism,"
identified as situations "where the different ethnic-cultural
communities are usually conveniently located or collected in
territorially distinct and separate, and self-contained, units of
the country." (Ibid.)

HORIZONTAL JUDICIAL FEDERALISM   Identified by Porter and
Tarr as "the patterns of influence among state supreme courts" in
the United States. (Porter and Tarr 1982, from the abstract)

HYBRID FEDERALISM   (1) In the United States, "[t]he hybrid
formulation"--partly national, partly federal--is said to indicate "a matrix model of American federalism with power distributed among multiple centers." (Rothman 1978:112)   (2) In a
comparative perspective, McWhinney equates hybrid federalism with
a mixed federal constitutional system.   The term is used when
there are grave doubts about the federal legitimacy of an actual
or proposed new system of dispersed power.   Thus he says that the
Government of Ireland Act of 1920, which still stands as the
foundation of the government of Northern Ireland,

> represents not so much an application of the
> federal idea in the sense of a process of
> imaginative devolution of legal power by a
> parent, Imperial authority [i.e., hybrid federalism];
> as a failure of the federal idea in a situation
> where the basic societal conditions in Ireland of
> religious and general ethnic-cultural diversity, or
> at least dualism, coupled with the logic of geog-
> raphy and economic interdependence of the two parts,
> all pointed to a constitutional solution in terms of
> political unity for Ireland under a federal consti-
> tution with appropriate institutional checks and
> balances and Bill of Rights-type guarantees weighted
> in favour of minority religious interests. (McWhinney
> 1966:75)

For other reasons Cyprus is cited also as an illustration of a
hybrid federal system.   See corporate federalism.

HYPHENATED FEDERALISM   This book is a book of hyphenated
federalisms.   Landau says that "many of our hyphenated
federalisms" are aimed at helping to place "borderline cases" of
alleged federalism "in one category or another." (Landau
1973:176)   A fuller discussion of the utility of hyphenated
federalisms appears in the Introductory Essay.   See also Stewart
1982.   It will suffice to say here, with Landau, that "[t]he
hyphenated phrases that we . . . use to describe its [the system's] behavior are indications of the extent of the system's
flexibility, of its equipotentiality. . . . Federalism, if the
concept is not reified, may be expressed in many ways." (Ibid.,
pp. 190-91.   It should be pointed out that Landau definitely does
not feel that federalism is an infinitely plastic concept.)

IDEAL FEDERALISM   (1) What Freeman identifies as the "federal ideal," the situation in which "each of the members of the Union [is] wholly independent in those matters which concern each member only," while on the other hand, "all [are] subject to a common power in those matters which concern the whole body of members collectively," is, he says, "so very refined and artificial, that it seems not to have been attained more than four or five times in the history of the world." (Freeman 1893:2,3)   (2) The German writer, Brie, in his work Der Bundesstaat, identified the "ideal federal state" as one in which the central goverment has full supremacy in foreign affairs and in specifically enumerated internal affairs of federation-wide concern." (Brie 1874:140, cited in Garner 1910:15)   The constituent units would have all remaining powers.   (3) Ideals for specific types of federal systems also are recognized.   McWhinney observes that, "Contemporary Switzerland is usually taken as the Continental European, Civil Law, ideal-type model of a multi-cultural community. . . . " (McWhinney 1966:16)

IDEOLOGICAL FEDERALISM   It is observed that "federation can be essentially an ideology or a methodology." (Franck 1968:26) (1) In a European setting, Duchacek points to "the use of federal terminology in political movements, when the aim is to forge unity out of ideological . . . diversity." (Duchacek 1970:190)   A modern illustration is the creation by Communists, socialists, radicals, and additional leftists of the Federation of a Democratic and Socialist Left in France.   The Comintern and Cominform demonstrate, for Duchacek, "an ideological union of territorial parties." (Ibid.)   (2) In the context of East Africa, Franck identified the ideological federalist as one who "pursue[d] federalism so far as possible or conceivable." (Franck 1968:26)   However, the supporters of ideological federalism were few.   Probably less than half of the old imperial government officials and white settlers generally "were in any sense ideologically committed to federalism." (Ibid.)   Support for federalism in East Africa was likely to come, in Franck's judgment, only from the Africans themselves, and there was too little time "in which to unbutton the fixed ideas of [previous] generations, and to make a clean, ideological distinction between the colonial-white-mercantilist federalism of the past and a new Africanized, unifying, ideological federalism of the future." (Ibid., p. 29.)

ILL FEDERALISM   Federalism which is functioning poorly ("Kranken Föderalismus," Deuerlein 1972:9).

IMPERFECT FEDERALISM   (1) This is a type of federalism discussed by Edward Freeman, Alexis de Tocqueville, John Stuart Mill, Alexander Hamilton, and James Madison, who identify an imperfect federal union as one which contains elements of confederatism. (Garner 1910:151)   It is organized more on the order of a confederation than a unitary system of government. Writing early in the twentieth century, Garner asserted that "most federal unions belong to the imperfect type; that is, they represent a mixture of federalism and confederatism." (Ibid.) (2) Brougham in 1844 identified the imperfect federal union as the situation "where two or more states, having their separate governments for domestic purposes, are united under a central government which controls each state and forms a part of its government for domestic purposes; in a word, where several states having separate political institutions are under one executive administration." (Brougham 1844:506) Examples included England, Scotland, and Ireland as joined in the seventeenth century and Great Britain and Ireland in the eighteenth. (3) In roughly the same time period as Garner, Bluntschli commented that "[t]he Union . . . of two or more States, either under one common ruler, or as a single new State . . . is always imperfect when it is merely personal. This [imperfect federal union] may be merely transitory if the same person happens to succeed to the thrones of two different States, and may afterwards cease if the succession falls again to two different persons." (Bluntschli 1892:271) The German Empire and Spain, when both were governed by Charles V, is cited as an example of an imperfect federal union. In Bluntschli's view imperfect federalism is "the lowest of all" forms of union. (Ibid., p. 272.)

IMPERIAL FEDERALISM   Numerous writers have discussed imperial federalism. (1) In the American Constitutional Convention of 1787, Martin says that "those representing the large states, seeking to gain particular powers over the other states," should properly be called imperialists. (Martin 1926:271)   (2) A modern interpretation of Althusius is that the empire was a federal union of states and free cities just as, at the base, "the village was for him a federal union of families. . . . " (Friedrich in Carney 1964:x-xi)   (3) Mogi believes that the 1860s signaled "the dawn of imperial federalism" because it was in that decade that the British North America Act was passed (1868) and Freeman's extremely influential History of Federal Government was published (1863). (Mogi 1931a:235)   Imperial federalism was a response to colonial separationists and held that "the grant of responsible government and the reform of the imperial parliament to allow the colonists to secure equal opportunity in the legislature of the empire . . . [was] essential for colonial unity." (Ibid., pp. 235-36.)   Most imperial federalists were "statesmen or business-men who were connected with colonial trade or industry, and their advocacy of federalism was more or less the result of their own interests, and not of theoretical aspirations." (Ibid., p. 236.) Prime Minister Disraeli supported imperial federalism in a speech in 1872 in which he called attention to the need for "the institution of some representative council in the metropolis which would have brought the colonies into constant and continuous relations with home government." (Disareli quoted in ibid., p. 238.) For Britain, however, "the ideal of imperial federalism . . remained a phantom, not a reality." (Ibid., p. 252.) (4) Bluntschli cited the German federal empire formed out of the North German Confederation as a "new and parallel form" of federalism alongside republican federations such as the United States. (Bluntschli 1892:270-71) (5) Peirce labeled "imperial federalism" the early behavior of President Reagan in "studiously ignor[ing] the calls of governors and local officials for full consultation for a sorting out of today's hopelessly intertwined and confused intergovernmental roles, and for a clear view of how much federal aid they can and can't expect." (Peirce 1982:7A) As the 1982 segment of his new federalism initiative was being more fully developed, however, the President asked for more counsel from state and local officials as well as members of Congress. He was also said to be in the mood for compromise.

IMPOSED FEDERALISM   A situation in which a federation is "established against the consent of the majority of the peoples involved." (De Blij 1967:461) The imposed federation is one of de Blij's five types of federal states, along with mutual interest, compromise, centralized, and shape. All are defined in this volume. De Blij cautions: "History has taught us that most imposed federations are short-lived," citing, specifically, the Mali Federation, the Central African Federation, and the West Indies Federation. (Ibid.)

IMPROBABLE FEDERATION   The chief minister of Jamaica, Norman Manley, called the West Indies "the most improbable federation ever conceived." (Quoted in Wallace 1961:444) Wallace explains the reasons for this designation in "The West Indies: Improbable Federation?" (Ibid., pp. 444-59.) Among them was the fact that, "In no other federation [was] half the population and therefore half the political strength . . . concentrated in a single unit [in this case, Jamaica." (Ibid., p. 444.) Further, Jamaica apparently always regarded "the decision to federate . . . . to be temporary and tentative." (Ibid., p. 446.)

IMPROPER FEDERALISM   Improper federalism is apparently identical with imperfect federalism. (Brougham 1844:506) Examples of improper (also imperfect) federalisms include the seventeenth century union of England, Scotland, and Ireland and the eighteenth century joining of Great Britain and Ireland.

IMPURE FEDERALISM   Impure federalism is synonymous with partial and imperfect federalism.

INCIPIENT FEDERALISM   The OUD defines incipient as an adjective which means "beginning; or coming into, or in an early stage of existence; in an initial stage." (1955 ed.) Sawer calls one of his chapters (IV), "Failed and Incipient Federalism." (Sawer 1969:56-63) In this discussion he identifies "several short-lived federations, or proposals for federations which came

to nothing. . . . " (Ibid.)   Specifically cited as "at most an
incipient federal system" is the British relationship to Northern
Ireland which, under the Government of Ireland Act of 1920, provides for a "Parliament and Government with a general power to
make laws for the peace, order and good government of the area,
subject to the reservation of the United Kingdom Parliament of
foreign affairs, defence, foreign trade, most forms of taxation
(including customs) and various other matters." (Ibid.)   This
system is only incipiently federal because of the comprehensive
authority of Britain over Northern Ireland.

INCOME FEDERALISM   Income federalism is identified by Colman as one of a number of concepts of federalism of particular
relevance to American cities.   The term presumably refers to
federal programs providing temporary or long-term support to the
incomes of urban-dwellers, particularly as in the Supplemental
Security Income programs. (See Colman 1975:308.)

INDEPENDENT FEDERALISM   A political system which is both
federated and independent of any colonial power. (Hicks 1978:124)

INDIVIDUALISTIC FEDERALISM   According to Garson, the
federalism of the American Unitarian leader William Ellery
Channing was "an individualist . . . federalism."   As Garson
interprets Channing, "government [should] be held to plain and
narrow bounds." (Garson 1975:8, 9)

INDUSTRIAL FEDERALISM   See particularly the discussion
above of economic federalism. Parrington identifies the coming
to greatness of industrial federalism in the United States as
occurring after the Civil War. (Parrington II, 1927:307) This
would be when the industrial revolution was in full swing. For
Parrington the term is an ideological one, not referring to an
association of industries but to the kind of policy favored by
industrialists from the federal government in terms of high tariffs and scant regulation and other favorable policies. These
industrialists could be identified as the philosophical descendants of the original Federalist partisans.

IN-STATE FEDERALISM   This expression was used syonymously
with intrastate federalism late in 1982. Karnig and associates
suggested a redistribution of functions between state and local
governments. Operating in the middle would be "a form of 'in-
state federalism,' with joint ventures between the state and local governments." (Karnig et al. 1982:497)

INSTITUTIONAL FEDERALISM   This concept has a postwar
European context. Contemporary European federalists felt that
the concern "should not be to replace national sovereignty with a
jealous, absolute, and 'indivisble' European sovereignty, but to

create different and appropriate institutions which correspond
in their jurisdiction and geographic scope to the different problems which arise." (Brugmans in Brugmans and Duclos 1963:59,
quoted in Hay 1966:93) Hay's interpretation of this statement is
that Brugmans "rejects federalism as an institutional concept. .
. . " (Ibid.) Instead, it seems that Brugmans is rejecting
federalism as a comprehensive institution in favor of many
federal institutions. Federal theorists usually have an interest
in all kinds of institutions which exist in a given territory.
Livingston points out that "[a] society . . . may possess a unitary set of institutions and employ them as though they were
federal in nature. [However,] [t]he institutions themselves do
not provide an accurate index of the federal nature of the
society that subtends them; they are only the surface manifestations of the deeper federal quality of the society that
lies beneath the surface." (Livingston 1956:2)

INSTRUMENTAL FEDERALISM   Landau argues that "if we set
aside the Newtonian image for the Darwinian, federalism is transformed into an instrument, a social invention, an adaptation that
is functional only for a specified set of conditions." (Landau
1973:178) For Landau federalism thus "loses its intrinsic value
and is to be applied as needs be." (Ibid.) "Under this model,"
he continues, "the universe is no longer closed; it is ever-
changing. Government becomes an organism, growing and evolving,
'modified by its environment, necessitated by its tasks, shaped
to its functions by the sheer pressures of life.'" (Woodrow Wilson quoted in ibid.) Wilson argued against a constitutional
formalism. Americans of the late nineteenth century were "many
years away from the paper pictures of the Constitution."
(Landau's paraphrase of Wilson) Landau's conclusion from this is
that "instrumental federalism has longed since ceased to be
functional . . . it has accomplished its task . . . it remains an
anachronism--a case of 'political lag.'" (Ibid., p. 178.)

INTEGRAL FEDERALISM   The integral federalist movement, a
French political phenomenon, is traced by Pentland to 1930s beginnings. It was "an eclectic mix of ideas from Proudhon, syndicalism, left-wing Catholicism and a number of other politically
eccentric sources. It emphasized the bankruptcy of 'formal' democracy, capitalism and the established ideologies of right and
left, [and] advocated a pluralistic or federal society of communal groups and interests." (Pentland 1973:160) Elazar identifies Alexandre Marc as "a founder and [presently the] leading
exponent of integral federalism. . . . " (Elazar 1979b:1) Marc
and his fellow-integral federalists "sought to turn Europe in a
different direction through the union of the continent on a
federal basis and the reformation of society along federal
principles, in the process developing a grand design which they
saw as right for all of humanity, based fully and entirely on
federal principles." (Ibid., p. 7.) Marc himself says that

integral federalism seeks to "capture Proudhon's vision of federalized society . . . including a federalized economy, and using the following scheme: at the base, 1) autonomy; at the second level, 2) competitive cooperation; at the third level, 3) subsidarity; and finally the principle that both fulfills and transcends previous levels, 4) participation." (Marc 1979:118) Integral federalism also seeks to spread the federal principle to science and philosophy. Thus, "conscious addition" may be said to be "the formula for integral federalism," that is, "federalism politique + socialism libertaire + personnalisme + philosophie et methodologie systemiques." (Ibid., p. 130.)

INTEGRATED FEDERALISM   (1) Integrated federalism is, for Sawer, the same phenomenon as organic federalism. It is the third stage in the continuing trend of centralization in the model federal system, following dual federalism and cooperative federalism. However, no specific system takes this path in any particular order or to any predetermined degree. (Sawer 1969:64-65)   (2) Schlesinger comments that, "Federalism . . . supposes some degree of equilibrium between the constituent parts in those fields where federalist integration is sought." (Schlesinger 1945:487)   But the integration in integrated federalism must not extend too far.

INTERCANTONAL COOPERATIVE FEDERALISM   This expression appears in Siegrist's title for his study in the mid-1970s of relations among the Swiss cantons, "Die schweizerische Verfassungsordnung als Grundlage und Schranke des interkantonalen kooperativen Föderalismus." (Siegrist 1976-78)

INTERCOMMUNAL FEDERALISM   Associations of little political units, looking toward formation of a national federation; used specifically with reference to France. Maxime Leroy sugged in La Ville francaise; institutions et libertes locales that "intercommunal federalism might . . . finish by giving us little by little, slowly, by successive empiricisms the territorial reconstruction which an inspired action from too high up so far revealed itself incapable of bringing about." (Leroy 1927:177 quoted in Gooch 1931:120-21)

INTERDEPENDENT FEDERALISM   (1) The originator of this expression is Alan K. Campbell, former Director of the U.S. Office for Personnel Management. It is used to express the belief that, "If past trends continue, the future will bring more extensive federal and state involvement in metropolitan and urban problems." (Duncombe 1966:248)   Duncombe was particularly interested in "contacts between federal and county personnel" and "ties between state and county officials. . . . " (Ibid.) He favored county home rule, not for the sake of county autonomy, "but [to provide] greater flexibility to serve as a more effective partner in a combined federal, state, and local effort to solve the serious urban and rural problems of our times."

(Ibid., p. 249.) Interdependent federalism recognizes "the growing interdependence of our federal system, and the necessity for the county to prepare itself for its role as a local government leader in this partnership." (Ibid.) (2) Duchacek uses interdependent federalism as one of many synonyms for cooperative federalism. (Duchacek 1970:318)

INTERLOCKED FEDERALISM   Thirty-five years ago Grodzins observed: "Building upon techniques and traditions of the past, the Federal system today [1949] is made up of tightly interlocking levels of government serving the same people." (U.S. Senate 1949:70.   Grodzins was writing for the Council of State Governments as part of a Hoover Commission task force study.) The term interlocked federalism is very briefly recognized by Duchacek 1970:318 as conveying the same meaning as cooperative federalism.

INTERNAL FEDERALISM   Basically, federalism within a single federal nation-state, as distinguished from international federalism.   (1) In the eighteenth century, Montesquieu and Rousseau "advocated internal federalism . . . [because of] their conviction that a federal government alone could preserve 'small republicanism' in a dangerous world of large, powerful monarchies." (Riley 1979b:61)   Internal federalism calls for the association and multiplication of societal unions as an instrument of human liberation.   The human spirit is crushed when there is an absence of intermediary bodies between the individual and the state. (Grand Larousse Encyclopedique, 1961 ed.)   However, Kant scorned internal federalism, but praised international federalism.   (2) In modern France the notion of internal federalism has been controversial.   Advocated by rightists but also by some leftists, "internal federalism . . . seemed obscene to most radicals and socialists . . . 'federalism' was synonymous with 'separatism' in the revolutionary vocabulary, and separatists had given help to the national enemies." (Brugmans in Yarbrough et al. 1972:86)   For some French intellectuals, particularly as their views found expression in the publication La federation, "internal federalism had to accompany or precede supranational federalism to overcome excessive nationalism." (Ibid., p. 89.) (3) Duclos believes "[i]nternal federalism (in the single federal nation-state) today often tends toward a unitary state. . . . " (Paraphrase in Hay 1966:94 of Duclos in Brugmans and Duclos 1963)

INTERNATIONAL FEDERALISM   (1) Before the twentieth century, international federalism found its best expression in the European peace leagues conceptualized by St. Pierre and Kant, put forward mostly as "reactions to one aspect or another of the triumph of the national state." (Riley 1976:18)   Specifically for Kant, "international federalism is . . . essential to the stability of states and their laws. . . . " (Riley 1979b:60-61)   (2) John Dewey favored international federalism and rejected "the

Hegelian philosophy of history as ignoring 'all future possibility of a genuinely international federation to which
isolated nationalism shall be subordinated.'" (Dewey 1942:134-35
quoted in Ostrom 1979:93-94)   (3) Friedrich defines an international federal order as one which "is sufficiently loose for
its members to have separate and autonomous relations with other
states, and at the same time, to develop or maintain joint relations." (Friedrich 1968:83)   Friedrich feels it is desirable
"both to recognize the existence of international federalism and
not to misunderstand it as a sharply defined alternative to
national federalism." (Ibid.)   (4) Duclos observed of postwar
Europe that "international federalism [was] growing, albeit so
far only in confederal institutional form." (View of Duclos in
Brugmans and Duclos 1963:59, reported in Hay 1966:94)

    INTERNATIONAL LAW COMMUNITY FEDERALISM   This is the
author's   translation   of   Dennewitz's   expression,
"volkerrechtsgemeinschaftliche Föderalismus."   He   refers   to
supranational   and   international   federalism.   (Dennewitz
1947:37ff.)

    INTERTWINED FEDERALISM   Another synonym for cooperative
federalism presented by Duchacek 1970:318 and otherwise un-
defined.

    INTRASTATE FEDERALISM   (1) Semblance of federalism which
may exist within an American state.   Beer observes that, "On the
basis of . . . the home rule provision of a state constitution .
. . [there may be established] a mild, but real, intrastate
federalism." (Beer 1973:50)   (2) Mallory, using Canada as his
point of reference, defines intrastate federalism as the situation "in which the major institutions of the central government
are constructed on a representative principle which reflects the
principal divisions of the country both by region and by religious and cultural differences." (Mallory 1977:151)

    ISOPOLITY FEDERALISM   Ancient Greek federations have, on
occasion, been classified into two categories, isopolities and
sympolities.   The first, "isopolity, or 'interchange citizenship,' [defines the situation in which] each citizen became a
member of other cities in the [ancient Greek] league but each
city continued to manage its own affairs." (Sinclair 1968:115
quoted in Schechter 1975:5)

    JEFFERSONIAN FEDERALISM   "The Pluralist federal system,"
McWhinney observes, "is Jeffersonian in character, with its faith
in enlightened self-government and cooperation at the local
level, and its distrust of centralized power." (McWhinney
1965:17)   While most writers on American government might feel
that the Jeffersonian model historically has had greatest
legitimacy, Paul Ylvisaker, Roscoe Martin, and Robert Wood "have
argued that the Jeffersonian model never existed except in a

few isolated atypical instances or as a historical construct."
(Views of these scholars are reported in Glendening and Reeves
1977:296.) Instead, they seem to feel that "the Madisonian model
of representative government is more in keeping with the American
tradition" than the heavily participatory Jeffersonian federalism. (Ibid.)

JOINT FEDERALISM   This term is used with reference to the
Canadian federal system, which has developed procedures whereby
functional agencies at the federal and provincial levels work
closely together in the formulation and administration of public
programs.   "The relative success of joint federalism," Meekison
believes, "can be attributed in part to the highly specific nature of the interactions which have developed; i.e., program
agencies could work closely together because their collaboration
did not depend on federal-provincial agreement on more comprehensive objectives." (Meekison 1968:286)

JUDICIAL COOPERATIVE FEDERALISM   Approach to American
cooperative federalism which focuses on contributions made to its
theory and practice by courts and judges, particularly in the
years since 1937.   Walker asserts that "the [American federal]
system needs more than a confectionary judicial theory of
cooperative federalism." (Walker 1981c:151)   Instead, in Walker's
view, "[i]t needs one that is rooted in the realities--political,
fiscal, administrative, programmatic, and procedural--of today's
intergovernmental relations."   "Above all," Walker strongly believes, "it needs a judicial approach that reflects a genuine
sense of reasonableness and balance." (Ibid.)

JUDICIAL DUAL FEDERALISM   During the period 1789-1860 in
American history, Walker believes, judicial dual federalism
dominated the Supreme Court.   The Marshall Court was judicially
dual federalist, Walker feels, because it "was protective of its
own institutional independence, assertive of its authority to
render ultimate judgment regarding unconstitutional actions of
the nation's political branches and of states, and selectively
protective of Congress's powers under the Constitution." (Walker
1981c:48-49) Perhaps surprisingly, "it also was mindful that the
national government's powers were by no means plenary; that the
states are 'for some purposes sovereign, and for some purposes
subordinate' . . . and that the relationship between the two
levels was essentially one of tension." (Ibid., p. 49.   The
internal quote is from Cohens v. Virginia, 19 U.S. (6 Wheaton)
264 (1821).) Ascription of judicial dual federalism to the successor Taney Court is much more accepted.   Under the Tenth Amendment, in Taney's view, the states had "complete, unqualified, and
exclusive" power to "provide for the public health, safety, and
good order" of their citizens. (Corwin in McCloskey 1962:200-01
quoted in Walker 1981c:50) Judicial dual federalism as practiced
by Chief Justice Taney also endorsed "national supremacy in its
own limited sphere . . . [and] the Court's fundamental role as

final judge of what is constitutionally permissible within the
state's sphere of action." (Ibid.) Judicial dual federalism did
not end, finally, Walker believes, until the late 1930s when the
Court, by approving the Farm Mortgage Act, the revised Railway
Labor acts, and the National Labor Relations and Social Security
acts, administered "last rites for judicial dual federalism. . .
. Dual federalism as it had been applied judicially was a dead
doctrine. . . . " (Ibid., pp. 69-70.) For the ideas of Daniel
Elazar relative to the viability of dual federalism on any front,
see the entry for cooperative federalism.

JUDICIAL FEDERALISM   To think of judicial federalism is to
think about "the general framework in which interjudicial relations take place." (Winkle 1980:2) Judicial federalism "sets
forth the structure and intersystem rules" and specifies "[t]he
division of authority between state and federal courts" in the
American federal system. (Ibid.) Leach says that what he terms
"the federalism of jurisprudence" specifies "the limits of action" within a federal system. (Leach 1973:17)

JURIDICAL FEDERALISM   While judicial means "of, pertaining
to, or proper to courts of law or to the administration of justice" (American Heritage Dictionary, 1971 ed.), juridical emphasizes more strongly the right of judges--jurists--to say what
the law is. Usually these participants in intergovernmental relations are more united than actors in other spheres, but Leach
openly wonders about "[w]hat kind of fissures"--clefts,
openings--"exist even in juridical federalism." (Leach
1973:16-17)

JURIDICO-POLITICAL FEDERALISM   Heraud credits Marc with expanding the vision of students of federalism beyond a narrow
juridico-political federalism. ("Federalisme juridico-politique,"
Heraud in "Reperes pour en federalisme . . . ," 1976:27) Thanks
to Marc the variables included within federal studies are now
much more numerous. And, even juridico-political federalism research has been made more substantial through the infusion of new
value and empirical considerations.

JURISTIC FEDERALISM   "Juristic" and "juridical" (as well as
"judicial," for that matter) differ little, actually. The choice
of modifiers of federalism is open to the commentator. (1) The
suffix "ist" indicates a "person who does . . . produces . . . a
specified thing." (American Heritage Dictionary, 1971 ed.)
Juristic federalism is the kind of federalism emanating from
jurists who produce outputs pertaining to the federal system.
(2) In a comparative perspective it is important to note that
"traditional juristic notions . . . [were] preoccupied with problems of sovereignty, of the distribution of competencies, and of
the structure of institutions." (Davis 1978:173) German jurists
have been frequent contributors to federal theory. Mogi identifies Hans Kelsen's model of juristic federalism as a

"complete system of the legal mechanism of our future ideal world," a world characterized by a "repudiation of the theory of the pre-eminence of the individual state-order" and "the renunciation of the sovereignty of the state." (Mogi 1931b:1054) In the United States, Edward S. Corwin has probably made the greatest contributions to the understanding of juristic federalism. (3) Neuman virtually emasculates juristic federalism when he uses the expression to denote only the bare bones of the federal system. The only element the assertedly federal systems of the United States, Canada, Australia, Switzerland, and the Soviet Union have in common, he contends, is the "juristic" one; that is, "in each, the citizen of the federal state is subject to two jurisdictions [emphasis added]: that of the federal government and that of the states." (Neuman in Macmahon 1955:44)

KALEIDOSCOPIC FEDERALISM   Fagin is reported as believing that "the [American federal] system cannot be described as a cake of any sort." Thus he prefers the kaleidoscope as a metaphor. (Fagin in Schnore and Fagin 1967, cited in Ranney 1969:61) The OUD identifies a kaleidoscope as "an optical instrument consisting of from two to four reflecting surfaces placed in a tube, at one end of which is a small compartment containing pieces of coloured glass; on looking through the tube, numerous reflections of these are seen, producing brighly-coloured . . . figures, which may be constantly altered by rotation of the instrument." (Oxford Universal Dictionary, 1955 ed.)

KAMIKAZE FEDERALISM   Federalism which is going to self-destruct unless course corrections are made. Sommer observed in the West Germany of the late 1960s that modernization of federalism was essential to a restoration of its health. "We have to make a useful working animal out of a holy cow," Sommer argued. "Not only the centralists endanger federalism; the federalists themselves, with their stubbornness, endanger federalism." (Quoted in Deuerlein 1972:281, tr. Petra Schuler)

KANT'S FEDERALISM   Several references to the federal thought of Immanuel Kant appear in this volume. (See the name index.) The most important fact about Kant's federalism is that it "moves mainly in one direction--beyond the national state." (Riley 1979b:43) Riley argues that Kant's particular variety of international federalism "was more important to [his] political theory . . . than to that of any other thinker, since for him the possibility of a public legal order on any plane was jeopardized by the absence of such an order on the broadest plane, the relations of independent states." (Ibid.)

KINGLY FEDERALISM   A kingly federalism is a federal system headed by a monarch. (Freeman 1893:74) The expression monarchic federation is more commonly used.

KROPOTKIN'S FEDERALISM   "The chief purpose of Kropotkin's federalism," King says, "was to secure a decentralization of power to the local, communal level, rather than the concentration of all significant initiatives at the centre." (King 1982:43, his footnote omitted) Kropotkin's bitterest remarks were directed at highly centralized parliamentary governments.

LAND FEDERALISM   Pertaining to public lands policies of the American federal government, particularly as revised during the Reagan Administration. In mid-1981 it was reported that the administration was "addressing itself to many of the western land issues." The Secretary of the Interior, James Watt, was said to be "drawing on the advice and input from many western Governors, Republican and Democratic, as he consider[ed] the possibility of batching lands and taking other initiatives which will provide greater effectiveness in utilizing Federal and state lands in the west." (Williamson 1981:12)

LATE FEDERALISM   This is another way in which federalism may be put in a general time perspective. Zeh writes of "Spätföderalismus" in West Germany. He prefers this time-frame term to cooperative federalism, which, because of the fusion of central and local authorities, he feels no longer is an accurate description. "Spätföderalismus" has no ideological basis and, also, the expression suggests that, with the passage of time, federalism will continue to undergo important changes, if it does not expire completely. (Zeh 1977:475, 476)

LAYER CAKE FEDERALISM   In an influential essay in 1960, Morton Grodzins observed: "The American form of government is often, but erroneously, symbolized by a three-layer cake." (Grodzins in U.S. President, Commission on National Goals, Goals for Americans, p. 265.) Grodzins (and his most famous pupil, Daniel Elazar) argued that, "The American federal system has never been a system of separated governmental activities," for which the image of a layer cake would be appropriate, because "[t]here has never been a time when it was possible to put neat labels on discrete 'federal,' 'state,' and 'local' functions." (Ibid., p. 268. See the entry for marble cake federalism.) Joseph E. McLean may have been the first to use the layer cake metaphor to explain what the American federal system was not like. (McLean 1952 quoted in Graves 1974:66) Wright feels that the metaphor best applies to the broad period in American history prior to 1937. "The chief concern of [this] conflict phase of IGR was the effort to identify and implement 'proper' boundaries for officials' actions." (Wright 1974:5) The "supposed separat- ism [of this period] . . . gave credence to the metaphor of 'layer cake federalism' as a crude means of describing national, state and local disconnectedness." (Ibid., pp. 6-7.)

LEAGUE FEDERALISM   The Greek associations of city- commonwealths are generally identified as federal. Taylor believes that "[c]areful analysis of the constitution of the Achaian League seems to have clearly established the fact that its government was in some important respects similar to that adopted by the United States in 1787. However, the Framers had little knowledge of such Greek league federations." (Taylor 1911:111-12) In the New York ratification debate, George Clinton identified three elements of every federal league:

> 1st. That as the States are the creative principle, the power of the confederacy must originate from and operate upon them. . . .
> 2d. That the states having equal rights to protect, ought to be equally represented.
> 3d. That it is the will of the states, which is to be expressed in the federal council as their interests arise . . . the delegates who are to express that will . . . ought to be subject to their appointment and controul. (Quoted in Anderson 1961:240)

LEGAL FEDERALISM (1) Federalism as indicated by a constitution. Martin says that "the legal federalism outlined in the [American] Constitution has permeated the practice of federal-state relations in every walk of public life." (Martin 1965:172) "For much of American history," as Loeb and Berman view this history, "federalism was viewed primarily as a legalistic concept. Supposedly, federalism meant that the national government had certain powers, but that the states were free to exercise all those powers not given to the central government." (Loeb and Berman 1975:346) According to this view, the Constitution should indicate "what kinds of powers properly belonged to each level of government. Or, if the Constitution failed to provide an explicit guide . . . the Supreme Court could . . . decide. . . . " (Ibid.) (2) The officially prescribed, perhaps as contrasted with the actual, patterns of intergovernmental relations. Cerny comments that, "Despite the discussions among constitutional lawyers German federalism in practice has been much more a 'political' than 'legal' federalism." (Cerny in Earle 1968:183) That is, such autonomy as the German lander are able to enjoy is more attributable to informal political factors than to formal legal guarantees provided in the Bonn Constitution. (3) The philosophical system of Hans Kelsen. (See Mogi 1931b:965.) For Kelsen, "the most important thing of all was the repudiation of the theory of the pre-eminence of the individual state order, or, in other words, the renunciation of the sovereignty of the state." (Ibid., p. 1054.)

LENINIST FEDERALISM The pre-1917 Lenin rejected federalism "for all stages of development as a pattern both for the structure of the Social Democratic Party and of the state." (Low 1958:105) It legitimated separation and this a true communist could not accept. More practically, it was juxtaposed to the

Bolshevik notion of democratic centralism. However, according to
Low, after the 1917 revolution "[t]he conception of federalism
played an increasingly important role in Communist theory" and
Lenin came grudgingly to accept federalism as necessary to
achieve full democratic centralism.   In Low's totally un-
sympathetic view, Lenin's concessions to federalism "were merely
sham concessions and [his] respect paid to it merely lip-service,
a farce designed to deceive the border nationalities" whose support he needed to maintain power. (Ibid., pp. 110-11.)   Yet,
Duchacek says that Lenin might have been anticipating "a federal
union of national communist dictatorships, founded on common
class interests and belief in Marxism, when he dreamed about an
ultimate Proletarian Federation of the World." (Duchacek
1970:332)

        LEXICAL FEDERALISM   Federalism as defined by a dictionary.
Landau observes that "the meaning of federalism has acquired a
lexical status.   If we turn to . . . the Oxford Universal (3rd
Edition) or the OED, we will find that the term 'federal' denotes
a form of government in which two or more states constitute a
political unity while they remain independent as to the control
of their internal affairs." (Landau 1973:174)   This volume
assumes the insufficiency of general dictionary definitions.

        LIBERAL FEDERALISM   A French source identifies de Tocque-
ville as an exponent of liberal federalism ("federalisme
liberal").   Liberal federalism would function as a counterbalance to the powerful state centralism associated with post-
Revolutionary France. (Dictionnaire Encyclopedique Ouillet, 1969
ed.)

        LIMITED FEDERALISM   An incomplete association of political
units for specifically identifiable purposes.   Writing about the
individual European Communities, for example coal and steel, Hay
expresses the view that their particular attributes "require . .
. a reevaluation of the concept of sovereignty and the recognition that sovereign powers can be transferred in part."
That is, "the Communities are limited federations to the extent
of their sovereign powers." (Hay 1966:89)   Hay defends "limited
federalism" as "accurate and acceptable . . . especially because
the qualification ('limited') removes the anomaly of several,
overlapping 'full' federations." (Ibid.)   Hay acknowledges "ob-
jections to this classification . . . [based on the fact] that
the limitation affects one of the essential elements of a federation, statehood, and that, like some [other] classifications . .
. it appears tailor-made for the particular phenomenon without
contributing to a broader conceptualization." (Ibid.)

        LINGUISTIC FEDERALISM   This term would describe a "federa-
tion on the basis of . . . linguistic states." (Jennings in
Hawkins 1965:2.   Jennings himself does not actually use the

expression "linguistic federalism." However, "linguistic federalism" is an appropriate expression to characterize the re-formed Indian federalism "on the basis of what they call linguistic states, i.e., states using different official languages. . . . ") Jennings feels that along with economic and communal problems, "the linguistic problem" may be one of the greatest a new federation will face. Switzerland can also be identified as an instance of linguistic federalism. McWhinney cites the Swiss Confederation as a "multi-lingual, multi-national, federal society." (McWhinney 1965:16) (2) In the late 1930s and early 1940s Clarence K. Streit, an American journalist, proposed an international linguistic and ideological federation composed of the most populous democratic countries. Its con-stitution would be similar to the U.S. Constitution. The name of the linguistic union would be the "Union of the Free." (Cited in Wynner and Lloyd 1944:340) (3) Currently operating federations concerned with language study include the International Federations for Modern Languages and Literature and the World Federation of Foreign-Language Teachers' Associations.

LIP-SERVICE FEDERALISM   Lieber dubbed the Federal Water Pollution Control Act of 1972 an exercise in "'lip-service federalism'--i.e., Congress used the rhetoric of cooperative federalism but never carried out its promise of a federal- state partnership in water pollution control." (View of Lieber 1972 cited in Hall et al. 1978:193)   Lip-service is defined as "insincere agreement or payment of respect." (American Heritage Dictionary, 1971 ed.)

LITERARY FEDERALISM   Deuerlein uses the expression literary federalism for the early twentieth-century Germans who advocated federalism but imp.acitcally so because they ignored the key variable--particularism--on which a workable federal system would have to be based. (Deuerlein 1972:186)

LITTLE FEDERALISM   (1) Traditionally the relationship be-tween the American state government and local governments has not been viewed as federal.   The standard interpretation of American state-local relations is that, in contrast with the states which have reserved powers pursuant to the Tenth Amendment of the Con-stitution, localities possess only those powers granted to them by the state in "express words" or "necessarily or fairly implied in or incident to the powers expressly granted" or "essential to the accomplishment of the declared objects" the local units of government were set up to achieve. This is Dillon's Rule. (See Dillon 1873:173.)   Thus the state-local relationship is clearly unitary. (2) The idea of little federalism is used with respect to state legislative apportionment prior to the reapportionment revolution of the 1960s. Glendening and Reeves noted that, "the long-established 'little federal system,' in which one house was apportioned on a basis other than population was no longer acceptable" after Reynolds v. Sims, 377 U.S. 533 (1964). (Glendening and Reeves 1973:79) (3) Little federalism also connotes a national federation the scope of whose activities is less than some of its proponents might have hoped for. Hicks says that in West Pakistan, following the secession of Bangladesh, "a new little federation was set up, perhaps viable, but a sad comedown from the plan for the federation of the entire subcontinent." (Hicks 1978:117) Indeed, the new little Pakistani federalism was established with only four provinces.

LIVING FEDERALISM   The flexibility of federalism, Saladin explains, is what furnishes its vitality. Genuine living federalism ("lebendiger Föderalismus") requires flexibility throughout the system if it is to stay alive and remain active. (Saladin 1978:407-08)

LOCAL FEDERALISM   Luther Gulick argued "the case for local federalism." (Gulick 1962:152) By this he meant "the assumption of the metropolitan responsibility by a more extended unit of government," through "the creation of a new local federated metropolitan government." (Ibid., p. 153.)

LOOSE FEDERALISM   Political union which cannot be tight because of the significant differences existing among its constituents. Hicks observes that the British, at the time of their exit from India, "tried hard to establish a single (although invariably loose) federation for the whole subcontinent." However, because of the heterogeneity of subcontinent populations and the diversity of cultural and political experience, this was not possible. (Hicks 1978:85)

MADISONIAN FEDERALISM   Greilsammer equates Madisonian federalism with Hamiltonian federalism. (Greilsammer in Elazar 1979a:112) See the entry for Hamiltonian federalism and the references to Madison in the name index.

MANAGERIAL FEDERALISM   In the managerial model of federalism, "the states and localities are cast in the roles of middle and lower echelons of management that cannot be trusted to follow orders without being paid off and reined in." In Schechter's view this is a distorted approach to American federalism because, with this interpretation, "[t]he political idea of states as polities and localities as communities has all but disappeared." (Schechter in Hawkins 1982:61)

MARBLE CAKE FEDERALISM   Morton Grodzins identified the
rainbow or marble cake as a "far more accurate image" of the
American federal system than the layer cake. The marble cake is
"characterized by an inseparable mingling of differently colored
ingredients, the colors appearing in vertical and diagonal
strands and unexpected whirls."   Drawing the parallel, Grodzins
said that, "As colors are mixed in the marble cake, so functions
are mixed in the American federal system." (Grodzins in U.S.
President, Commission on National Goals, Goals for Americans, p.
265.) He further explained to a broad readership that,
"Functions are not neatly parceled out among the many
governments. They are shared functions. It is difficult to find
any governmental activity which does not involve three of the
so-called 'levels' of the federal system." (Ibid., p. 266.) The
association of the American federal system with a marble cake may
have been made orignally by Joseph E. McLean. (McLean 1952 quoted
in Graves 1974:46)
     In the view of the ACIR, "An extraordinary degree of
'marbleization' has become the overwhelmingly dominant trait of
contemporary intergovernmental relations." (ACIR, 1976:65 and
1981a:40) Walker says the "'marble cake' [was] . . . baked during these three decades"--1930-60. Of that, "there can be little
doubt." (Walker 1981c:84) He feels that the marble cake metaphor
particularly "capture[d] the relatively structured, simple, and
stabilized, though obviously somewhat complex pattern of the
[1950s] . . . The 'ingredients,' . . . were almost wholly the
federal government and the states; the chocolate and vanila."
(Ibid., p. 91.)
     "The renewed interest in functional reassignment during the
1970s," the editor of the National Civic Review (Joan A. Casey)
believes, "has largely been a reflection of mounting concern
about accountability stemming from what has become a 'super-
marbleized' and overloaded federal system." ("The Overloaded System," 1980:305) Duchacek uses "marble cake" as a synonym for
cooperative federalism. (Duchacek 1970:318)

MARGINAL FEDERALISM   Federalism so weak that the system to
which the expression "marginally federal" is applied might just
as well be identified as a unitary system. Hicks says that "the
Constitution which [India] adopted in 1947 (essentially drawn up
by the British in 1935 for a different purpose) can only be
called marginally federal or quasi-federal." (Hicks 1978:85)
Hicks contends that the development of India since independence
has shown it to be even less federal than at the time of its
marginally federal beginnings.

MARKETPLACE FEDERALISM   This is a metaphorical, diffusive,
futuristic model for American federalism. It represents the opposite of a total nationalization of governmental functions. In
a pragmatic marketplace federalism, briefly described but dis-
missed as unlikely to be adopted (in Leach in Yarbrough et al.
1972:82), there would be tens of thousands of jurisdictions with

power to exercise significant choices on behalf of their constituents. Neighborhood councils would proliferate in large
cities. This conceptualization is closely related to public
choice theory.

MARSHALLIAN FEDERALISM   "[I]n terms of American constitutional history . . . a federal constitutional system in
which the nation is dominant in relation to each and all of the
member-states is Marshallian in character, after the great early
Chief Justice [John] Marshall of the United States who did so
much to build a strong national authority out of the factionalism
of the individual states." (McWhinney 1965:17)

MASONRY WALL FEDERALISM   According to President Ronald Reagan, "The [American] founding fathers saw the federal system constructed something like a masonry wall."   "The states are the
bricks," the President explained," and "the national government
is the mortar."   "For the structure to stand plum with the Constitution, there must be a proper mix of brick and mortar."
(Quoted in Hawkins 1982:79)   "Unfortunately," in Reagan's view,
"over the years, many people have come . . . to believe that
Washington is the whole wall, a wall that incidentally leans,
sags, and bulges under its own weight." (Ibid.)

MATRIX FEDERALISM   According to Elazar, "the basis of American governmental organization from its original perspective,"
that is, "the fundamental distribution of powers among multiple
centers," involves a sharing "across [a] matrix, not the devolution of powers from a single center down a pyramid." (Elazar
1976:12)   For Elazar, "each cell in the matrix represents an
independent political actor and an arena for political action."
Although, "some cells are larger and some smaller and the powers
assigned to each may reflect that difference," nevertheless,
"none is 'higher' or 'lower' in importance than any other."   This
matrix model of American federalism "also clearly delineates the
separation of powers among coequal branches of government (executive, legislative, judicial) within each cell. We call that
matrix federalism." (Ibid.)   Rothman says that the original
"hybrid formulation" devised at the Constitutional Convention--
partly national, partly federal--"suggests a matrix model of
American federalism with power distributed among multiple centers." (Rothman 1978:112)

MATURE FEDERALISM   This expression is most familiarly re-
called from the title of the book edited by Macmahon in 1955,
Federalism, Mature and Emergent. Essays in the book are said to
portray "the realities of a maturing federal system at work . . .
drawn from . . . [several] field[s] of policy and administration." (Macmahon 1955:vii)   Part Two of the Macmahon work is
"Basic Controls in a Maturing System."   The dictionary definition
of mature is "complete and finished in natural growth or development."   To be maturing is "to evolve toward full development." (American Heritage Dictionary, 1971 ed.)

MAXIMAL FEDERALISM   This is an ideal type description of
Riker for those situations in which "the ruler(s) of the federation [would usually] make decisions without consulting the rulers
of the member governments." (Riker 1964:6)   He suggests that
"[t]he Soviet Union may be an example of a federation at the maximum . . . [since] the guarantee of independence to constituent
units seems only nominal, except, perhaps in the area of . . .
the cultural life of linguistic and ethnic minorities around whom
the union republics are constructed." (Ibid.) Federations "which
are closer to the maximum than to the minimum [Riker describes]
as centralized"; "those closer to the minimum than to the maximum
are [for him] peripheralized." (Ibid.)

MEDIEVAL-CONSTITUTIONALIST FEDERALISM   Riley applies this
label to one of two strands (the other is democratic federalism)
of the federalist thought of Montesquieu. (Riley 1978:77)   He
feels Montesquieu's medieval-constitutionalist federalism was
more important for the French political theorist than his democratic federalism.   Parrington says that it was "from the
Federalists of the Montesquieu school" that John C. Calhoun "drew
his theory of static government, resulting from exactly balanced
powers. . . . " (Parrington II, 1927:69)   This is the essence of
medieval-constitutionalist federalism.

MEDIEVAL-CORPORATIVE FEDERALISM   Riley says, in an essay on
Kant, that "the property of the nobility and churches . . . had
sustained that form of corporatism that one might call 'medieval
federalism.'"   (Riley 1979a:16)   "The   Kantian   state   . . .
[claimed] a right to 'inspect' the influence of [the] great corporate bodies" which were the basic units of medieval-corporative
federalism. (Ibid.)

MERCANTILIST FEDERALISM   This expression is used by Franck
in his discussions of efforts of predominantly white business
interests in Africa to bring about economic unity. His research
shows that, "The determined and persistent, if unsuccessful,
mercantilist-federalist campaign reached its climax between 1925
and 1955." (Franck 1968:27)   But "mercantilist-federalism had
[not] been purely a white-man's policy."   Franck observes that,
"When the negotiations for East African federation began in 1963,
it was wrongly   assumed by Kenyans and Tanganyikans that
mercantilist-federalism" had   only   white   interests   in   view.
(Ibid., p. 30.)

MERE FEDERALISM   Federalism only in the limited sense in
which it was defined at the time of the American Constitutional
Convention, that is, a confederation. Tansill notes that, "At
the outset of the [Philadelphia] debates it became clear that the
aim of many delegates was not confederation [mere federalism] but
a strong national government." (Tansill 1927:927, quoted in Anderson 1961:178) Edmond Randolph urged his fellow-delegates to

agree to the proposition, "That a union of the States merely foederal will not accomplish the object proposed by the articles of confederation, namely, 'common defence, security of liberty, and general welfare.'" (Quoted in Anderson 1961:178)

META-FEDERALISM   It has been suggested that the European Economic Community may represent an instance of a meta-federal governmental structure. (Stein 1979:898 citing the thinking of Covey T. Oliver)   The prefix "meta" denotes change, transformation, or transcendence. (American Heritage Dictionary, 1971 ed.)   Thus a meta-federal system is one which exhibits traditional federal principles but in very innovative ways.

METHODOLOGICAL FEDERALISM   Franck points out that "federation can be essentially an ideology or a methodology. . . . The methodological federalist pursues unity [Franck was writing with specific reference to East Africa] only so far as is necessary to achieve his limited objective," e.g., "cheaper railroad fares or a power grid." (Franck 1968:26)   "The origins of federalism in East Africa," Franck believes, were "methodological."   From the most critical perspective, federalism was simply "a device to develop [as independence neared] a white mercantile hegemony throughout East Africa similar to the one in Kenya and, later, in the Federation of Rhodesia and Nyasaland." (Ibid., pp. 26-27.)

METROPOLITAN FEDERALISM   Metropolitan federalism is one of the remedies proposed for dealing with the numerous problems of sprawling urban areas containing numerous local governmental jurisdictions.   There would not be an amalgamation of all local governments into one, but instead a federation of governments, with areawide problems being handled by the new local-federal government while more restricted problems remained the responsibility of the smaller governments.   Toronto and Miami are examples of metropolitan federalism.   The principal technical difficulty in implementing metropolitan federalism is deciding which functions are local, which are areawide.   Graves observes that this approach "is in effect a partial city-county consolidation . . . [but] does not require that either city or county surrender its identity and is, therefore, more feasible from a political point of view." (Graves 1964:643)   The Toronto metropolitan federation dates from 1952, the Miami experiment from 1957.   The pioneer public administration scholar, Luther Gulick, has asserted that "for most large, sprawling metropolitan areas the only practicable choice is a new metropolitan federation of some sort." (Gulick 1962:153)

MILITARY FEDERALISM   Riker stresses the significance of a military situation or external threat to the creation of federalism.   For example, the West German federal system "was a proposed bargain in the face of the Soviet military threat . . . " (Riker 1964:37 quoted in Dikshit 1971:185)   Further, behind the

Austrian federal system "stands the fact of anschluss, the ever-present fear of an aggressive Germany." (Riker 1964:38 quoted in ibid., p. 187.) Dikshit disagrees with Riker's strong emphasis on the military origins of federalism. He believes that "an external military threat, which is in most cases an important agent in bringing discordant units together into a federation, is nevertheless [particularly in modern times] not a necessary condition for the origin of federal unions under all circumstances." (Ibid., pp. 188-89.)

MINIATURE FEDERALISM   The federal concept of intergovernmental relations also has been suggested as a means of understanding intracounty contacts. For example, "County commissioners [in the United States] . . . govern federal republics in 'miniature,'" according to Marando and Thomas. Besides legislating for county residents living in unincorporated areas, "Commissioners must also operate as middlemen between state and city on many activities . . . [and] administer state services to city residents. In addition, they must coordinate many services, such as law enforcement and road construction, which overlap city boundaries." (All Marando and Thomas 1977:135)

MINIFEDERALISM   A federal union which is small, both in the objects toward which the union is directed and probably also the size of the constituent units. The expression "mini federation" is derived from Hicks who speculates about a federation composed of Dominica, St. Lucia, and perhaps other small islands in the Windward group, bordered on the west by the Caribbean Sea and on the east by the Atlantic Ocean. (Hicks 1978:62)

MINIMAL FEDERALISM   This condition is, for Riker, one in which "the ruler(s) of the federation can make decisions in only one narrowly constructed category of action without obtaining the approval of the rulers of the constituent units." (Riker 1964:5-6) He explains that "[t]he minimum is one category of action, not zero, because if the ruler(s) of the federation rule nothing, neither a federation nor even a government can be said to exist." (Ibid., p. 6.) Like maximal federalism, this is essentially an analytical, not a descriptive, category. Even so, federations of ancient states are classifiable as minimal in those situations where the "rulers were authorized to make decisions independently only about military tactics and then only during the course of a battle." (Ibid.)

MIXED FEDERALISM   This term McWhinney uses synonymously with hybrid federal system. Chapter 5 of McWhinney 1966 is entitled, "Mixed or 'Hybrid' Federal Constitutional Systems." See entry for hybrid federalism.

MODERN FEDERALISM   (1) Elazar identifies as the sires of modern federalism the framers of the U.S. Constitution who "bypass[ed] . . . the sovereignty issue by vesting sovereignty in

the people and making all governments simply the trustees of
those powers specifically delegated to them by the people through
proper constitutional mechanisms." "This," in Elazar's opinion,
"is the basis of modern federalism, the great American invention
of the 18th century." (Elazar 1979b:5) Bone says that, "the modern concept of federalism emerged from the Constitutional Convention at Philadelphia in 1787." (Bone 1972:387) Wheare observes that, "the modern idea of what federal government is has
been determined by the United States of America. . . . Many consider it the most important and the most successful example."
(Wheare 1953:1 quoted in ibid. See also Elazar 1972, "Modern
Federalism," pp. 13-19.) Mogi notes that "American federalism
was first put before the American public in the . . . Federalist,
which was the first foreshadowing of modern federalism." (Mogi
1931a:238) Diamond regards modern federalism and American
federalism as synonymous. (Diamond 1973:134) Most recently modern federalism was used in a U.S. Senate speech by Senator
William V. Roth of Delaware when he introduced a resolution pro-
posing a National Conference on Federalism to try to do something
about the "confusing and impenetrable maze" which is "modern
federalism" in the United States. ("Convocation on Federalism
Gains Congressional Support," 1980:5) Such a convocation has not
been held. (2) According to Elazar, Althusius should be regarded
as "the godfather of modern federalism." (Elazar 1979b:1) (3) In
the European context, Riley identifies "the modern federal state"
as one critical response to "the triumph of the national state,"
since modern federalism stands against "absolute concentration of
power at the expense of territorial autonomy. . . . " (Riley
1976:18)

MONARCHIC FEDERALISM   A federation headed by one or more
monarchs. Freeman suggested late in the nineteenth century that
"the decaying Ottoman Empire . . . afford[ed] a most tempting
field for the experiment of some form or other of monarchic
Federation." (Freeman 1893:85) He cautioned, however, that while
"there is not abstract absurdity in supposing that a league of
monarchies, especially constitutional monarchies, might assume
the true Federal form . . . such a constitution has never existed; it would be a political machine even more delicate and
hard to work than a Federation of Republics." (Ibid., pp. 74,
75.) The United Arab Emirates could be regarded as a contemporary manifestation of monarchic federalism.

MONISTIC FEDERALISM   "For purposes of useful classification
and analysis of the various federal constitutional systems,"
McWhinney calls "a constitutional system characterized by
increasingly centripetal tendencies in terms of effective location of policy-making" one which "is monist in emphasis . . .
this, we might say, is Monistic federalism." (McWhinney
1965:16-17)

MONOETHNIC FEDERALISM   Monoethnic federalism describes a situation in which internal boundaries can be drawn without reference to the geographic location of ethnic, tribal, or linguistic groups. (Duchacek 1970:293)   Duchacek offers the United States, Australian, West German, Austrian, and Latin American federations as examples of "somewhat monoethnic federations." (Ibid.) In each there is one predominant ethnic group.

MONTESQUIEUEAN FEDERALISM   What Riley calls "Montesquieuean 'foderalism,'" using the archaic spelling, at its best emphasized the living of the good life in small political jurisdictions. (Riley 1978:94)   The framers of the U.S. Constitution, as their views found expression in the Federalist Papers, believed they had developed "a new conception of republicanism which made Montesquieuean 'foderalism' unnecessary and undesirable. . . . " (Ibid.) They believed they had found a way by which sovereignty could be divided in such a manner as to bring about the advantages simultaneously of centralized and noncentralized political authority.   See the name index for other references to the federal thought of Montesquieu.

MORE PERFECT FEDERALISM   In "the more perfect mode of federalism"--as understood in the mid-nineteenth century--"every citizen of each particular state owe[d] obedience to two governments--that of his own state, and that of the federation." The United States was identified as an instance of more perfect federalism, a key aspect of which was "a court of justice [the Supreme Court] . . . [which was] supreme over the various governments, both state and federal," and had "the right to declare that any new law made, or act done by them, exceeds the powers assigned to them by the federal constitution, and in consequence has no legal validity." (All John Stuart Mill quoted in Bouvier 1867:765)

MULTICENTERED FEDERALISM   In a multicentered federal system, according to Elazar, "politics [remain] noncentralized"; the multicentered system functions "through the separation of powers and a continued reliance on checks and balances."   Elazar rejects the "adaptation of managerial devices and ideas [as hostile] to a multicentered federal system. . . . " (Elazar 1981b:19)

MULTIDIMENSIONAL FEDERALISM   This expression is one of several applied by Djordjevic to modern Yugoslav federalism.   He writes: "The creation of multi-dimensional federalism is a result of the contemporary epoch, full of the struggles of classes of peoples, and of groups and individuals to overcome the apparatus and cult of the State including centralism, political monism, hierarchy and the contradiction between the whole and its parts." (Djordjevic 1975:80-81)   Most federal systems are multidimensional, including more than a central-provincial relation.

MULTINATIONAL FEDERALISM   This descriptive term denotes federations containing multiple ethnic and lingual groups. Thus "[i]n the Soviet Union . . . the internal federal boundaries divided the country into fifteen union republics, each dominantly inhabited by a different ethnic and lingual group and each endowed with territorial autonomy and equal representation by twenty-five deputies each in the Supreme Soviet." (Duchacek 1970:294) Furthermore, "ethnic subdivisions within each of the fifteen union republics are also endowed with territorial autonomy and direct representation. . . . " (Ibid.) India is another case of multinational federalism.

MUNICIPAL FEDERALISM   This is the Grant-Nixon label for what is more commonly termed metropolitan federalism. These authors cite as "examples of municipal federalism" the two-tiered structures of London, Toronto, and Miami. The first two are regarded as better expressions of municipal federalism than is Miami. (Grant and Nixon 1982:396-98)

MUTUAL FEDERALISM   A reference to the work, primarily, of Pierre-Joseph Proudhon (1809-65). "The essence of the economic order," as Barker interprets Proudhon, "was a federal essence: the order . . . was by its nature une federation mutualiste, composed of occupational groups freely formed for the purpose of production and exchange and benefit." (Barker 1951:35) Society for Proudhon is naturally "a federal society of complementary occupations." (Ibid., p. 37.) The word "mutual" is the equivalent of "synidcal." "Each autonomous group of producers freely exchang[es] its products for those of other groups on a just basis of reciprocal equality. . . . " (Ibid.)

MUTUAL INTEREST FEDERALISM   A federation whose "population is bound together by common ethnic origins, a single language, a joint economic effort, and shared political objectives." (De Blij 1967:450) Another case of mutual interest federalism would be where "peoples who differ in several important respects may temporarily be faced by the same enemy, and their mutual interest may lie in warding off that danger" through federation. De Blij identifies the American federal Constitution as an instance of this type of mutual interest federalism, observing that "while the joint concern of the original thirteen states no longer faces the United States today, the strength and eminence of the country are based upon contributions made by all; thus every state has a stake in its perpetuation." (All ibid.)

NATIONAL FEDERALISM   (1) Federalism at the level of the nation-state. (2) Wright attributes one important use of the expression "national federalism" to James L. Sundquist. (Wright 1978:19) Perhaps the most vigorous defense of national federalism, however, was made by then-Senator Joseph S. Clark of Pennsylvania in 1960. Clark argued for "national federalism" in the belief that, "We will solve the problems of providing adequate local public services when we evolve new concepts of Federalism in line with the reality of modern life--and not until then." (The Federal Government and the Cities, 1961:40) "Our traditional concept of Federalism," in Clark's view, was "outmoded in the last century by the urbanization of our society. . . . " (Ibid., p. 49.) "Federalism," for Clark, was an instance "of political lag which urgently deserve[d] our attention." (Ibid.) Yet, even Clark recognized the power in the word federalism and chose in his term "national federalism" to modify but not to obliterate it, even if its traditional meanings would be almost destroyed. Landau attributes this tendency to attach modifiers which do more than slightly alter customary conceptualizations to the fact that "'federalism' possesses powerful persuasive (valuational) connotations in addition to its descriptive properties. . . . To say that 'federalism is dead,' that it is no longer applicable to the present circumstances, [would] be equivalent to saying that a cherished and enduring value is dead. Unwilling to do so we invent . . . national . . . federalism--and say only that dual federalism is dead." (Landau 1973:178-79. Landau names several other varieties of federalism besides national which have been offered as possible substitutes for the old dual federalism.)

NATIONAL-SUPREMACY FEDERALISM   Approach to federalism attributed to Chief Justice John Marshall by Belz. According to Belz, Marshall's distinct approach to federalism consisted in the fact that, "though recognizing state powers, [he] expounded a theory of national-supremacy federalism which held that federal power properly exercised could in case of conflict supersede state power and control any person in American territory." (Belz 1978:xiv)

NATION-CENTERED FEDERALISM   Corwin believed that in the span of years from 1789-1860 nation-centered and state-centered concepts of American federalism vied for dominance. (Corwin in McCloskey 1962:188-89.   View cited in Walker 1981c:47) "From Hamilton as the first Secretary of the Treasury to John Marshall as Chief Justice of The Supreme Court (1800-1835), and thence to Daniel Webster in the Senate in the 1830s and 1840s," Walker notes, "a nationalist theory of the Union was enunciated." (Ibid.) This nationalist theory consisted of these key elements:

[1] "The Constitution was interpreted . . . as the people's great charter.
[2]. "It was supreme as law, and created a national government whose enumerated powers were buttressed by a broad reserve of implied powers.
[3] In combination, these powers were adequate to meet the most diverse demands placed on the Union government." (Ibid.)

Leach says that, "The nation-centered theory of federalism posits the idea that the Constitution is a document emanating from and ratified by the American people as a whole," and this is probably the most common theme when the concept of nation-centered federalism is broached. (Leach 1970:10) Beer elaborates on the "national theory of American federalism" by presenting its claim that "a single sovereign power, the people of the United States, created both the federal and state governments, delegating to each a certain limited authority. . . . " (Beer 1978:12) "[P]opular sovereignty [thus] appears as a single national will acting as the constituent power." (Ibid.) (2) Nation-centered federalism is also appropriate to discussions of Canadian federalism. What Black calls the centralist concept "centers [Canadian] federalism on the government in Ottawa and embodies the idea that the whole people of Canada is the sole source of political authority in the nation." (View of Black 1975 noted in Leach 1977:127)

NATURAL FEDERALISM   (1) Spontaneously occuring federalism; not specifically provided for by conscious governmental or private decision. This concept of federalism is associated with the German writer Friedrich Tonnies who, in Community and Society, emphasized "what might be called the 'naturally federated' texture of pre-industrial life. Federalism here is not principally a political instrumentality but rather a social patchwork arising spontaneously from the autonomy of many social associations and the cooperation that naturally arises between them." (View cited in Susser 1979:105) Natural federalism is "spontaneously social, autonomously communal, and [possesses a] structurally variegated character. . . . " (Ibid.) (2) Natural federalism may also be used synonymously with the usual pattern of federalism.   Marc says that "it was the American Revolution . . . leading to the establishment of the present Constitution of the United States, which provided the historical opportunity for territorial, political federalism to be expressed in a two-level model so miraculously equilibrated and successful that it has come to be considered the 'natural' form of federalism." (Marc 1979:118)

NECESSARY FEDERALISM   This notion relates to "Federal action in the area of fundamental rights [in the United States] regardless of whether welcomed by the State--Necessary federalism." For Shuman civil rights legislation in the 1960s exemplified necessary federalism in that it involved essential but undesired intergovernmental relations. (Shuman 1968:12)

NEGATIVE FEDERALISM   American federalists in the 1960s were, from one perspective, categorized by Deuerlein into negative and positive federalists. The negative federalists opposed all central government actions which challenged the power of individual states and localities. Senator Barry Goldwater, the Republican presidential candidate in 1964, was a leading negative federalist. (Deuerlein 1972:293)

NEIGHBORHOOD FEDERALISM   (1) Mary Parker Follett analyzed political forces operative at the neighborhood level which were federal in character. Elliott says her book The New State was a provocative "attempt to decentralize with the neighborhood group as the unit. . . . The community principle of the neighborhood group she hope[d] to make the unit of political association." (Elliott 1928:433.   Elliott believed Follett did not, however, make clear how this new federalism of the neighborhoods was to take place.)   (2) Also enlightening is the discussion of "Inter-communalism: Neighborhood Cooperation" by Morris and Hess (1975).   In this model a "neighborhood assembly or government [would] . . . symbolize [the] cohesion [of the organized neighborhood], and [represent] the community in its dealings with the city . . . Neighborhood corporations [would negotiate] with the city to take over service operations on a contractual basis for the neighborhood. . . ." (Ibid., p. 145.)   Also federal in character are the "strong links [which develop] among many com-munities, reinforcing each other in their struggles." (Ibid.)

NEO-FEDERALISM   See also new federalism. Posey 1965 has a chapter section heading, "Neo-Federalism," in which he discusses the "increase in importance of [the American] federal govern-ment."   This increase he attributes to two principal factors: (1) "the enlarged circuit of economic activity . . . [associated with] [t]he industrial revolution [which] brought an ever-increasing specialization of enterprise, resulting in an ever-enlarging radius of economic activity" and (2) "the doctrine of implied powers . . . [which enables] the national government [to] exercise any power that can be reasonably implied from the ex-pressly granted powers, [which] has brought about an expansion in federal jurisdiction." (All Posey 1965:200)

NEW FEDERALISM (GENERAL)   This is probably the most frequently used but also it is among the most generalized of the federalism   descriptors   presented   in   this   volume.   The bibliography will indicate more uses than can be presented here. Following is a brief sample of usages of new federalism in modern scholarly literature. They are arranged chronologically based on the period with which the writer was concerned.
The federal union proposed by the Constitution of 1787 is referred to as a new federalism. Kenyon says this new federalism was not appreciated by the antifederalists, some of whom pro-fessed to believe that, "Either the new government would collapse or it would endeavor to stamp out diversity and level all citizens to a new uniformity in order to survive." (Kenyon in Roche 1967:201)   Kenyon believes that "men of little faith" who thought like this "fail[ed] to grasp the principles of the new federalism . . . [a] proposed government [which was] one of limited, enumerated powers."   Instead, "They constantly spoke and wrote as if the scope and extent of its powers would be the same as those of the respective state governments, or of a unified national government." (Ibid.)

W. Y. Elliott spoke in 1928 of "a new federalism, not
directed as federalism used to be, toward the integration of
several small states into a larger whole, but rather toward the
disintegration of the great State into small national groups on
which large powers are to be conferred by way of devolution."
(Elliott 1928:92)

Noting that there was "a basic change" in the American
federal system during the Great Depression of the 1930s, Gilbert
and Smith believe "it is probably correct to speak of a 'new
federalism,'" particularly as a result of the Social Security Act
of 1935 which "redistributed . . . responsibility for programs
formerly considered state and local . . . it shifted the fiscal
balance of federalism so that federal grants became more of a
necessity than a supplement in most state programs. . . . "
(Gilbert and Smith in Stedman 1968:136) Jane Perry Clark identified cooperative federalism as the new federalism in her 1938
study, The Rise of a New Federalism.

Berle felt that the "steady evolution of economic organization [was] forcing a new federalism [in 1955]. . . ." (Berle in
Macmahon 1955:70) The elements of the new federalist economics
included

> [1] industries national in scope [which] have
> steadily gravitated towards governmental and even
> central governmental control . . . [2] industries
> providing products or services deemed necessary by the
> community, and dominated by so small a group of
> enterprises that a measure of national planning and
> control, set up by or in cooperation with government,
> has been found necessary by the community or by
> industry, or both . . . [3] a group of enterprises . .
> . brought into existence by and largely conditioned
> upon the needs and desires of government. (Ibid.)

Writing in the Eisenhower era (1957), Lerner observed that
it was "characteristic of the American temper that after each extension of the Federal power, a new equilibrium is struck at the
higher level. Hence the 'new federalism' of the present generation, which runs toward the return of power to the local units."
(Lerner 1957:403)

Ferry enunciated a new federalism for black Americans.
Blacks, Ferry declared, were not looking for "a New Jerusalem,"
nor were they anticipating an integrated national community. Instead, they had, in the late 1960s, "a vision of a new federalism
that will give 10 percent of our citizens the chance they are
seeking to make whatever they want to make of themselves, their
culture, and their community." (Ferry 1968:17 quoted in Leach in
Yarbrough et al. 1972:74) Black communities should be, in
Ferry's view, set up as autonomous political entities.

Drucker seemed to visualize elements of cooperative federalism and its extension into creative and direct federalism

in his 1971 perception of a new federalism. Whereas, "Traditional federalism [saw] relationships of coexistence and competition between the federal government and the various states . . . in the New Federalism other political units in addition to the states (especially the metropolitan areas) are directly in relation with the federal government and work directly with it." "More important," from Drucker's point of view, was the fact that "institutions that are not 'government' but private increasingly become the agents of government in the fulfillment of public functions. . . . " (All Drucker 1971:69)

New federalism is, of course, used frequently in other federal systems to characterize changes in course. The earliest use of new federalism encountered in the research for this publication was by Baumgartner in 1851 in the Swiss publication, Schweizerspiegel. (Cited in Frenkel 1975:727)

Starr wrote in 1977 of Australia's "two new federalisms." He referred to the federal policies of Prime Minister Gough Whitlam initiated in December 1972 and those of Prime Minister Malcolm Fraser begun in November 1975. (Starr 1977:7-26) Whitlam's Liberal party policies were criticized by opponents as "contradictions of federal constitutional arrangements in such a way that the role of the Commonwealth [central government] would be enhanced." (Ibid., pp. 12-13.) In contrast, Liberal policies (as offered by Fraser) were said to be "more in step with the interests of State parliamentarians, who tend (irrespective of party allegiance) to be reluctant to surrender their prestige and power." (Ibid., p. 26.) Cranston identifies "[t]he major element of the 'new federalism' . . . [as] the 'handing back' to the States of a fixed share of the revenue derived from personal income tax, coupled with a reduction of specific purpose grants. . . . " (Cranston 1979:136)

NEW FEDERALISM (NIXON)   The new federalism of Richard Nixon apparently started from a largely unnoticed Nixon radio address from Williamsburg during the 1968 presidential campaign. (Walker 1981c:101) As President, Richard Nixon announced his ideas for a new federalism in a speech telecast nationwide on August 8, 1969. He repeated the thrust of his remarks in an address to the Governors Conference the next month. The dominant idea was to shift back "power, funds and authority . . . increasingly to those governments closest to the people . . . to help regain control of our national destiny by returning a greater share of control to state and local authorities." (Nixon quoted in Leach 1970:16) In the television speech, Nixon added that, "For a third of a century power and responsibility have flowed toward Washington . . . We intend to reverse this tide, and to turn back to the states a greater measure of responsibility." This turn back would not be "a way of avoiding problems, but . . . a better way of solving problems." ("Text of Nixon's Address to the Nation . . . " 1969:10c) Michael Reagan identified Nixon's new federalism label as an "attempt at labeling the system for the purposes of both description and prescription. . . . " (M. Reagan

1972:163)   The President indicated four essential elements of
the new federalism:

[1] a complete replacement of the present welfare
system;
[2] a comprehensive new job training and placement
program;
[3] a revamping of the Office of Economic Opportunity;
and
[4] a start on the sharing of Federal tax revenues with
the states. ("Text of Nixon's Address," 1969:10c)

Colman saw the new federalism of the Nixon (and Ford) years as
comprehending the following elements:

Decentralization of governmental decision-making on
domestic issues; for strictly federal programs . . .
more decisions should be made in regional offices and
fewer in Washington headquarters; for decisions
involving matters of combined federal-state-local
concern or of federal aid, the federal government
should make decisions in broader terms, leaving much
more flexibility to states and localities. To implement the decentralization policy, federal aid should be
dispensed in broader terms . . . [The federal government should] [p]rovid[e] funds instead of services to
needy people. . . . (Colman 1975:328)

A 1980 retrospective view of new federalism said its goals were
to

[1] reverse the flow of power, funds and responsibilities away from the federal government and toward
the states, localities, and general public;
[2] reduce the size and power of the federal
bureaucracy;
[3] simplify intergovernmental administrative
machinery; and
[4] bolster the authority of elected officials of
general purpose governmental units and curb that of
private nonprofit organizations, special districts,
and other so-called 'paragovernments.' ("The Overloaded System," 1980:304)

Richard Nathan, speaking for the Nixon Administration, said "the
key idea of the new federalism [was] the need to sort out
governmental functions more carefully, to rationalize the role
and responsibilities of the different levels of Government. .
. . " (Congress, Senate, Hearings, 1973:88-89)
A 1981 ACIR study identified three major successes for
Nixonian new federalism in its structural efforts to shift previously federal responsibilities to states and localities.

These were passage of the General Revenue Sharing program in
1972, the Comprehensive Employment and Training Act (CETA) of
1973, and the Community Development Block Grant Program (CDBG) in
1974. (ACIR, 1981a:117. All but general revenue sharing were
finally enacted during the Ford Administration.) Walker notes
that, "While none of the special revenue sharing proposals were
enacted in their original form, [the] Nixon initiatives did lay
the groundwork for block-grant compromises." (Walker 1981c:105)
     Walker finds the following pardoxes in Nixonian new federal-
ism:

     [1] A conscious presidential effort to curb cate-
gorical grants . . . yet their number only multiplied.
     [2] A serious presidential drive . . . to 'devolve'
greater decisionmaking authority . . . yet intrusive
conditions . . . increased.
     [3] Most [of the new forms of federal aid which
emerged] came to resemble the older, categorical form.
     [4] Greater managerial confusion [actually] resulted
[from the effort to streamline the grant delivery
system]--thanks to more programs, more recipients,
and more conditions. . . .
     [5] Generalists and general aovernments were favored by
presidential efforts, yet . . . no effort [was made] to
distinguish among subnational governments that were
genuinely general. . . .
     [6] Some sorting out of governmental functions was
contemplated . . but the overall tendency was a
massively expanded commingling of governmental
functions. (Ibid., pp. 112-13.)

Elazar saw in Nixonian new federalism an attempt to supplant
traditional notions of American federalism (which he interprets
using the matrix analogy) with the corporate model for the exercise of power. Key decisions would be made in Washington and
states and localities would have only the freedom to adopt the
specific techniques they would use to conform to policies unilaterally established above them. (Elazar 1973b:257) In Nixonian
new federalism the pyramid, not the matrix, becomes the appropriate federalism analogy. (Elazar 1981b:7) Decentralization is
substituted for noncentralization. But Peirce says Nixon's new
federalism was "a policy designed to counteract the flood of narrow categorical aid programs under Lyndon Johnson's 'Great
Society.'" However, he adds that "the promised devolution of
power to states and localities proved chimerical" since "Congress[,] during the '70s[,] added some 150 new categorical aid
programs" and "[r]evenue sharing and other block grants of the
New Federalist era, intended to come with less strings, became
hemmed." (Peirce 1980:5)
     New York Times columnist Richard Madden said that new
federalism did not have more success because the President's
primary interests were in foreign affairs; also, the Democrats

controlled both houses of Congress. (Madden 1974:4)   It should
be remembered that the new federalism initiative was undertaken
three years before Watergate.   After Watergate, however, there
was even less Democratic congressional willingness to support
Nixon-sponsored measures in any field.   In a restrained rebuttal
to the President, Democratic Congressman Thomas Ashley criticized
"[t]he fiscal tools of New Federalism," because they were "designed to strengthen very small units of government, thus sub-
sidizing fragmentation rather than using resources to improve local capability through consolidation of overlapping and duplica-
tory   areas   of   jurisdictions."   (Congressional   Record,
1973:H10645-46) Ashley also felt that, "[T]he Federal Government
[should] not abandon its role in establishing national policy.
Otherwise we will further fragment [the] national effort and dis-
sipate the national resources of this country. . . . " (Ibid.)
Ashley favored the definition of national goals and then the
orchestration of "the different levels of government to meet
effectively specific objectives." (Ibid.)
     Wildavsky cited approvingly the research of Hudson who found
that, "Instead of promoting local autonomy, the New Federalism
grants . . . helped [in the case of the community Hudson studied]
to reduce city government autonomy." Indeed, "Since the early
1970s . . . dependence on federal funds as a source of revenue .
. . increased dramatically, local officials [became] politically
dependent on continued high levels of federal funding, and
federal 'strings' in the form of federal mandates affect[ed] local government activities more than ever before."   Thus, in
Hudson's view, "the New Federalism . . . reduced rather than
increased the city's independence from Washington." (Hudson
1980:91 cited in Wildavsky n.d.:70-71)

     NEW FEDERALISM (REAGAN)   President Ronald Reagan said in
his inauguaral address on January 20, 1981, that it was his
"intention to demand recognition of the distinction between the
powers granted to the Federal Government and those reserved to
the states and to the people." "All of us need to be reminded,"
he continued, "that the Federal Government did not create the
states; the states created the Federal Government." (Quoted in
Ayres 1981b:A13)
     Safire found the origins of the new federalism in Reagan
speeches in the mid-1970s (while he was Governor of California)
dealing with the idea of transferring federal programs to the
state and local levels. (Safire 1982:A5) Specifically, he suggested transferring $90 billion in federal programs to state and
local governments. However, he was criticized for omitting identification of sources for subnational funding of these programs.
     The President established a presidential advisory committee
on federalism by executive order on April 8, 1981. He also set up
a coordinating task force on federalism at the same time.   The
former was staffed primarily with elected public officials at all
levels; the latter with White House and Cabinet operatives.   In

this same period, speaking to governors assembled at the White
House, the President said that inauguration of a new federalism
was a principal goal of his administration.   As part of this
initiative he would try to convert as many categorical grants as
possible into block grants. (Ayres 1981a:3)   Columnist Neal
Peirce identified the new federalism initiative as "the highest
level effort in U.S. history to address reform of the federal
system." (Quoted in "Intergovernmental Focus," 1981:4)
     The principal enunciation of the new federalism came on
January 26, 1982, in his state of the Union address.   Reagan said
he would ask Congress to transfer to the states programs currently being administered by the federal government, programs estimated to cost $49 billion by fiscal year 1987.   "In a single
stroke," Reagan said, "we will be accomplishing a realignment
that will end cumbersome administration and spiraling costs of
the Federal level while we insure these programs will be more responsive to both the people they are meant to help and the people
who pay for them." (Quoted in "Text of President's Message . .
. ," 1982:A16)
     As originally proposed, Washington would take over the cost
of the Medicaid program.   States would get the full burden of Aid
to Families with Dependent Children (AFDC) and food stamps.   In
later versions, the federal government was assigned food stamps.
A temporary trust fund of $28 billion would be established to fi-
nance the shifted programs.   The fund would be filled with pro-
ceeds from oil windfall-profits taxes and gasoline, liquor, and
tobacco excise taxes.   States would have the option of continuing
or not continuing the transferred programs.   The trust fund would
gradually recede as federal taxes were reduced, then eliminated,
leaving revenues for the states to tap as they saw the need to do
so.   By 1991 the states would have either to raise additional revenue on their own or drop some of the programs which had been
shifted to them.   A minimum of 15 percent of the funds received
by the states in lieu of continuing old programs would have to be
passed on to the local level.   By 1988 states would have complete
responsibility for all programs involved in the swap.
     Weissert identified the following "key assumptions" which
seemed to be at the base of the new federalism:

     [1] "grass roots" governments are best equipped to
     diagnose and deal with problems;
     [2] states are willing and able to assume greater
     responsibility for the administration and financing of
     social programs;
     [3] state and local officials will cooperate and col-
     laborate more closely than in the past and will be able
     to "get their acts together" in the near future;
     [4] the appropriate roles of different levels of gov-
     ernment can be identified and functions can be reassigned
     in a reasonably systematic manner. (Weissert 1982:4)

Naftalin, not a supporter of the new federalism, identified the following aspects:

[1] sharp reduction in the federal funding of grant programs, abandoning some, decreasing others;
[2] substantial shift to state governments of responsibility for managing federally aided programs, with the federal government presumably relinquishing some tax source[s] that states can take as a tradeoff for the loss of federal money;
[3] encouragement of corporations, foundations, voluntary associations and individuals to substitute their resources and energies for the federal support being discontinued;
[4] tax incentives to stimulate investment that will create employment opportunities and reduce the need for programs of economic assistance; and
[5] a general lowering of expectations so that less is demanded of government. (Naftalin 1982:136-37)

Naftalin objected to the new federalism because of "its pervasively negative view concerning our capability as a nation to deal with domestic problems" and "[i]ts deep distrust of government [which] is tending to immobilize us, making it increasingly difficult to develop constructive initiatives." (Ibid., p. 139.)

Liberals generally found fault with the new federalism because of their conviction that middle and upper income taxpayers have much more political clout at state and local levels than less privileged groups. (View reported in Calkins and Shannon 1982:29) Constituencies representing minorities, central cities, and social welfare interests generally tend to be more strongly represented in Washington.

Elazar supported Reagan's efforts to bolster the position of the states in the American federal system and "thereby strengthen the system as a whole." (Elazar in Hawkins 1982:37) However, he felt that Reagan new federalism placed too much "reliance on simple notions of separating federal and state functions as a basis for policymaking rather than on strengthening the states by restoring classic patterns of intergovernmental cooperation." (Ibid., p. 38.)

New Feudalism   This is a derivative of new federalism. It has been employed in response to several new federalisms. In 1982, Georgia State Senator Julian Bond identified the new federalism of Ronald Reagan as "the new feudalism." It would divide rather than unite the nation. It would make very difficult national movements toward national goals, particularly in the areas of civil rights and social and economic programs. ("New Federalism," 1982:5) New York Democratic Governor Hugh Carey said that the new federalism was actually "a 'new feudalism,' which will pit states against each other and cities against their state capitals as all struggle anew for a fair share of dwindling federal funds or jockey to protect their own economic interests." ("New Federalism or Feudalism?" 1982:19)

NEW JUDICIAL FEDERALISM   Federalism in the judicial arena
in the United States in the Nixon years and immediately following
was identified as a new judicial federalism. (Weinberg
1977:1191-1244) This new model "requir[ed] deferences to state
administration and state adjudication that only yesterday were
thought unnecessary or unwise." (Ibid., pp. 1192-94. Her footnotes omitted) Two cases which well illustrated the deference
inherent in the new judicial federalism were Younger v. Harris
(401 U.S. 37 (1971)) and Rizzo v. Goode (423 U.S. 6 (1976)). The
former case, Weinberg says on the basis of her survey, "is almost
universally understood to have worked a revolution in the
availability of federal injunctions against state proceedings."
(Ibid., p. 1100. See also our federalism.) Henceforth, they
would be much more difficult to secure. In the latter case the
Supreme Court disallowed a federal injunction in a situation
involving alleged police misconduct. A federal judge had sought
to require Philadelphia to prepare and submit plans for improving
the processing of citizen complaints against the police and to
revise training programs and manuals subject to his veto. This
the Supreme Court, pursuant to the new judicial federalism, found
to be ill-conceived federal interference into essentially local
affairs.

NEW-MODELED FEDERALISM   Parrington summarizes the thought
of Francis Lieber under the heading, "new-modeled federalism."
This is the federalism of "an evolving state that draws all lesser sovereignties into its orbit by the law of attraction." (Parrington II, 1927:89) "Applying German liberalism to American
constitutionalism," Lieber succeeded, Parrington believes, "in
new-modeling the Federalism of Hamilton and sending it forth to
meet the needs of an imperializing generation." Although Lieber
associated himself with Webster as concerns "the organic nature
of the federal compact," Lieber "went further and elaborated a
theory of the state as an historical development that receives
its form and spirit from the impress of social needs." "In the
hands of Theodore Woolsey and John W. Burgess," Parrington concludes, Lieber's new-modeled federalism was "a structure that . .
. came to overtop all local and state sovereignties." (Ibid.)

NEW NEW FEDERALISM   (1) Because, in the 1960s, they saw
that "the social services [were] changing rapidly in response to
both poverty and affluence in America," Gilbert and Smith asserted that "a 'new, new' and a 'new, new, new' federalism [were]
now in evidence. By these [they] mean[t] the direct federalism
of grants to local governments, and the private federalism of
grants to individuals and non-governmental institutions."
(Gilbert and Smith in Stedman 1968:136) (2) Safire used this expression to distinguish between Reagan new federalism and Nixon
new federalism. "Reagan's new New Federalism is simpler and
more daring than old New Federalism," Safire said. (Safire
1982:A5) Nixon's new federalism was more centralist in that it

amounted to "national goals [being] set at the national level by the Congress and the president . . . with localities making decisions about how this national policy was to be carried out. Thus, the feds would say to the locals, 'do it your way,' . . . 'but do it.'" (Ibid.)

NEW-STYLE FEDERALISM   This variety of federalism Michael Reagan identifies as "a political and pragmatic concept, stressing the actual interdependence and sharing of functions between Washington and the states, and focusing on the mutual leverage that each level is able to exert on the other." (M. Reagan 1972:3)   It is synonymous with intergovernmental relations. (Ostrom interpretation of M. Reagan in Ostrom 1976:26)   In the United States, Professor Reagan's focus of analysis, new-style federalism is hastened by "the general cultural homogenization occurring through the media of communications and the ease of transportation. . . . " (M. Reagan 1972:156)

NEW URBAN FEDERALISM   The new urban federalism, according to Colman, stresses direct federal-local relationships, without an important intermediary role for the states.   The new urban federalism he dates principally from the passage of the Housing Act of 1937, in which "Congress squarely confronted the issue of whether federal funds should flow through the state government or whether they could go directly to localities," and resolved the question in favor of direct federal-local relations. (Colman 1975:320)   Most of Colman's discussion of federal-local relations goes under the label, "direct federalism."

NOMINAL FEDERALISM   (1) "Nominal" denotes a governmental system in which "the states and their localities are governing entities in name only." (Wright 1978:25)   Wright says that "those [observers] who have focused on the capacities or incapacities of the states" feel comfortable with this descriptive label for the American federal system. (Ibid.)   (2) In a broader perspective, Dunn places Yugoslavia among the "nominally federal systems"-- that is, federal systems "in name only"--but prefers to assign it a "special status," because of legitimate decentralizing procedures. (Dunn 1975:149)

NONCENTRALIZED FEDERALISM   From the perspective of the axis of the American federal system, Elazar prefers the expression noncentralized federalism over decentralized federalism.   Elazar believes that "the organizational expression of federalism is noncentralization, the constitutional diffusion and sharing of powers among many centers." (Elazar 1981b:14)   "Non-centralization," he explains, "is not the same as de-centralization," because the latter term "implies the existence of a central authority, a central government that can decentralize or recentralize as it desires."   In the case of "decentralized systems, the diffusion of power is actually a matter of grace, not right"; in contrast, "[i]n a noncentralized political system, power is so diffused that it cannot be legitimately centralized or concentrated without breaking the structure and spirit of the constitution." (Ibid. This is a recurrent theme in Elazar's writings. The reader will find it frequently in the Elazar references in the bibliography.)

NONFEDERALISM   Absence of federalism. If federalism consisted of a number of simply defined attributes, it would be possible quickly to distinguish federalism from nonfederalism. If not easily, at least a "skilled inspector of federal systems" could "take hold of a federal or purportedly federal system, subject its constitution and its political-constitutional practice to a battery of test questions, satisfy himself to what extent the . . . criteria are satisfied, strike a balance between the total pattern of conformity and the total pattern of deviation, and locate the given system on the spectrum of federalism and nonfederalism." (Davis 1978:163) Davis is specifically critiquing here Wheare and his criteria of federalism which are, Davis feels, presented as a kind of "analytical kit." In fact, no analytical kit is available to the inspector of federal systems.

NONPOLITICAL FEDERALISM   Duchacek points out that "the term federalism is often . . . used in [a] nonpolitical . . . [context]. . . . " (Duchacek 1970:189) Included among nonpolitical federalisms would be ecumenical organizations and "commercial or industrial complexes that have been created by association of previously independent companies whose autonomy and identity have not been obliterated but guaranteed in [a] merger. . . . " (Ibid.)

NONTERRITORIAL FEDERALISM   (1) Zylstra says Harold Laski felt "[f]ederalism . . . must not be thought of in terms of territorial contiguity, but [as] 'a division of functions upon some rough basis of useful performance.'" (Zylstra 1968:73 quoting Laski)   Thus Laski essentially held to a concept of nonterritorial federalism.   (2) But Livingston believes that without territoriality a "society cannot be said to be federalism. . . . [I]t becomes functionalism, pluralism, or some form of corporativism." (Livingston 1956:2)

NOT-FULL FEDERALISM   The not-full federation is one in which the aligning states have "retain[ed] their sovereign rights, their jura majestatis." (Friedrich in Carney 1964:x) This conceptualization was supposedly developed by Althusius, but Riley contends that, "for him, 'not-full' federation meant mere alliance or treaty relations, while 'full' federation meant complete consolidation of two polities." (Riley 1976:36)

NOVANGLIAN FEDERALISM   This is Schneider's designation for one of "two schools [the other was the republican school] of Federalist philosophy current during the American Enlightenment, and [which] eventually . . . faced each other bitterly in civil war." Novanglian federalism "flourished in New England [and]

found its fullest exposition in the writings of John Adams,"
who, in one series of exchanges with his political opponents in
the Revolutionary War era, took the pen name Novangulus.
(Schneider 1963:73) This constitutional school "served to give a
common front to the vested interests of landed and commercial
aristocrats, first against British mercantilism, then against
Southern agrarianism, and finally against the urban propertyless
classes, whose interests were thought by the wealthy to be con-
temptible because they were not 'fixed.'" (Ibid.)

OCCUPATIONAL FEDERALISM   Federalism in postwar Germany was
said to be the creation, principally, of the occupying powers
("Besatzungs-Foderalismus," Deuerlein 1972:230-31)   In the late
1940s some Germans felt that this federalism would have to be
overcome if independence was to be regained and excessive particularism was to be curbed.

OFFSHORE FEDERALISM   This is a special policy-oriented
federalism which is most concerned with the jurisdictional status
of marginal sea exploitation.   The subject was treated in a 1976
law review article from the American and Canadian perspectives.
(See Swan 1976b:296-322.) Swan feels that "the danger of international rivalries over marginal sea area exploitation . . . ren-
ders persuasive an energetic federal government role in the
marginal sea [policy] arena." (Ibid., p. 322.)

OLD FEDERALISM   (1) Anderson equated old federalism in the
United States with legalism. But, nearly 40 years ago, he could
proclaim that, "The old federalism that was legalism is dead."
(Anderson in MacDonald 1949:79)   (2) Leach, in 1970, associated
"old federalism" with a degenerate cooperative federalism of
"disparate programs, policies, and administrative procedures. . .
. " (Leach 1970:221. He felt much postitive movement had been
made away from this "old federalism.")   (3) Presumably the immediate ancestor of what is contemporaneously regarded as the
"new" federalism can be referred to as "old" federalism. Colman
points out that, "The continually changing character of
federal-state-local relations suggests that the New Federalism of
today may be the old federalism of yesterday." (Colman 1975:320)
(4) From a comparative perspective, Lower observes that, "Under
the heat and pressure generated by social and economic change in
the twentieth century, the distinct strata of the older
federalism[s] have begun to melt and flow into one another."
(Lower et. al. 1958:122)

OLD-LINE FEDERALISM   The old-line federalism McWhinney
identifies as "two dimensional" (federal and state only) and
"horizontal." The old-line federally organized society does not
have major problems of conflicts of interests among its territorially dispersed constituent groups. (McWhinney 1965:7)

OLD NEW FEDERALISM   See this expression as used in the entry for new new federalism.

OLD-STYLE FEDERALISM   Chandler and Plano assert that,
"Throughout the 1800s, traditional 'old style' federalism was
concerned with defining the separate spheres of authority and
jurisdiction between national and state governments." (Chandler
and Plano 1982:62) This term is employed by Michael Reagan in
much the same manner as dual federalism. (M. Reagan 1972:3, 156)

OLD URBAN FEDERALISM   Under the old urban federalism such
dealings as the American national government had with localities
went through the states. The federal government was not directly
connected to cities. However, as Colman notes, "Beginning with
the public housing legislation of 1937, the [old] pattern of
intergovernmental relations--namely, a strictly federal-state
relationship--began to be modified."   Thus the Roosevelt
Administration is credited with revolutionizing American intergovernmental relations by virtue of the tremendous increase in
direct federal-local ties. Yet, quantitatively, expansion of the
federal-local partnership was even greater during the Kennedy and
especially the Johnson years. (All Colman 1975:320-21)

OLIGARCHIC FEDERALISM   A federal system in which a minority
of the constituent units dominates the majority of units. The
United States would be an illustration of oligarchic federalism,
"if the twelve [most populated] states were politically to gang
up against the less-populated thirty-eight states." The twelve
would be "an imperial oligarchy in the Federal union of fifty
states." (Duchacek 1970:282. Duchacek uses this as an illustration of "(wild) theory.") More seriously, Duchacek says that
Michels's ideas about the "inevitable tendency to oligarchy" hold
substantially true for numerous federal systems. (Ibid., pp. 285,
286.) Duchacek identifies as a "variant of oligarchic federation
. . . tilted to the advantage of component units," the "'feudal
federalism' . . . experienced by Brazil after 1889 when the revolution replaced monarchy by a federal republic." (Ibid., p.
333.)

ONE-DIMENSIONAL FEDERALISM   One-dimensional federalism, according to Djordjevic, is political only.   In contrast, his
multidimensional federalism represents "an intertwining of
political and functional interests and powers [and] a transcendence of the traditional principle of [one-dimensional]
federalism, which only applies to the political sphere."
(Djordjevic 1975:78) The Yugoslav writer feels that contemporary

society is evolving from the old, one-dimensional federalism to the new polyvalent federalism.

ONTOLOGICAL FEDERALISM   Ontology is that aspect of philosophy which concerns being. Marc says that "the economic and social and . . . even the epistemological and ontological federalism, pursued by [his] school, reveals the same isomorphic pattern that is embodied in American political federalism." (Marc 1979:130) Federalism has genuine existence in the structures of society and is, for Marc, a principal weapon in "the struggle against the blind forces of domination, exploitation, covetousness, and sadistic quest for power. . . . " (Ibid., p. 129.)

OPERATIONAL FEDERALISM   This term refers to the actual as contrasted with the merely theorized pattern of relationships of governments and governmental actors within the federal system, with specific reference here to the American system. Operational federalism is most frequently considered from the perspective of federal aid administrators. (Walker 1981c:102) In Walker's view, the objective observer of the contemporary governmental scene in the United States would have to come up with an "operational theory of federalism" which recognizes "an increasingly overburdened and dysfunctional federalism wherein intergovernmental relations have become more pervasive, more expansive, less manageable, less effective, and above all less accountable." (Ibid., p. 225.) Incisive commentators on recent American operational federalism include Gawthrop 1969 and Lindblom 1965. (Cited in Boschken 1979:20) Leach identifies the model cities program as a key "innovation in operational federalism" introduced by Washington in the mid-1960s. (Leach 1970:234) The most recent surveys of aid officials revealed less of a "commitment to stand-pat positions . . . greater flexibility in confronting broad managerial and interlocal issues . . . much more moderate professional concerns regarding state and local counterpart personnel. . . . " (Walker 1977:17) From empirical data derived from administrators an "operational theory of federalism" as opposed to a merely abstract and deductive model can be constructed.

OPTIMAL FEDERALISM   Etheredge employs this term in his presentation of research related to the impact on the American federal system and the citizenry of the heightened role and visibility of government. Etheredge says that when government is large, does much, and is easily seen, relations of psychological dependence may be strengthened. Etheredge's "model of self-conceptions and emotional syndromes characteristic of the two parties in a dependency relationship predicts there will be objectively inconsistent and unrealistic expectations and demands by both parties, inadequate rationality and program evaluation, and mutual frustration, and disillusionment." (Etheredge 1977:161, from the abstract) As Etheredge observes trends in

American politics he finds the potential for an increasing dependency subculture which, in turn, will generate additional political and administrative problems with which the federal system will have to cope.

ORGANIC FEDERALISM   (1) In the World War II era Young asserted that, "Organic federal association between the democracies [was] their only hope." (Young 1941:15)   But the unity required for organic association would require considerable time. (2) This variety of federalism is defined by Sawer as one "in which the Centre has such extensive powers, and gives such a strong lead to Regions in the most important areas of their individual as well as their co-operative activities, that the political taxonomist may hesitate to describe the result as federal at all . . . the organic stage begins to develop as the Regions lose any substantial bargaining capacity in relation to the Centre." (Sawer 1969:125)   Sawer names Austria as the principal example of an organic federal system since "[t]he Centre dominates every aspect of policy, supervises the administration, and holds the whip of possible dissolution over the Region legislatures." Presumably, Austria nevertheless merits some type of federal designation, however, since "there is some region autonomy." (Ibid.)   The U.S. could develop into an organic federalism because "[t]he restraint of judicial doctrine on Centre power is relatively weak." Preservation of state autonomy might, in Sawer's opinion, "be drastically altered by mass movements, deriving from military defeat or humiliation and internal disorder produced by the color situation." (Ibid., pp. 126-27.)   Sawer wrote during the civil rights revolution of the 1960s.

ORGANIZATIONAL FEDERALISM   The unlikely user of this expression was Joseph Stalin in 1913.   In a collection of his speeches presented under the title Marxism and the National Question, Stalin discusses several options for dealing with nationalities in party and state under socialist rule.   His proposed solution, particularly for the Caucasus (and favored by Social Democrats elsewhere), was organizational federalism.   "The national problem in the Caucasus," Stalin explained, "can be solved only by drawing the backward nations and peoples into the common stream of a higher culture." (Stalin 1942:55-56) Regional autonomy, that is, organizational federalism, was acceptable to Stalin because "it draws the backward nations into the common cultural development; it helps them to cast off the shell of isolation peculiar to small nationalities." (Ibid.)

ORRERETIC FEDERALISM   The Federal Orrery was the name of an American Federalist party periodical published during the 1790s. An orrery is "a piece of mechanism devised to represent the motions of the planets about the sun by means of clockwork." (Oxford Universal Dictionary, 1955 ed.) This mechanistic model was the most common image of the American federal system during this period.

ORTHODOX FEDERALISM   (1) Basically an ideological expression of federalism.   Mogi asserts that traditional political federalism is based on an unfair distribution of economic resources.   However, in the 1930s, Mogi said he "believe[d] that [he saw] the decay of orthodox federalism [and] the last phase of the existing [economically undemocratic] regime." (Mogi 1931b:1115) In its place "the true federal idea [would] shine in the future as the guiding star of truth, pointing the way to the attainment of that real democratic community which mankind is endeavoring to secure without the misery of dictatorship or the catastrophe of anarchy in this age of transition to the new social order." (Ibid.)   (2) Logically, the expression orthodox federalism could be used to characterize the generally accepted theory and practice associated with any federal system.

OUR FEDERALISM   An expression for American federalism coined by Supreme Court Justice Hugo Black. The enunciation came in 1971 when Justice Black spoke of "Our Federalism" in the context of the presumed need to understand that "the entire country is made up of a Union of separate state governments." (Younger v. Harris, 401 U.S. 37 (1971)), cited in Walker 1981c:136)   In the view Black stated at this time, "the National Government [would] fare best if the States and their institutions [were] left free to perform their separate functions in their separate ways." (Ibid.)   As applied to the criminal justice area, "Our Federalism" meant that "only in extraordinary circumstances may federal courts enjoin state criminal proceedings." (Interpretation of Younger v. Harris made by Winkle 1980:7-8)   Koury observed in a 1979 law review article that there was "no doctrine in the federal courts which presently elicits more controversy than 'Our Federalism.'" (Koury 1979:709)

OUTCOME-ORIENTED FEDERALISM   Schechter says that "there is what might be termed an 'outcome-oriented' view of federalism and managerialism in which emphasis is placed more on the 'substantive results' of the policy-making process than on the process itself and for its own sake." (Schechter 1981:136)   He attributes this orientation to contemporary American political scientists David J. Olson and Philip Meyer. Olson and Meyer were more concerned with democracy than federalism.)

PACIFIC FEDERALISM   Immanuel Kant makes the contention in Eternal Peace that unless there is a "universal foedus pacificum ('pacific federation') of 'republics' there is no security anywhere for 'public legal justice.'" (Kant in Riley 1979b:43)   According to Riley, "a federal 'eternal peace' does not merely fit into but actually is the culmination of Kant's whole political and moral schema. . . . " (Ibid., p. 44.)   It should be noted that Kant's pacific federalism envisions a community of communities, "not a society of individual persons." (Ibid., p. 54.)

PANFEDERALISM   For example, Pan-African federalism. "Pan"
means all and in this usage refers to the hopes for a federation
consisting of all of the peoples occupying a particular
continent. Franck comments on the problems faced by Pan-African
federalism. (Franck 1968:29)

PAPER-FEDERALISM   Federalism in writing but not in reality.
Elazar observes that, "In West Africa the short-lived and mainly
'paper-federalism' between Ghana, Guinea and Mali is [an] example
of federal experimentation in Africa." (Elazar 1979a:178)

PARLIAMENTARY FEDERALISM   (1) The essence of parliamentary
federalism is cabinet government collectively responsible in a
political system organized on the basis of federal principles.
It has been adapted, for example, in the case of Canada, Australia, and South Africa from the British Westminster model. (2)
King notes Saint-Simon's advocacy of "a distinctly European parliamentary federation" because "only an overall political union
of the continent--starting with England and France--could inhibit
the recurrence of war, lay the foundations for an enduring peace,
and thereby generate significant economic development." (King
1982:30)

PARTIAL FEDERALISM   (1) Grant and Nixon identify as partial
federalism the Miami-Dade County, Florida, "two-[tier] form of
metropolitan government which incorporates, to a limited degree,
the principle of federation" in its "retention of the existing
municipalities . . . for the performance of 'purely local'
activities [and] the allocation of authority to Dade County [of]
those governmental activities which are 'essentially
metropolitan' in nature." (Grant and Nixon 1982:397) (2) It
signifies federal arrangements in which the sovereign powers of
theretofore independent states are transferred only in part. (See
Hay 1966:89.) Davis identifies as a nineteenth-century methodology the arrangement of "unions or leagues of states in a
dichotomous federal scheme of perfect/imperfect, pure/impure, or
total/partial. . . . " (Davis 1978:207)

PARTICIPATORY FEDERALISM   This would be a federalism
characterized by a wide sharing of influence. It would be essentially a partnership, a fellowship. Djordjevic argues that,
"Human society is in a process of transition from 'traditional'
(territorial and political) federalism to a 'new federalism' that
is . . . participatory," as well as social and functional.
(Djorjdjevic 1975:77)

PARTICULARIST FEDERALISM   (1) One of the earliest
associations to which the term particularist federalism has been
applied was the German union of 1815. It was set in motion by
the Congress of Vienna which aimed, by encouraging an already
strongly independent spirit among many small German states, to
rebuild the balance of political power in Europe. (Dennewitz

1947:118-19) (2) States rights model of federalism associated with German thinkers Konrad Beyerle and Max Seydel. Beyerle was in the National Assembly of Weimar and, in this chamber, "clearly expounded the Bavarian attitude which was still largely influenced by the theory of confederation of Max Seydel," a theory which Mogi feels is most appropriately identified as particularist federalism. Particularist federalism defended "the system of 'reserved rights' for . . . [states] and the federative basis of the new [Weimar] constitution. . . . " (Mogi 1931b:940-41) The Brockahus Enzyklopadie says that a particularist federation is one in which there are powerful separatist sentiments among the components of the union. (1968 ed.) (3) In the United States, Germanophile Francis Lieber criticized states-rights adherents for looking for liberty in particularism. "In magnifying the individual commonwealth," Parrington interprets Lieber, the states rights advocates "overlooked the more vital units of self-government," such as families, churches, exchanges, scientific associations, etc. (Parrington II, 1927:93)

PARTNERSHIP FEDERALISM   This term should be associated with cooperative federalism. Elazar is most notable for associating American federalism with the concept of partnership. His first major work sought "to demonstrate that the pattern of American federalism--the American partnership--has been a constant one since the early days of the Republic"; that is, "virtually all the activities of government in the nineteenth-century United States were cooperative endeavors, shared by federal and state agencies in much the same manner as government programs are shared in the twentieth century." (Elazar 1962:1) The concept of American federalism as a partnership is also captured in the subtitle of the 1955 book by Anderson, The Nation and the States: Rivals or Partners?

PERFECT FEDERALISM   Freeman identifies two conditions as "necessary to constitute a Federal Government in . . . its most perfect form." First, "each of the members must be wholly independent in those matters which concern each member only." Second, "all must be subject to a common power in those matters which concern the whole body of members collectively." (Freeman 1893:2) Davis questions whether the Achaean League was an example of perfect federalism. It would have been "perfect" if the federal power had had direct authority over the citizenry of the union, a precondition "which, in modern politics, is held more than anything else to distinguish an Imperfect from a Perfect Federation." (Freeman 1863 quoted in Davis 1978:31)

PERIPHERALIZED FEDERALISM   One of the principal variants of federalism identified by Riker. Riker developed a method for establishing the dimensions of models of peripheralized and centralized federalism which provokes "the assertion that the proximate cause of variations in the degree of centralization (or peripheralization) in the constitutional structure of federalism is the variation in the degree of party centralization." (Riker 1964:129, quoted in Kuic in Yarbrough et al. 1972:13) Riker cites the American Articles of Confederation as an illustration of peripheralized federalism. "The chief criticism . . . of the peripheralized federalism of the Articles was," he contends, "that the system . . . was inadequate for war and the prospect of war." (Riker 1964:16ff., quoted in Davis 1978:134)

PERMISSIVE FEDERALISM   This adjectival federalism is suggested by American political scientist Michael Reagan.   "The notion that phrase conveys," he trusts, "is that there is a sharing of powers and authority between the national and state governments, but that the state's share rests upon the permission and permissiveness of the national government." (M. Reagan 1977:163) However, Landau submits that "[i]f . . . there is a modicum of stability attached to the meaning of the term 'federal'--and both the ordinary language and textbook usage affirm that this is so--then the concept 'permissive federalism' is entirely inconsistent." (Landau 1973:174)

PERPETUAL FEDERALISM   The concept of a "perpetuo Foedere" is employed by Pufendorf in Of the Law of Nature and Nations.   In French the expression is "la Confederation perpetuelle." Pufendorf writes of a "type of composite state which comes out of the perpetual federation of several states." (Pufendorf quoted in Davis 1978:60; trans. for present author by Gregory de Rocher) Perpetual federalism is to be contrasted with a temporary military alliance.

PERSONALIST FEDERALISM   The chief exponents of personalist federalism are Robert Aron and Alexandre Marc.   Nelson says that these French theorists typically "go to some pains to stress the incompatibility of personalist federalism and Marxism.   They support a Proudhonian method of balancing antinomies against the Hegelian and Marxist synthesis." (Nelson 1957:57)   As Nelson interprets it, "personalist philosophy . . . is not a system in the sense of a deductive construction, but an attempt to show the implications in the major areas of human activity--cultural, religious, political, inter-personal relations--of the meaning of personal existence." (Ibid., p. 54.)   Kinsky notes that, "Personalism envisages a general application of federalist principles in all areas of society and even in the methodology of knowledge." (Kinsky 1979:153)   Based on his survey of personalist/integral federalism literature, Kinsky sees a federalist society founded in these principles:

1) In the political field, demonopolization of the
national state internally through a regionalization and
a redefinition of the local commune, with a view to
dismanteling the urban centers which have become
unlivable; externally through the construction of a
federal Europe and the transformation of the U.N. into

a world federation. 2) In the economic and social
field . . . a series of institutions designed to ensure
the autonomy and fulfillment of the person: a minimum guaranteed social wage, public service, bi-zonal
planning, etc. [Kinsky footnotes omitted] Federalist
personalism cannot subscribe to the separation of
politics and economics. . . . To wish to restrict
liberty and democratic participation to the nonexistent
realm of pure politics means taking away one of the
fundamental dimensions of the human person . . . 3) In
the cultural field . . . respect of the diversity of
languages and cultures which form the richness of
European heritage. (Ibid., pp. 153-54.)

The personalists were "agreed that man was above all not an
'individual.' He is a 'person,' that is both responsible and
free, committed and autonomous, a being in himself, but related
to his fellowmen by his responsibility." (Ibid., p. 133.) "Personalism," Kinsky concludes, "seeks to reestablish the equilibrium between the four dialectical tensions of man confronted with
the world, his neighbour, society and destiny." (Ibid., p. 150.)

PICK AND CHOOSE FEDERALISM A critical interpretation of
Reagan new federalism noted by Utah Governor Scott M. Matheson.
(Matheson 1982:506) Supposedly, the federal government would
"pick and choose" the programs which it would shift to state and
local governments. The implication was that the shift would
prove costly to these governments and that the programs decentralized would not necessarily be those which the subnational
levels would have selected.

PICKET FENCE FEDERALISM The coiner of this adjectival
federalism was former Governor Terry Sanford of North Carolina,
presently Chancellor of Duke University. (Sanford 1970:80, cited
in Walker 1981c:125) Wright observes that, "It was not by
happenstance that the originator of 'picket fence federalism' was
Governor Terry Sanford." As Governor, Sanford and his aides were
"[c]aught in the matrix of expanding federal programs of the
1960s" and found this metaphorical expression "a handy way of describing the scene of activity." (Wright 1978:210-11) Like other
such expressions, picket fence federalism is not useful as a
"precise guide to policy and administrative actions." Yet, this
modifier "dramatizes the need for powerful assertions of
gubernatorial influence if state policies and programs are to be
more than a hodgepodge of independent professional and functional
fiefdoms." (Ibid., p. 211.) Colman describes the kinds of conditions which led to picket fence federalism, particularly the
"rapid rise in functional government, with lines of ideas,
authority, and money flowing through functional rather than overall policy-political-governance channels." (Colman 1975:323)
Walker equates picket fence federalism with what he terms

bureaucratic federalism. (The reader should see especially Walker 1981c:102, 124-25.) He notes that the "'picket fence' theory with all of its rigid, vertical functionalism . . . was endorsed by three-quarters of the respondents" to a 1964 survey of the Senate subcommittee on intergovernmental relations. (Ibid., p. 128.)

PIECEMEAL FEDERALISM   Federal relationships may be characterized as "piecemeal" where "two or more independent states . . . draw closer together, establishing first, in terms of probable development, piecemeal federal relationships with regard to matters where, as between them . . . tensions exist." This, Hay explains, "is a functional-federal relationship. . . . " (Hay 1966:92)

PINWHEEL FEDERALISM   A contemporary interpretation of American federalism, which takes note of the fact that, "Out from the Washington bureaucracy's many departments go spigots to state, to county, to city, to school districts and special districts. Rarely is the fund flow coordinated in Washington, or in the states and localities." (Peirce 1980:8, reporting the thinking of David Walker)   A further description of pinwheel federalism sees "all actors--states, areawides, counties, cities, townships, not-for-profit agencies, and others--[as] essentially equal shafts revolving around Washington as the 'pin.'" (Weissert 1980:19)

PLURALISTIC FEDERALISM   A federal system is obviously pluralistic when its predominant tendencies are centrifugal rather than centripetal; that is, decentralizing rather than centralizing. (McWhinney 1965:16-17)   Logically, any federal system must be pluralistic. Pluralistic federalism, McWhinney explains, "is Jeffersonian in character, with its faith in enlightened self-government and co-operation at the local level, and its distrust of centralized power." (Ibid., p. 17.)   In literature, the most eloquent support for a kind of pluralistic federalism probably occurs in the writings of Walt Whitman. Elazar notes that Leaves of Grass "is permeated with explicit expressions of the federal pluralism of the American people." (Elazar 1979b:6)   Vile says that "[t]he federal structure of the United States has, from the beginning, been an instrument in battles which were not necessarily geographically concentrated, but which were pluralist interests, that is different groups within the population who have seen the Federal government or the States respectively as defenders of class or plural interests." (Vile 1961:36-37, quoted in Hay 1966:9 at n. 51)

POLAR FEDERALISM   An interpretation of American federalism which focuses on representative institutions responding to opposing interests. Thus Eulau contends that, "The political order envisaged by The Federalist is one of polar federalism rather than dual federalism.   Polar federalism is predicated on the

complementarity of institutions and especially of representational institutions." Polar federalism focuses on more
than the relationship between federal and state governments.
"What is obviously needed," Eulau feels, "is an elaboration of
polar federalism in the perspective of representation as the process by which government can be made responsive to the people."
(All Eulau 1973:168)

POLIS-FEDERALISM   Federalism of the ancient Greeks, as
characterized by Diamond. "This term," Diamond feels, "conveys
of itself everything necessary to explain why the Greeks did not
move forward to 'a firm union.' Their approach to federalism
rests upon the Greek view that the worthwhile life could be lived
only in very small communities," that is, the polis. (Diamond
1973:131) Although "any effort truly to enlarge the political
community . . . necessarily made life less worthwhile," still,
union was essential for defensive purposes so the Greeks
"invented federalism. . . . " (Ibid.)   Polis-federalism was,
therefore, "only a way to have certain minimal functions performed among a group of otherwise quite autonomous small countries. . . . " (Ibid.)

POLITICAL FEDERALISM   (1) Jenkin says that the principal
concern of political federalism is with "the problems of political power and interests that are associated with modern federalism in distinction to the problems of operating a system in which
the claims to power generally have been met." (Jenkin n.d.:1)
Jenkin complains that "the political base of our [i.e., the Amer-
ican] system has been taken for granted. . . . ‾‾(Ibid.)   He
attributes this to the fact that "the basic questions of political relations are more apt to be raised at the inception of a
federal system or in the case of profound dissatisfaction with it
than when the system is operating satisfactorily." (Ibid., p. 2.)
Miller believes that in contemporary American society "the factory community operates as the recipient of delegated power to
carry out important societal functions" and "is the economic
counterpart--and superior, be it said--of the unit of political
federalism, the forty-eight [now 50] state governments." (Miller
1958:634 and 637, quoted in Wright 1978:26)   Berle entitles his
chapter in Macmahon 1955:68ff., "Evolving Capitalism and Political Federalism." Normally, federalism is thought of in political
terms rather than primarily from social, functional, or participatory perspectives. (But see Djordjevic 1975:77.)   In a
1981 report the ACIR recommended "[s]trengthening political
federalism through the party system." (ACIR, 1981a:137)   This
would be done by the parties and federal and state legislative
bodies approving "measures which [would] strengthen the parties
as forums for the regular consideration of major policy issues by
public officials at all levels of government as well as by
citizen party members. . . . " (ACIR, 1980:41)   Marc criticizes
American theorists for restricting their concern to political
federalism.   They "cling to political federalism" because,

"whether they are conscious of it or not, they want to keep faith with the Founding Fathers." (Marc 1979:124) (2) For Proudhon political federalism denoted forces of persuasion rather than formal constitutional guarantees. In his view, "'autonomous' communes and 'sovereign' provinces" were appropriate corollaries to the "natural and spontaneous federalism of the economic order." (Barker 1951:36) Proudhon's political opinions are, in Mogi's view, summarized in "political federalism or decentralization." (Mogi 1931b:1114) (3) German federalism has been much more a "political" than a "legal" federalism. That is, such powers as units of government away from Bonn have been able to exercise have rested on informal factors rather than on formal legal guarantees. (Cerny in Earle 1968:183)

POLITY FEDERALISM A polity is defined as "an organized society; a state." (Oxford Universal Dictionary, 1955 ed.) Polity federalism would thus denote federalism as applied governmentally rather than in, for example, a civic club. Sharma and Choudhry entitle their 1967 study, Federal Polity.

POLYETHNIC FEDERALISM A federal system consisting of multiple groups possessing diverse religious, linguistic, ancestral, etc., characteristics. Duchacek comments that where "internal boundaries in a federation are made to coincide with the ethnic, tribal, or linguistic ones . . . [t]his is . . . a polyethnic federalism, as adopted by India, Burma, the Soviet Union, Yugoslavia, Czechoslovakia (since 1968), but only partly by Switzerland and Canada. . . . " (Duchacek 1970:293)

POLYVALENT FEDERALISM This variant of federalism (as illustrated in Yugoslavia) is defined as the "intertwining of political and functional interests and powers," which "represents a transcendence of the traditional principle of federalism, which only applies to the political sphere, and its extension to social, cultural, and economic spheres. . . . " (Djordjevic 1975:78) The polyvalent federal system, which represents a break from strictly territorial/political conceptualizations of federalism, consists not only of territorial communities (including communes, republics, and autonomous provinces), but also nationalities and nonterritorial, functional groups (for example self-managing worker associations). (Schechter 1975:12) Djordjevic argues that, "Modern society is in a process of transition from political federative association, from territorially-based community to a functionally-based community, from a mechanistic constitutional model to an organic constitutional model." (Djordjevic 1975:78-79) Polyvalent federalism is not only social and functional but strongly participatory.

PORTFOLIO FEDERALISM "We have," in the view of Ronald Reagan's former principal economic adviser Murray L. Weidenbaum, a Federal system of government which is, in effect, a portfolio designed by our Constitutional forefathers." Weidenbaum urges American leaders of the present day "to recognize the growing need for a 'portfolio' or diversification approach to an increasing number of our economic, regulatory and social problems." Like foolish investors, Weidenbaum analogizes, "policymakers at the Federal level . . . often identify a real social or regulatory problem, but then foolishly commit [themselves] to a single course of action--much as if [they] were [investors] committed to a single common stock." What is needed, in contrast, are "[i]ndependent actions by strong State and local governments . . . to 'diversify' the Nation's portfolio of policy actions." (Weidenbaum 1981:8-9)

POSITIVE FEDERALISM   American federalists in the 1960s (according to one scheme) could be classified as positive or negative.   Positive federalists advocated the division of the country into small political units with real problem-solving capability so as to bring about a renaissance in local self-government.   Deuerlein identifies then-New York Governor Nelson Rockefeller as a positive federalist. (Deuerlein 1972:293)

POST-COACH FEDERALISM   An apparently derogatory term for the federalism of postwar West Germany applied by critics who actually would prefer a unitary state.   Post-coach federalism ("Postkutschenföderalismus"), that is, "mail car federalism," may stand for a federal system whose functions are too limited and, in the case of West Germany, reflect too much the particularist and separatist sentiments of Bavarians and Hanoverians, Catholics, and political romantics. (Deuerlein 1972:299)

POST-COLONIAL FEDERALISM This is one of a number of paradigms of federalism cited by Davis to indicate "the evolution of the 'federal' concept. . . . " (Davis 1978:215) Numerous entries in this volume relate to post-colonial federalism.

POST-FEDERALISM   After federalism.   Thus, in the case of Indonesia, Schiller writes of, "The Post-federal Period." (Schiller 1955:332-36) In this section he discusses the transfer of sovereignty from the United States of Indonesia set up in 1945 to the unitary Republik Indonesia Serikat in 1949, after only four years of federalism.

POST-MODERN FEDERALISM   Federalism of the future. Althusius has been called a forerunner of modern federalism, Martin Buber of post-modern federalism.   See Buber's federalism entry (and other references to Buber as given in the name index) for a brief discussion of the ideas supposed to characterize post-modern federalism.

POST-SECOND-WORLD-WAR FEDERALISM Simply those federal systems which have been founded since 1945.   Hicks identifies the post-Second-World-War federations as including Nigeria, "particularly important," East Africa (Kenya, Tanzania, Uganda), the Caribbean islands, the federation of Malaysia and Singapore, the British Central African federation, and federalism in the Indian subcontinent. (Hicks 1978:119) Most of the post-Second-World-War federations were unsuccessful.

POST-TECHNOCRATIC FEDERALISM   This futuristic model for American federalism was used by Elazar in a 1973 article.   A technocracy is defined as "a government and social system controlled by scientific technicians." (American Heritage Dictionary, 1971 ed.)   In the corporate realm, after the death of entrepreneurs such as Ford and Rockefeller, technocrats became the governing agents; that is, "management teams that, in effect, became oligarchies sitting on top of each corporate pyramid." (Elazar 1973b:257) Power was diffused to an extent but was capable of being recentralized at any time. The technocratic philosophy found its "fullest embodiment in the conglomerates, whereby centralized decision-making authority is partially devolved to units lower down the hierarchy so long as they conform to the overall policies set unilaterally at the top." (Ibid.) This "new kind of decentralization," Elazar charged in 1973, was "what we now see reflected in President Nixon's 'New Federalism.'" (Ibid.) However, Elazar argued that the political realm could function better without the use of technocratic principles.   Thus he advocated a post-technocratic federalism in which "political communities scaled in ways suited to the tasks they must perform" have the key decision-making roles. The federal government would function as their servant, not as their master. This rescaling might "involve some compromise in the technical quality of services delivered but, in the long rung," Elazar believed, would be "likely to enhance the most important concerns to which the 'delivery of services' problem is supposedly addressing itself"; that is, "enabling government to serve as an instrumentality that enables people to build a good society." (Ibid., pp. 290-91.)

PRACTICAL FEDERALISM   Practical federalism is illustrated in the case of a "federal [union] in which there [is] no clear and precise constitutinal division of powers, although practically the parts [retain] their independence, while effectively united in a larger whole." (Sidgwick 1919:532 at n. 1) "[A] modern state might be practically federal, without a precise and stable division of powers, if the substantial autonomy of the parts were maintained by custom and opinion," Sidgwick observes. But he much prefers explicit enunciation of federal principles since practical federalism only "involves an obvious risk of friction and conflict between the government of the parts and the government of the whole." (Ibid.)

PRAGMATIC FEDERALISM   (1) Beck identifies American federalism as essentially pragmatic. "The genius with which the federal principle was developed in the Constitution," he feels, probably is attributable first and foremost to the American pragmatic temperament. (Beck 1956:114)   A leading textbook in American intergovernmental relations is <u>Pragmatic Federalism</u>. The title means that, "As each problem involving more than a single governmental jurisdiction arises, it is dealt with in a pragmatic fashion; an individual solution is devised for it without reference to any general theory of intergovernmental relations." (Glendening and Reeves 1977:6) Pragmatic federalism, according to these authors, is not a new phenomenon.   It had its origins in the Constitutional Convention "compromises of 1787 [which] were the beginnings of a system of pragmatic federalism which places responsibilities on each successive generation to make similar practical adjustments to keep alive the bargain struck between centralization and decentralization." (Ibid., p. 312.)

Elazar challenges the adequacy of pragmatic approaches to American federalism.   In his opinion, "Federalism in the United States was at its strongest when it fit within an American grand design and was not relegated to the vicissitudes of an un- reflective 'pragmaticsm' designed to respond only to the per- ceived needs of the hour." (Elazar 1979b:8) (2) Federalism which is altered incrementally on a functional basis. This is the us- age of Franck who notes the hope that in East Africa a successful "legacy of common services . . . [would build] up a mass follow- ing for pragmatic federalism" among Africans predisposed to be antifederalists because of the exploitative federalizing efforts of white mercantilists. (Franck 1968:29) Mitrany is thinking of federalism pragmatically when he urges that approach to integra- tion whereby "activities [are] . . . selected specifically and organized separately--each according to its nature, to the con- ditions under which it has to operate, and to the needs of the moment." (Mitrany 1966:70)

PREFECTORIAL FEDERALISM   Elazar uses prefect as "a metaphor for the assumption widely prevalent, if erroneous, that the [American] federal system is properly a pyramid and inter- governmental relations are best conducted in an appropriately hierarchical manner." (Elazar 1981a:1) Prefectorial federalism is Elazar's shorthand designation for "the problem of hierarchi- cal, interventionist management" in the United States in recent years. (Ibid.) He dates the rise of prefectorial administration from the Johnson Administration of the 1960s. Although neither the President nor his aides ever "articulated [a] doctrine of prefectorial administration . . . [they] did recommend the ap- pointment of a federal 'coordinator' in every metropolitan area." (Elazar 1981b:6-7) This suggestion was not implemented. Elazar attributes to the Nixon Administration initiation of an articulated "justification of prefectorial administration, if not a doctrine, as part of its 'New Federalism.'" (Ibid., p. 7.)

Elazar says that "it is the essence of the prefectorial approach that hierarchical decision making, executed through a bureaucratic structure, should not only establish a chain-of-command but a power pyramid which comes to a single point at the top." (Ibid.) In his interpretation of recent American history, "The gradual acceptance of the idea of prefectorial administration came through a convergence of . . . the spread of the managerial idea among American businessmen, public administrators, and political reformers . . . coupled with the perhaps more subtle spread of Jacobin and corollary Marxist ideas among American academics and intellectuals." (Ibid., p. 11.)

PREMIER FEDERALISM   Karve identifies the Swiss federal system as the "premier federation" because it is "the oldest, the most continuous and one of the most developed of the existent federal states." (Karve 1932:74)

PRE-MODERN FEDERALISM   This is one method of classifying federal systems from a time dimension. Elazar uses this category along with pre-federal, semi-integrated confederacies, and twentieth century failed federations. (See Elazar 1972:tables 1 through 5.)

PRIMARY FEDERALISM   The lower level of a system of federations. The Afrique Occidentale Francaise (AEF), composed of Senegal, Guinea, Upper Volta, Dahomey, Ivory Coast, Niger, the Sudan, and Mauritania, was a primary federation within the secondary federal French Union of the Fourth Republic. (Neuberger in Elazar 1979a:171-72)

PRIVATE FEDERALISM   Private federalism is federalism which features among its constituent units more than simply governments. Gilbert and Smith do not believe that "'private' federalism" is "strictly speaking . . . federalism at all." (Gilbert and Smith in Stedman 1968:140) Glendening and Reeves point to the feeling that the growth of private federalism "substantially weaken[s] the ability of the states to maintain long-established patterns of relations with their political subdivisions." (Glendening and Reeves 1976:169)

PROCESS-ORIENTED FEDERALISM   (1) Schechter says that "there is what might be termed a 'process-oriented' view of federalism and managerialism in which emphasis is placed on the ordering of power or program relationships because of the distinct costs and benefits, both political and economic, that accrue from the very way things are done or persons interact." (Schechter 1981:136. He attributes articulation of process- and outcome-oriented notions of democracy to contemporary American political scientists David J. Olson and Philip Meyer.)   (2) Pentland notes that latter-day federal thought "has been concerned less with the stark juxtaposition of international disorder and federal order,

and more with how systems move toward the latter condition."
This new orientation is said to be very indebted to Friedrich's
advocacy of a process-oriented federalism. (Pentland 1973:61)
Process-oriented federalism also has been equated with functional
federalism. (McWhinney and Pescatore 1973:1)

PROCUSTREAN FEDERALISM   That approach to federalism which
"seeks to apply national approaches to the great variation in the
organizational patterns and arrangements of American state and
local government," involves, in Nathan's view, "the serious risk
of becoming, in point of fact, a kind of Procustrean federalism."
This adjectival federalism is derived from "Procustres, a bandit
of Greek mythology, [who] sought to design the perfect bed.   To
do so, he forced people to lie in beds which often did not fit
them.   For those who were too large, he sawed off their feet;
those who were too small were stretched on the rack." (All Nathan
1975:125)   To force state and local governments uniformly to com-
ply with identical national regulations "could be equally painful," according to Nathan. (Ibid.)

PROFESSIONAL FEDERALISM   Characterization of the relations
of vocational activity groups to the American federal government.
"Because   many   operational   relations   involve   professional
people--doctors, lawyers, and the like--we may," Martin suggests,
"think in terms of professional federalism." (Martin in Bailey
1965:171-72)

PROFESSIONALIZED   FEDERALISM   "The   growing   professionalization of government" has given rise to what Beer identifies as "a new type of centralizing coalition and a new stage
in the development of American intergovernmental relations that
may be called professionalized or technocratic federalism." (Beer
1973:79-80)   With professionalized federalism, "the relation of
federal and state governments is continuous with the cooperative
federalism of the previous generation insofar as the federal
government, often through a categorical grant program, continues
to use the states as instruments of national policy." (Ibid.)
However, "[a] significant difference arises from the quite
different manner in which the knowledge now being applied in
policy making has originated."   The "theory-oriented research"
which "often underlies the design of programs today" frequently
is the product of a "research elite and its associated professionals." (Ibid.)

PROFESSORIAL FEDERALISM   Use of this expression would
amount to criticism of a federal system so designated.   McWhinney
characterized the Cypriot Constitution of 1960 as "a 'professorial' federal constitution."   The "degree of correspondence
between law and societal facts" was scant indeed and thus the
federal system so stipulated was "doomed to be an exercise in
constitutional futility." (McWhinney 1966:76)   Professorial
federalism would be merely "an exercise in rationalized

constitutionalism--in the postulation of an 'ideal-type' model
for the institutional moderation of power" which could never be
operationalized. (Ibid.) The Cypriot Constitution sought to
pacify both Greeks and Turks through very elaborate divisions of
power and apportionments of offices.

PROLETARIAN FEDERALISM   Proletarian federalism is illustrated in "political movements when the aim is to forge unity
out of ideological, not territorial, diversity. (Duchacek
1970:190) Specifically from the proletarian perspective,
Duchacek notes that, in France, in the post-World War II period,
Communists, socialists, radicals, and other left-wing associations created the Federation of a Democratic and Socialist
left. A century earlier, in 1874, and then a little later, in
1889, the first and second Socialist Internationals expressed,
even in their anthem, "the hope that ultimately the proletarian
federation [might] transform itself into one single international
party with one uniform socialist creed." (Ibid.)

PROLIFERATED FEDERALISM   One of two principal metaphorical
expressions used by Wright to characterize Johnsonian Great
Society notions as actually practiced (along with fused-
foliated). The Johnson years were filled with irony, Wright believes, because while "the theory called for convergence, consent, and concord," actually "there was much grantsmanship which
was not necessarily to the good." (Wright 1974:11) The essence
of the paradox is the simultaneous emphasis on "convergence, consent, and concord" and the practice of "proliferation, participation, and pluralism." (Ibid.)

PROPER FEDERALISM   A proper federal union, according to an
1844 study, exists "where two or more states, having their separate governments for all domestic purposes, are united by a central government, which regulates their mutual relations as member
of a political community, but does not interfere with the
functions of the several governments, and their authority over
the individuals who are their subjects, unless in so far as those
functions and the authority may affect the federal relation."
(Brougham 1844:505-06) "It is of the essence of this proper
federal union," Brougham continues, "that its different members
should have equal rights, and that all should bear a part in the
central administration." (Ibid., p. 506.)

PROPRIETARY FEDERALISM   Federalism as it pertains to
governmental dealings with business interests. The expression
was created by Schechter who said that the controversy over "the
Concorde [supersonic plane] . . . rais[ed] a serious question as
to whether the right mix--of airport noise, aircraft commercial
concerns--[was] best served by [the] peculiar system of 'proprietary federalism.'" (Schechter 1978:137) But, "[b]arring the
unlikely prospect that Congress will preempt the field, airport
noise regulation will remain an important variation of

'cooperative federalism' which most closely approximates a 'dele- gated partnership' primarily between the federal government, airport proprietors, and the aeronautics industry." (Ibid., p. 155.)

PROTEAN FEDERALISM   Protean means with indefinite form, subject to dramatic growth and change. Federalism is susceptible to infinite forms as it is shaped under widely varying con- ditions. Macmahon in 1955 referred to the "protean nature of federalism" which enables it to operate from the crudest to the most complex "levels of political association." (Macmahon 1955:vii) Because of its protean nature, federalism tempts scholars from many disciplines to study it.

PROTOFEDERALISM   This is federalism at a very early stage of development. Elazar used the expression in this way: "The proto-federalism of the United Provinces and the Swiss cantons coming at the outset of the age of nationalism . . . stimulated the first serious efforts to formulate federal theories based on modern political principles." (Elazar 1972:12)   Contemporary European regionalism is a kind of protofederalism. (Elazar 1979a:6)

PROUDHON'S FEDERALISM   Other entries in this volume iden- tify particular aspects of Pierre-Joseph Proudhon's federalist thought. This personalized expression summarizes Proudhon's "anti-statist federative model." (Djordjevic 1975:75-88)   The state cannot be permitted to monopolize power; politics and ec- onomics cannot be separated. (Kinsky 1979:132)   There should be "a series of institutions designed to ensure the autonomy and fulfillment of the person." (Ibid.)

PROVINCIALLY-ORIENTED FEDERALISM   Engelmann and Schwartz apply this term to contemporary Austria, observing that "[t]he Socialists have tried to rework their image in a more provincial direction," particularly since 1967. Chancellor Bruno Kreisky rose politically with "a base in the Lower Austrian provincial organization and managed to become national leader by means of an anti-Vienese provincial party coalition." It was "[t]his per- sonal history which sensitized [Kreisky] to the virtues of a provincially-oriented federalism far beyond the party norm." (All Engelmann and Schwartz 1981:86-87)

PSEUDO-FEDERALISM   Not actually federal although claiming to be. (1) Stevenson identifies Czechoslovakia and Venezuela as "pseudo-federal states." (Stevenson 1973:236)   (2) Constantin Franz, a nineteenth-century German writer and activist, called the North German Union "pseudo-federative" because of its hegemonial, militaristic, and centralizing features. (View cited in Deuerlein 1972:158)   According to Elazar, "pseudo-federal" systems are notable because they only appear to employ "federal principles but actually violate the essence of the federal idea. . . . " (Elazar 1972:8)

PUBLIC FEDERALISM   Governmental federalism and public
federalism are presumably the same. Traditionally in the United
States federal theory has focused on public federalism and the
relationships between public entities. In recent years, however,
"[t]he support of private organizations with public funds within
unique jurisdictions, and the building of special constituencies," has posed a challenge to public federalism.
(Gilbert and Smith in Stedman 1968:141)

PUBLIUS'S FEDERALISM   Federal ideas of the authors of the
Federalist Papers, Alexander Hamilton, James Madison, and John
Jay.   Boschken argues that "we are perhaps at a turning point
where conditions are emerging similar to those surrounding development of Publius' federalism." (Boschken 1979:34) There is a
need, in his view, once again "to focus on [non-]bureaucratic
[and non-]hierarchical solutions" to public problems.   He takes
issue with those who would argue that "Publius' federalism is at
best 'a governmental device of limited utility, unrelated to the
"real" problems of the day except insofar as it gets in the way
of "solving" them.'" (Ibid., citing approvingly the criticisms of
Elazar 1973c:2)   Like Madison, latter-day Publian federalists believe that "in a world of great diversity in wants, ex-
pectatations and life styles, [federalism] is a way to obviate
the necessity for too much uniformity--the kind that would be required if the body politic were to be treated as if it were one
undifferentiated piece." (Elazar, 1973b:295, cited in Boschken
1979:36)

PURE FEDERALISM   (1) "Purely federal" as used in the American Constitutional Convention of 1787 meant what is now referred to as a confederation.   Thus, on June 14, 1787, delegate
William Paterson of New Jersey "asked that debate on the report
of the committee [of the whole] be postponed to permit his group
[the small states] time to prepare a plan 'purely federal, and
contradistinguished from the reported plan,'" that is, the
Randolph or large-state plan. (Anderson 1961:185, excerpting from
Tansill 1927:204-07)   Joseph Story acknowledged in his Commentaries that "[t]he articles of confederation although in some
few respects national, were mainly of a pure federative
character, and were treated as stipulations between states for
many purposes independent and sovereign." (Wright 1929:493, quoting Story)   Thomas Jefferson said that he "consider[ed] the pure
federalist as a republican who would prefer a stronger Executive;
and the republican as one more willing to trust the Legislature
as a broader representation of the people, and a safer deposit of
power. . . . " (Quoted in Foley 1900:333) (2) Pure federalism is
defined as "the principle of organization whereby a compromise is
achieved between concurrent demands for union and for territorial
diversity within a society, by the establishment of a single
political system, within which, general and regional governments
are assigned co-ordinate authority such that neither level of

government is legally or politically subordinate to the other."
Yet, Watts, who presents this definition, says it "does not provide only one pure federal model, for a whole range of
institutional variations implementing the principle of co-
ordinate authority is possible." (All Watts 1966:13. Punctuation
is presented as it is in the original.)

PURPORTED FEDERALISM   Perhaps stronger than pseudo-
federalism but still more apparently than really federal. Watts
in 1966 called West Germany, Yugoslavia, Brazil (Charter of
1946), Venezuela (1947), and Argentina "purported federations."
(Watts 1966 cited in Davis 1978:218)

QUASI-FEDERALISM   (1) American colonies in the eighteenth
century are said to have had "quasi-federal institutions" which
gave rise to a one-sided (colonists only) view that the "relationship [of the colonies] to the British Government was
federal even though London entertained no such notion." (Elazar
1972:14)   The United States today is not generally identified as
quasi-federal despite strong centralizing trends.   Walker believes that the American system "is still a recognizably federal
system"; that the prefix "quasi" is not warranted because "various factors (legal, political, bureaucratic, and attitudinal)
continue to check the emergence of one hierarchical system."
(Walker 1978:115)   (2) The term quasi-federal might be applied to
relationships within American states, specifically to relationships between state and local governments.   Martin observes
that, Dillon's Rule notwithstanding, "[s]omething quite like
[i.e., the meaning of quasi] a federal system has grown up within
the states; for while the law calls for state supremacy, practice
has produced a considerable measure of municipal autonomy. . . .
[D]e jure the state is supreme, de facto the cities enjoy considerable autonomy." (Martin 1965:32)   (3) Freeman identifies ancient Rome as a quasi-federal system and "to [the] quasi-Federal
elements she largely owed her greatness and permanence." (Freeman
1893:572)   (4) In the sixteenth and seventeenth centuries, Riley
notes, the Holy Roman Empire was decaying, and this decay had as
one of its manifestations "a quasi-federal league of real
States." (Riley 1976:17)   Between approximately 1650-1700, Riley
finds that the Empire was, in fact, "in a state of quasi-federal
equilibrium between the rapidly declining central power and the
rapidly rising power of regional states such as Prussia, Bavaria,
and Saxony. . . . " (Ibid., pp. 29-30.)   (5) Montesquieu is cited
as a supporter of "quasi-federal institutions (such as the par-
lements)" in an attempt "to guard against despotism everywhere."
(Riley 1978:78)   (6) Quasi-federalism defines a situation where
"the central authority exercises some degree of control, in
specific matters, over the constituent elements."   This is one
interpretation of quasi-federalism, offered by Wheare, who places
Canada in the quasi-federal category. (Classification cited in
Barker 1951:51-52)   Wheare's reason for identifying Canada as

quasi-federal is that "the British North America Act provides
for so strong a federal government that the provinces should be
considered hardly more than the beneficiaries of constitutional
decentralization." (View of Wheare reported in Elazar 1977:3)
Recent events in Canada render Wheare's categorization of Canada
now highly suspect. Quasi-federal states are, for Wheare, middle
categories between fully federal and fully unitary states.
(Wheare 1964:19,24 cited in Teune in Earle 1968:214) To identify
a system as only quasi-federal is to call attention to "mere
appearance of something that is seemingly so and is in fact different from what it appears to be." (Aiyar 1961:9) Either from
the beginning, or in later development, social, economic, political, ideological, and other forces foreclose a true federal
character. (Ibid., p. 10.) (7) Sugg is reluctant to identify the
Soviet Union as quasi-federal. The expression "quasi-federal,"
in his view, "is far from connoting the actual relations between
the union republic and the autonomous entities," which involve
far less autonomy than the notion of federalism, even quasi-
federalism, should convey. (Sugg in Yarbrough et al. 1972:117)
(9) In Aiyar's opinion the Indian Constitution should not be
identified as quasi-federal. (Aiyar 1961:9) Hitchner and Levine,
however, apparently place India in the quasi-federal category because "[t]he powers of the central government . . . are so far
superior to those of the states that . . . [i]n time of emergency
the central government may virtually suspend the federal system."
(Hitchner and Levine 1968:51) (9) Duchacek says that Uganda,
Libya, and Cameroon began their lives as independent states with
"quasi-federal structures" but, in time, were converted by
authoritarian regimes into very centralized political systems.
(Duchacek 1970:293) (10) Franck believes the modifier quasi-
federal may properly be used "to include any form of association
between states [a] in which the relationship is a continuing one;
[b] regulated by an established system of normative rules and
roles; [and] [c] executed in an impartial and flexible manner
consonant with those rules and roles. . . . " (Franck 1968:192)
For the future, Franck is supportive of efforts of developing
states "to create quasi-federal regulation of trade within a free
trade area, to market common products jointly, and to encourage
the growth of market and money areas large enough to attract
investment and credit." (Ibid.) (11) Franck identifies NATO as
an example of a "functional quasi-federal experiment." (Ibid., p.
194.)

RACIAL FEDERALISM A racial federalism is a plural society
in which the dispersion of power among population groups, inter-
mingled within the society, is more significant than the allocation among territories. Cf. territorial federalism. Watts in
1966 identified Malaya and Rhodesia and Nyasaland, as then constituted, as racial federations. (Watts 1966:114, citing particularly the work of Carnell 1961:49-53) Watts does not believe
the difference between territorial and racial federations

is dramatic.   In territorial unions, racial groups may in fact
be congregated in particular areas; in racial associtions, they
may also be clustered.   Watts believes personally that, "The difference between territorial and racial federations, although by
no means insignificant," therefore, "is more one of degree than
of kind."   (Watts 1966:115)   In racial federations regional units
are   more   likely   to   be   ethnically   heterogeneous.   In 1919,
Sidgwick suggested that while, "Theoretically we should perhaps
include the case in which parts divided by race or religion, and
not by locality or habitation, [and which] have a substantial
autonomy," among federal systems, "the term 'federal' is not usually applied to such combinations." (Sidgwick 1919:533)   By 1966,
the term, with the help of an adjective, was being applied, however.

REAGAN FEDERALISM   The ideas of President Ronald Reagan relative to the American federal system are mostly presented in the
entry   new   federalism   (Reagan).   Only   a   few   illustrations   are
offered at this point to show how the presidential initiatives of
the early 1980s were personalized with Reagan's own name, particularly by some of his staff members.
Richard S. Williamson, the President's principal assistant
for intergovernmental affairs, said that "Reagan federalism . . .
entail[ed] providing significant regulatory relief to state and
local governments." (Williamson 1981:13) He identified these as
the highlights of <u>Reagan</u> federalism:

[1] Washington does not have a monopoly on wisdom as
how best to serve the American people.
[2] State, local and county officials are in a better
position to know and understand the needs of the people
than officials at the national level.
[3] Washington should be a partner with state, local
and county governments in helping solve the problems
facing the people.
[4] The Reagan Administration's budget reflects a shift
in federal priorities to truly national needs.
[5] Consolidation of categorical grant programs into a
comprehensive system of block grants underscores
President Reagan's belief that authority and responsibility should be returned to state and local governments.
[6] Regulatory reform will provide significant relief
to state and local governments.
[7] The reduction of federal taxes will allow more
revenue sources to be available to state and local
governments.
[8] President Reagan . . . established a Federalism
Advisory Committee . . . [to] provide a forum for
replenishing the intellectual capital of federalism and
to give specific guidance on programs. (Undated White
House statement)

Reagan federalism was also employed by others not in the President's official family. Colman said that "Reagan federalism [was] directed toward a reduced role of the national government and an increased role for state and local governments." (Colman 1982:126) Generally, the expression Reagan federalism was not used as much as new federalism either inside or outside the White House following delivery of the President's January, 1982, state of the Union message.

REAL FEDERALISM (1) In 1973, Stevenson asserted that there were only five "real federal states," that is, "states in which there is a true distribution of independent powers among the central government and the governments of the largest subdivisions." (Stevenson 1973:235) These, he said, were Canada, the United States, Australia, West Germany, and Switzerland. (2) Freeman says that ancient Rome did not exhibit "real Federalism" because "the relation of the Tribes to each other was not a Federal relation" and "because all the Tribes were members of the one ruling commonwealth and did not form sovereign communities themselves." (Freeman 1893:574) (3) Real federalism, according to several sources, requires a union composed of previously independent political unions. Thus, as Duchacek observes, "Some authors tend to consider subsequent or simultaneous creation of new units in a federation . . . not real federalism." (Duchacek 1970:240-41) Lord Haldane is reported as feeling, for example, that Canada's constitution, the British North America Act of 1867, "was not a federal constitution because it had created a central government simultaneously with the provincial governments." (Attorney General for the Commonwealth of Australia v. Colonial Sugar Refining Co., Ltd., 1914, cited in Duchacek 1970:241) (4) Dennewitz says that real federalism requires that the union be voluntary and that the components have equal legal status. (Dennewitz 1947:46) Dictated federalism and hegemonial federalism are not real federalism. (5) "Real unions" constitute one of several classifications of unions or political combinations identified by Sharma and Choudhry. (Sharma and Choudhry 1967:13) It is not a federation since "the uniting states . . . lose their separate characters even in their internal autonomy and become a unitary state. . . . " (Ibid.) Bluntschli says that "the so-called Real Union . . . is related to Federation," but, in this political combination, "the United States may . . . have a relative independence, [and] within certain limits they may have special legislatures and executives, but the whole state is one organism, and its highest interests are concentrated in the same hands." (Bluntschli 1892:272-73) Bluntschli cites Austria pursuant to the fundamental law of 1849 and the Constitution of 1861 as exemplifying real union. Generally, in the most important policy areas, the uniting states shared common ministries.

REALIGNED FEDERALISM   Merriam saw in the Reagan federalism initiative "the last great chance to sort out or decongest the overloaded national platter of programs." (Merriam 1982:123)   A realigned federalism, reallocating functions among governmental sectors, was essential because of "the cumulative effect of the burgeoning categorical grant programs, coupled with the cross-cutting general legislative mandates, plus the regulatory developments and court decisions [which had] created confusion, overlapping, and waste of alarming proportions." (Ibid.)

REBALANCED FEDERALISM   This is what Ronald Reagan was said to be trying to achieve with his new federalism initiative.   Lawson and Stenberg noted in 1982 that "intergovernmental relations in the United States [were] undergoing dramatic and rapid change unparalleled in recent history," and attributed this change to "effort[s] to 'rebalance' federalism [which] could well have drastic and lasting effects on the role, functions, and powers" of the federal government and state and local governments. (Lawson and Stenberg 1982:40)   Using Elazar's phrase "keystones of the governmental arch," these authors predicted that the states would "bear much of the burden for keeping a balanced intergovernmental system in place during the 1980s." (Ibid.)

REBORN FEDERALISM Attempting to drastically change federalism is said to be the equivalent of seeing it born again. Journalist Neil Peirce, writing of the Reagan new federalism efforts, said "the moral of [the] first saga of federalism reborn" was that a "Pandora's box of vital issues [was] being opened" and "the [American federal] system [was getting] its most thorough airing in decades." No one could then "predict where the ball [would] stop rolling." (Peirce 1982:7A)

REFORMED FEDERALISM   This adjective has been applied, along with renewed federalism, to the Canadian federation in recent years as the relationship of Ottawa and the provinces, under the pressure of Quebec separatist efforts, has been reconsidered. Smiley pointed in 1978 to "the failure of Ottawa and the provinces with English-speaking majorities to agree on the nature of a reformed federalism," to say nothing of Quebec and Ottawa. (Smiley 1978:234)

REGIONAL FEDERALISM   (1) The expression regional federalism has been applied in the United States to economic development and natural resources programs involving multiple agencies and the federal government.   The prime example is the Appalachian Regional Commission. (Gilbert and Smith in Stedman 1968:150)   (2) In Africa, Franck identifies efforts of white-dominated governments to unite countries in the same geographical area to promote economic progress.   These efforts were unsuccessful at the time they were initially made, Franck feels, because this kind of regional federalism could not be squared with the more ambitious pan-African federalism. Time was inadequate "to make a clean, ideological distinction between the colonial-white-mercantilist federalism of the past and a new Africanized, unifying, ideological federalism of the future," and because "the 'wrong' [i.e., white-dominated] African governments . . . were in power." (Franck 1968:29) Franck says that the negotiations for an East African federation which began in 1963 "revealed the lack of an explicit idea of regional federalism and disclosed powerful pockets of continued support for a nonideological mercantilist association, one which could call itself 'federal' only because the concept had been given no meaning." (Ibid., p. 30.)

REGULATORY FEDERALISM   This is how Kettl characterizes the efforts of the federal government to govern the behavior of subnational American governments, particularly through the use of conditions attached to financial aid.   "The tendency toward regulatory federalism," Kettl feels, stemmed in part from "a lack of patience" on the part of federal officials to allow cities particularly to correct deficiencies in their administration of public programs. (Kettl 1981:124)   Ironically, the regulations which made up regulatory federalism "imposed political and administrative burdens on the cities that made achievement of the [financially aided] programs' more general goals far more difficult." (Ibid.) While "Nixon's New Federalism had the virtue of assigning clear responsibility to subnational governments for the pursuit of [a program's] goals," Kettl indicts the "regulatory federalism that has evolved" from Nixonian new federalism because it "has blurred the lines of responsibility and has made a patchwork of accountability for intergovernmental policy." (Ibid., p. 125.)

RELIGIOUS FEDERALISM   The influence of religious patterns of governance on secular forms is treated in Garson 1975. Sidgwick points out that while, "Theoretically we should perhaps include the case in which parts divided by race or religion, and not by locality or habitation, [and which] have a substantial autonomy" among the universe of federalisms, in fact, "the term 'federal' is not usually applied to such combinations." (Sidgwick 1919:533)   Not that Sidgwick was writing 65 years ago.

RENEWED FEDERALISM   (1) Bebout, criticizing Reagan new federalism, argued that, "What we need . . . is neither a brand new federalism, nor an old federalism masquerading as new, but a constantly renewing federalism, serving the basic purposes of the preamble [to the U.S. Constitution] by adapting actions in their pursuit to the requirements of a changing world." (Bebout 1982:529)   (2) Premier Pierre-Elliott Trudeau's preferred expression for his efforts to provide new unity for a Canadian federation torn both by Quebec separatism and the increasing restlessness of the energy-rich, English-speaking provinces of the west is renewed federalism. One news report noted that, "Many in Quebec and elsewhere in Canada saw the PQ [Parti Quebecois] defeat in the [May 20, 1980] referendum as a victory for [Premier Trudeau's] middle road of 'renewed federalism.'" ("Separationists Lose Vote," 1980:3)

REPRESENTATIONAL FEDERALISM   This is federalism viewed from the perspective of the American voter who is governed "through two different governments," and who is, therefore, encouraged to see "the political world from two perspectives, one shaped by the social pluralism of the general government, and the other shaped by the territorial pluralism of the state government." (Beer 1978:15.   Beer credits the origin of the expression "representational federalism" to Eulau 1973.)   Beer feels that the contentions of the dissidents in pre-Revolutionary American struggles basically stressed "self-government, and that accordingly the meaning they gave to federalism was primarily representational, not dual." (Ibid., p. 11.)   He sees as "[t]he essence of the invention of 1787 [the American Constitution] . . . the use of the same electorate to choose two sets of governments, each with constitutional protection. . . . [T]he people were to maintain the balance for free government by casting their weight in one or the other scale . . . [T]he medium of interaction was the common electorate." (Ibid., pp. 14-15.) Of course, Beer cautions that, "In his political life, as a member of one nation, [the voter] does not separate from one another the two perspectives and the interests each elicits. . . . " (Ibid., p. 15.)

REPUBLICAN FEDERALISM   It is generally assumed that a federal system will be republican.   The German Empire of the late nineteenth and early twentieth centuries, however, was not republican but monarchical.   See Bluntschli 1892:271.   A republican federalism would be a federal union the central and constituent governments of which were governed by the people's elected representatives, not by hereditary rulers.

RESPONSIVE FEDERALISM   This expression was used in Responsive Federalism: A Report to the President on the Federal Assistance Review Project (1973).   It has no distinctive content. It is simply another positive word associated with federalism to try to show how it could be improved, here with the making of certain improvements in administrative procedures.   Burgess identified the theme of most studies in this time period (early in Nixon's second term) as an emphasis on "'jurisdictions' rather than 'functions' and the corresponding emphasis on the role of the elected official in the domestic policy process." (Burgess 1975:705)

RESTORED FEDERALISM   To get back to the federalism of the past when, presumably, there was a sharper differentiation in governmental roles and the American national government's role was less pervasive than it had come to be two-thirds of the way through the twentieth century. Moore argued for "restoring federalism" but he believed that "it [would] be very hard to make progress in restoring federalism without more than an inclination on the part of the [Reagan] White House to be sensitive to state and local power." A restored federalism would be "a sound, historically based notion of federalism. . . . " (Moore in Hawkins 1982:242)

RETRENCHMENT FEDERALISM   A negative depiction of Reagan new federalism. (Its use was noted in Matheson 1982:506.) The implication is that rather than seeking restoration of a rightful balance of power between federal and state governments, the Republican administration's principal aim was to cut back on expensive social programs and let states and localities take the brunt of citizen discontent with fewer public services.

REVISED FEDERALISM   As evidenced by the entries in this volume, federalism continually is being revised. One illustration of the use of the expression "revised federalism" will be presented. Mason notes that the U.S. Supreme Court, under Roger B. Taney's chief justiceship, created a "revised federalism" according to which "the Constitution was a compact of sovereign states, not [as under Chief Justice John Marshall] an ordinance of the people." (Mason in Earle 1968:24)

REVITALIZED FEDERALISM   Very generalized descriptor for the Ronald Reagan approach to federalism. The President, in remarks to his advisory commission on federalism, asserted that "one of his 'cornerstone commitments' was a 'revitalized federalism' in which power, authority and revenue sources would be shifted from Washington to state and local governments." (Quoted in Ayres 1981:B8) According to his assistant for intergovernmental affairs, Richard Williamson, Reagan wanted to base his Presidency on budget cuts, regulatory reform, "revitalized federalism," and only a few other public policy issues. (View cited in Peirce 1981b:785-88) "To fashion a revitalized federalism, a system that works," the President would "draw on the knowledge and expertise of local leaders. . . . " (Williamson 1981:17)

REVOLUTIONARY FEDERALISM   This is identified as one aspect of Marc's federalist thought. (See the name index for other aspects.) The revolutionary level of federalism, according to Marc, is characterized by invention and synthesis. It denotes the movement from the syncrete to the concrete, in the direction of praxis, or projection on action. (Summarized from Heraud 1976:29-30)

ROMAN FEDERALISM   The Roman model is one of the basic federal paradigms. (Davis 1978:215) Schechter, examining ancient applications of federal concepts, looks to the Roman republic to portray "yet another application of federal pacts as an empire-building instrument to neutralize those peoples too powerful or too valuable to subjugate. . . . " (Schechter 1975:5. Schechter finds particularly helpful on the Roman experience Fustel de Coulanges 1956:37-38.) Freeman observes that while "Rome was a city-commonwealth . . . it differed in many points from the city-commonwealths of Greece, and all the points in which it differed are approaches to the Federal type." (Freeman 1893:572) The tribes shared in the supreme power of Rome; the allies retained their individual local governments. (Ibid., p. 575.)

ROMANTIC FEDERALISM   The name of Hegel is not generally as-sociated with federalism.   However, Dennewitz makes the linkage in this context: The highest authority for Hegel was the will of the nation organized into a state. But the state should not ex-press an undifferentiated mass.   Instead, the state power should be erected on the foundation of the cooperation of the parts of the state.   The essentially unitary attitude of Hegel, for Den-newitz, represents some sort of combination of romanticism and federalism ("romantisch-föderalistisch"). (Dennewitz 1947:114)

SECONDARY FEDERALISM   The upper level of a system of federations.   In the Fourth French Republic the French Union ex-emplified secondary federalism, the Afrique Occidentale Francaise (AOF) and the Afrique Equatoriale Francaise (AEF) primary federalism. (Neuberger in Elazar 1979a:171-72)

SECULAR FEDERALISM   In essence, this is federalism outside a religious context.   Schechter points to the absence of ex-aminations of "the 'early modern' connections between Federal Theology (and Puritan practice) and 'secular' models of federal-ism in America, Switzerland and the Netherlands." (Schechter 1975:4)   Most entries in this volume can be classified as instances of secular federalism. For the most part they do not relate to the church or spiritual affairs.

SELF-MANAGED FEDERALISM   This is Spadijer's label for the worker-based federalism of Yugoslavia. ("Samoupravnog federlizma," Spadijer 1972:27)   The further development of this federalism "will enable the working class to become the basic so-cial [agency] and the prime moving force of the whole political system." (Ibid., p. 40.   Trans. Marshall Winokur)   Self-managed federalism is opposed both to anticommunist and antirevolutionary forces and neocentralist, technocratic, and state-oriented mono-polistic forces. (Ibid., pp. 40-41.   See other references to Yugoslavia in the geographical index and the entry for polyvalent federalism.)

SEMI-ANTAGONISTIC FEDERALISM   According to Wildavsky, today's American federalism is not wholly cooperative but neither is it wholly antagonistic.   It is "semi-cooperative and semi-antagonistic . . . varying, to the frustration of neat categorizers, with the policy areas, the time, the technology, and other factors . . . " (Wildavsky 1980:27)

SEMI-COOPERATIVE FEDERALISM   See semi-antagonistic federalism immediately above.

SEMI-FEDERALISM   Partially federal, not exactly half-federal.   Davis says that the ancient Grecian symmachies were "semi-federal alliances of states theoretically free and autonomous." (Davis 1978:13) Symmachia is literally translated "fellowship in fighting."   As the ancients used the term, it denoted informal working together in wartime, treaties of alliance, and confederations of potential military allies (e.g., military alliances, security pacts). (Ibid., pp. 13-14.)

SEPARATIST FEDERALISM   This is de Grazia's label for what most scholars would probably call dual federalism.   It, along with cooperative federalism, is one of "[t]wo major theories of federalism [which] have influenced American government since the beginning."   De Grazia says "'separatist federalism' . . . visualizes a maximum separation and isolation of state and nation." (De Grazia 1962:248)   The author associates Jeffersonians and Jacksonians with "an extreme separatist-federalist position" and argues that "[t]heir views dominated American legal and political thought, despite the effects of the Civil War, until World War I." (Ibid.)

SERVICE FEDERALISM   Colman identifies service federalism as one of a number of different varieties of federalism related to American cities.   He does not formally define the expression but, apparently, it refers to an emphasis on close intergovernmental relationships in the provision of a wide variety of services for residents of urban areas. (Colman 1975:308)

SHAM FEDERALISM   The U.S.S.R., Yugoslavia, and Czechoslovakia have been labeled "sham federal states" because "the federal structure is nullified by the omnipotence of the central organization of the Communist Party in each state."   Outside the Soviet sphere, for Burma, Zaire, and Brazil, "the [federal] constitution is a sham." (All Stevenson 1973:235) Apparently sham federalism is the same as pseudo-federalism. (Ibid., p. 236.)

SHAPE FEDERALISM   The fifth of the five types of federal states put forward by de Blij, along with mutual interest, compromise, centralized, and imposed.   De Blij concedes that "no one would argue that shape alone would produce a federal arrangement in any state."   Even so, "shape characteristics of some states have contributed greatly to that choice of politicoterritorial organization," e.g., federalism.   Pakistan probably would not have opted for federalism had it not been separated (prior to the

departure of Bangladesh) into two principal units. "Other
Islamic states," de Blij notes, "are unitary and highly centralized." (All de Blij 1967:463) De Blij accurately, as it
turned out, questioned "the chances of Pakistan to survive as a
unified political entity," given the thousand-mile division of
the federal state. (Ibid., p. 465.)

SHARED FEDERALISM This is a synonym for the more familiar
cooperative federalism when employed by Duchacek. (Duchacek
1970:318) Davis suggests that "the 'federalism of sharing,' like
'cooperative federalism,' [may] simply betoken an adjustment in
our vocabulary," to maintain the illusion that federalism per-
sists when it actually does not. (Davis 1978:185)   "Sharing
federalism," in Davis's view, represents an attempt by Americans
"to explain their own federal experience" and, if necessary, to
revise this experience in the process. (Ibid., p. 201.)

SHELL-GAME FEDERALISM   When Congress "enact[s] more and
more prorgrams, and then . . . cut[s] the staff of the agencies
that are supposed to administer the programs and the conditions
attached to them at the state level . . . [t]his is the old shell
game." (Walker in Katz and Schuster 1979:38) Thus emerged "a new
phrase for today's system--'shell-game federalism,'" a federalism
which amounts to "pretense in terms of monitoring, supervising,
and looking over peoples' shoulders . . . [h]ence the shell game
metaphor and all that it suggests by way of irresponsibility."
(Ibid.)

SIMPLE FEDERALISM   English translation of foedus simplex.
The basic meaning is "a simple alliance," particularly for military purposes. (Davis 1978:39, 60) Foedus simplex is most applicable to ancient Greek military associations.

SMALL-CITY FEDERALISM   This expression was suggested by
Green to point out that, in his view, "there is no clear [or]
consistent national policy of assistance designed to address the
variety of needs in [the] smaller cities" of the United States.
(Green 1979:1) The optimum solution would be a "comprehensive
attempt to restructure the current duplication of grant programs.
. . . "   But since that "would be tantamount to a revolution in
fiscal federalism," he suggests "the establishment of a more
equitable national policy which would include and address the
needs of smaller cities." (Ibid., p. 15.)

SMALL-REPUBLIC FEDERALISM   The architect of what is referred to as small-republic federalism was the Baron de Montesquieu, who perceived the smallness of a country to be "the
precondition of republicanism and republican liberty." (Diamond
1973:133) The motive for holding onto the autonomy of a small
territorial area through federal association is to defend republicanism and republican liberty, values which would be less

tenuously held to in consolidated systems or strongly
centralized federal settings. Yet, Diamond says, the Framers of
1787 were able to convince American disciples of Montesquieuean
small-group federalism that "the republican form of government
could . . . be made secure in a large country," governed by an
expanded federal authority." (Ibid., pp. 133-34.)

SOCIAL FEDERALISM   (1) "In every society in which a balance
in the respect for the right of the individual and the demand of
society occurs," Deuerlein explains, "social federalism ("gesell-
schaftlicher Föderalismus") is protected." (Deuerlein 1972:328;
tr. Mary Gray Porter)   Federal structures are not of primary
importance. What is significant is that whatever structures are
in place contribute to the individual-society balance. (2) Approach to federalism which sees an "intertwining of political and
functional interests and powers," which goes beyond "the
traditional principle of federalism, which only applies to the
political sphere. . . . " (Djordjevic 1975:78) Social federalism
extends the federal principle to social as well as cultural and
economic domains. Djordjevic argues that his "'model' of social
federalism has already had an impact on thinking in the field of
international organization helping to overcome the fear of the
'supranational state.' . . . " (Ibid., p. 79.)

SOCIALIST FEDERALISM   (1) In Western Europe, "federal
socialism is [presented] as a different kind of socialism . . .
far removed from the stifling collectivism of the Soviet description. . . . " (Marc 1979:124) In Marc's model of federalist
socialism "some enterprises are 'public' and some more 'private,'" but "[a]ll enterprises produce for and serve both [a
free] market and the plan," which is essential to ensure
"constructive competition" and "to reconcile private and local
initiative with over-all control." (Ibid., pp. 126, 127, 128.)
(2) Yugoslavia is identified as an example of socialist
federalism by Friedrich; that is, a socialist country which also
exhibits federal qualities. He was encouraged by growth in an
emphasis on the rule of law which might, in time, furnish a
meaningful check on "the centralized monolith of the extremes of
totalitarianism." (Friedrich 1968:165, 167)

SOCIETARY FEDERALISM   This type of federalism ("sozietarem
Föderalismus") is defined as that situation in which the
individual does not predominate over society nor does society
predominate over the individual. According to Deuerlein, "the
individual can become what he is only through society and in
society, the substance of which is determined by the substance of
the individual." (Deuerlein 1972:328; tr. Mary Gray Porter)

SOCIO-CULTURAL FEDERALISM   This theory of federalism was
developed by Livingston in 1952.   Tarlton observes that
Livingston felt, after introducing his socio-cultural theory of

federalism, that he could arrange societies in some kind of meaningful order "according to the degree to which they are more or less basically federal." (Tarlton 1965:866 citing Livingston 1952)

SOCIOLOGICAL FEDERALISM   "The sociological concept of federalism," Pentland believes, derives from such movements as integral federalism "which emerged in the 1930s as an eclectic mix of ideas from Proudhon, syndicalism, left-wing Catholicism and a number of other politically eccentric sources."   The sociological approach "emphasized the bankruptcy of 'formal' democracy, capitalism and the established ideologies of right and left, and advocated & pluralistic or federal society of communal groups and interests." (Ibid.)

SPAGHETTI FEDERALISM   A "crude metaphor" for the kind of American federalism which emerged as a result of Lyndon Johnson's Great Society programs.   The image of spaghetti comes from simultaneous trends of diversity and convergence. (Wright 1974:11) Spaghetti was suggested by "the scores of specific and discrete categorical grants" initiated in the Johnson years.

SPONTANEOUS FEDERALISM   Federalism occuring without conscious design. For Proudhon, an economic order "composed of occupational groups freely formed for the purpose of production and exchange and freely cohering in virtue of their mutual service and benefit" results "by its nature in an economic rule of right . . . of reciprocal service and proportional exchange between its constitute groups. . . . " (Barker 1951:35-36) This economic system, for Barker, is best identified as "natural and spontaneous federalism." (Ibid., p. 36.)

STATE-CENTERED FEDERALISM   Leach says, "State-centered federalism developed in resistance to the nationalism of Hamilton and Marshall and was first articulated in the Virginia and Kentucky Resolutions of 1798" (Leach 1970:12):

[1] The Constitution was a compact in that 'each state acceded as a State,' implying that ultimate sovereignty still resided with the latter.
[2] The powers of the national government were to be bound by 'the plain sense and implication' of the Constitution and were not to be construed broadly.
[3] The national government had no exclusive right to judge the scope of its powers while the states had an obligation to 'interpose' in any unconstitutional efforts to extend federal authority. (Walker 1981c:47-48 citing Kelly and Harbison 1976:199-200)

The years 1789-1860 were years in which "nation-centered and state-centered theories of federalism contended with one another." (Corwin in McCloskey 1962:188-89)

In the pre-Civil War period "the full-blown theory of state-centered federalism was polished and perfected, particularly by southerners, as its usefulness in rationalizing the differences between that section of the country and the rest of the nation became more apparent." (Ibid.) Belz uses this expression in the context of an historical analysis of post-Civil War U.S. politics. He says the initial efforts of southern states to restore race relations as closely as possible to their ante bellum condition aroused northerners and "provoked concern for state-centered federalism." In the Republican view "the nation consisted of states, and evils in one state did injury to all the states." Pursuant to this feeling, "to preserve the integrity of the states, and thereby the nation . . . Congress . . . exclude[d] southern delegates and form[ed] a Joint Committee on Reconstruction. . . . " (Belz 1978:100) Belz believes that, "The persistence of . . . state-centered federalism in Congressional thinking was evidence of the kind of constitutional conservatism that kept reconstruction policy from veering off into revolutionary radicalism." (Ibid., p. 106.) Well past the middle of the twentieth century, "the State-based federalism of America has served as a vehicle (or cloak) for a competition of regional or sectional interests." (Livingston in Earle 1968:95)

STATE-FEDERALISM   This is Furman's label for what Riker calls peripheralized federalism. Furman's primary concern was with grants-in-aid and to "identify the level of government (National or State) whose objectives are more successfully promoted by the distribution of grants. . . . " (Furman 1974:10) In the model he designates as state-federalism, grants are most influenced by the objectives of state political systems. In contrast, in the cooperative federalism model grants reflect national and state goals jointly; in centralized- or national-federalism models, national goals are strongly emphasized.

STATE-ORIENTED FEDERALISM   In 1981, President Reagan's principal domestic policy adviser, Martin Anderson, was identified as "the main architect of the new state-oriented federalism." Reagan, Anderson, Edwin Meese (counselor to the President), and David Stockman (Director of the Office of Management and Budget) were said to "have spoken as one in denying that," in enunciation of the new Reagan state-oriented federalism, "the Administration [would] adopt the racial bias of the old states' rights advocates." (Raines 1981:A24)

STATES RIGHTS FEDERALISM   The emphasis of the American federal system during much of its history. Beer argues that in "the Jacksonian period of 'states rights federalism,' . . . the states were the principal instruments of social choice while the federal government languished and declined. . . . " (Beer 1973:69)

STIMULUS-RESPONSE FEDERALISM   This is the title of a 1979 article by Rosenfeld.   For him, stimulus-response federalism involves "the relation between Supreme Court deference and state court justice." (Rosenfeld in Dailey 1979:113) While he supports some deference to state courts, he feels the Burger Court has gone too far. The stimuli of unsatisfactory state court systems producing frequently insensitive outputs (from his point of view) do not merit the response of a Supreme Court yielding to state court justice. "If [a] state court lacks the capacity or will to fulfill [its] duties," Rosenfeld believes, "the occasion for deference ceases to exist." (Ibid., p. 132. Rosenfeld's footnotes omitted)

SUBNATIONAL FEDERALISM   Federalism within the nation-state. (Brugmans in Yarbrough et al. 1972:87)

SUMMIT FEDERALISM   This term applies to Canadian federalism and was originated by J. S. Dupre.   According to a professional administrator, Anthony Careless,

> Summit federalism describes that federal-provincial
> interaction whereby initiative directions are
> established by those at the political summit of
> each administration, i.e., the First Minister
> (Premier or Prime Minister) rather than functional
> ministers. (Letter to author from Anthony Careless,
> Ministry of Intergovernmental Affairs, June 30,
> 1982)

This form of federalism, Careless continues, "involves inter-actions between tightly-controlled hierarchies at each level, such that the policy direction of each government in inter-governmental relations is distributive rather than aggregative." That is, it is "determined by a top-down rather than bottom-up process." Bureaucrats must work inside summit-established para-meters.

SUPPLY-SIDE FEDERALISM   A synonym for the economic aspects of Reagan federalism. Wildavsky questions the wisdom of federal assumption of medical insurance, energy, food, and other needs of clients on a greatly expanded welfare roll. "Why," he asks, "begin 'supply-side' federalism by increasing the federal share?" (Wildavsky in Hawkins 1982:189)   "[B]ig government," Wildavsky believes, "is antithetical to federalism because it preempts re-sources for the national government and because it causes virtu-ally every activity to mix the levels of government." (Ibid.)

SUPRANATIONAL FEDERALISM   The opposite of subnational federalism; federalism beyond the national state. Brugmans as-serts that "these two approaches to federalism--subnational

decentralization and supranational federation--are not contradictory," but complementary. (Brugmans in Yarbrough et al.
1972:87)   Subnational federalism helps "overcome excessive
nationalism" while supranational federalism would combat too much
localism. (Ibid., p. 89.)

SWEET AND SOUR FEDERALISM   Federal aid is sweet. The conditions attached to the grants received by state and local
governments in the United States may be sour.   Cappalli particularly objects to the proliferation of secondary conditions,
generally unrelated to the major objectives of grant-aided programs.   These conditions are cross-cutting, applying to multiple
programs.   Examples include requirements relating to non-
discrimination, environmental protection, worker safety, freedom
of information, and many other subjects. (Cappalli 1981:143-57)

SYMBIOTIC FEDERALISM   (1) Althusius writes of the universal
symbiotic association, a confederation which consists of public
symbiotic associations at lower levels, principally provinces,
cities, villages, and towns. Its constituents are not individual
persons. (Althusius, Politics, Carney ed., 1964:62) Sovereignty
inheres ultimately in the people collectively who through their
public societies delegate the power to exercise it to this
principal political association.   No individual or association
has more power than the universal confederation. Symbiotics is
synonymous with politics for Althusius. (Friedrich in Carney
1964:ix) (2) In biology, symbiosis refers to the living together
of two species of organisms in a union which is beneficial to
both. Symbiotic federalism is a concept suggested by Wildavsky
who pictures the contemporary American federal system as one in
which "the participants wrestle" but "it proves impossible to
separate them." The wrestling is not aimed at injury. The relationship of the intergovernmental participants is probably
"symbiotic . . . they live off one another . . . more for one at
hour 'x' leads to more for both at hour 'y.'" (Wildavsky 1980:11)

SYMMETRICAL FEDERALISM   "[T]he notion of symmetry," Tarlton
explains in the principal exposition of symmetrical federalism,
"refers to the extent to which component states share in the conditions and thereby the concerns more or less common to the
federal system as a whole." (Tarlton 1965:861) The more members
of the federal union possess the same social, cultural, economic,
and political attributes, the more symmetrical the union is. The
quality of symmetricalness "shap[es] [a state's] relations with
other component states and with the national authority." (Ibid.)
"The overall extent to which the federal system is characterized
by a harmonious pattern of states partaking of the general
features of the federal nation is at the core of the symmetry of
federalism." (Ibid., p. 867.)   Tarlton identifies "[a]n ideal
symmetrical federal system" as "one composed of political units
comprised of equal territory and population, similar economic

features, climatic conditions, cultural patterns, social
groupings, and political institutions." In short, "each of the
separate poltical units [is] in effect [a] miniature reflection
of the important aspects of the whole federal system." (Ibid., p.
868.) Of course, no ideal symmetrical federalism exists. And,
even should a given system approach the ideal, its components
would still have "general problems of [their] own in the solution
of which local authority would be thought to be best suited. The
federal authority would, in the main, be limited to . . . problems either common to the federal system qua system . . . or requiring system-wide attention and resources for solution."
(Ibid., pp. 868-69.)

SYMPOLITY FEDERALISM   A type of federation present in ancient Greece.   (See isopolity federalism.)   In the sympolity
"each citizen in addition to remaining a member of his own city
became a member of a larger body which was organized as a federal
union." (Schechter 1975:5)

SYNDICAL FEDERALISM   Syndicalism is one of the sources of
contemporary integral federalism. (Pentland 1973:160)   Barker
identifies Proudhon as its chief prophet.   Proudhon was foremost
in exclaiming that "the economic order was anterior in time and
superior in importance to the political. . . . That droit economique, based upon and constituted by the principle of mutua-
lite, was similarly anterior and superior to droit politique,
which ought to be deduced from, and should be a reflection of,
the economic principle of mutuality.   The essence of the economic order was a federal essence. . . . " (Barker 1951:35)   As
Barker interprets syndicalism, it envisioned "a federal society
of complementary occupations" which stands in stark contrast with
the contemporary Marxian image of "a warring society (which is
not a society) of colliding classes." (Ibid., p. 37.)

TAX FEDERALISM   Without elaboration, Frenkel cites tax
federalism ("Steuerföderalismus") as one of a number of informal
models of federalism related to public policy which one en-
counters frequently in the Swiss daily press. (Frenkel 1975:726)

TECHNOCRATIC FEDERALISM   This is "a new phase of [the] centralizing process" which, for many years, has been going on "[i]n
the United States, as in other modernizing societies, . . . [in
which] the general historical record has spelled centralization."
(Beer 1973:52)   This kind of federalism is technocratic federalism because "the main reasons for . . . change are not to be
found in the personal, partisan or ideological preferences of
office-holders, but in the new forces produced by an advanced
modernity."   Beer feels that the "growing professionalization of
government has created a new type of centralizing coalition" and
that this coalition's expression in intergovernmental relations

is best termed professionalized or technocratic federalism."
(Ibid., pp. 52, 79-80.) In technocratic federalism
"theory-oriented research . . . often underlies the design of new
programs . . . [T]he research elite and its associated professionals," most heavily represented in the federal government,
help to give the central government "a near monopoly of innovation." (Ibid., pp. 79-80. See the entry for post-technocratic
federalism for a presentation of Elazar's ideas on this subject.)

TECHNOLOGICAL FEDERALISM   This expression, "technological
federalism," was employed in a 1972 study of developments in
federalism. (See Warren and Wescher in Yarbrough et al.
1972:61-72.) Warren and Wescher are interested particularly in
urban governments which, they feel, need to make much greater use
of modern technologies in their problem-solving activities.
Federal assistance is mandatory and the best approach toward
technological federalism is "a mixed strategy, which includes
local initiative, as well as federal involvement." (Ibid., p.
67.) These authors are convinced that a research and development
system too heavily influenced by federal agencies will be much
less productive than a system in which problems are solved
through cooperative technological efforts, in which urban
governments also play an important input role.

TERRITORIAL FEDERALISM   (1) Federalism is generally conceived of in territorial terms when applied to the political
sphere. If the social diversities which justify a division of
authority "are not grouped territorially," Livingston says
flatly, "the society cannot be said to be federal. . . . [I]t becomes functionalism, pluralism, or some form of corporativism."
(Livingston 1956:2) In Area and Power federalism is viewed as an
"areal division of power." (Maass 1959:16) Watts observes that,
"the distinction between territorially diverse societies and
plural societies has led to the suggestion that among the new
federations a contrast can be drawn between territorial
federations such as India, Pakistan [pre-division], Nigeria, and
the West Indies, and racial federations such as Malaya and
Rhodesia and Nyasaland." (Watts 1966:114) Racial federations
seem to be even more shaky than territorial federations. (2) Using the Canada of the early federal period (post-1867) as his
point of reference, Mallory defines a territorial federation as
"one strongly governed from the centre in which the provinces
[which were essentially newly opened territories] . . . had only
a modest role in the process of government." Indeed, the early
Confederation "was more of an imperial system, governed from Ottawa, than a true federation." (Mallory 1977:151)

THEOLOGICAL FEDERALISM   Elazar points out that, "In its
original form, the federal idea was a theological concept that
defined the relationship between God and man as one in which both
were linked by covenant in a partnership designed to make them
jointly responsible for the world's welfare." This theological

federalism was "[f]irst formulated in the covenant theory of the
Hebrew Bible as the basis for God's relationship with Israel."
(Elazar 1972:1-2) Later "this conception of federalism was re-
vived   by   the   Bible-centered   'federal   theologians'   of
seventeenth-century Britain and New England who coined the
term'federal,'" an English word "derived from the Latin foedus
(covenant)--to describe the system of holy and enduring covenants
between God and man which lay at the foundation of their world
view." (Ibid., p. 2.)   A vital aspect of theological federalism
is the belief that God voluntarily "restrict[ed] his otherwise
omnipotent powers under the terms of the covenant [and] granted
man a significant measure of freedom," because, from this aspect,
"developed the concept of 'federal liberty.'" (Ibid.)   New England colonies and churches were structured along federal lines.

TIGHT FEDERALISM   Federalism characterized by a powerful
central government.   Hicks says that in Nigeria in 1966 the
leaders of the country, with the conclusion of civil war, felt
that the "right thing" would be to establish "a tight federation
with a strong centre but which would allow for diversities . . .
in respect of the great number of tribes and peoples (estimated
to be about 250) and . . . [to] get rid of regional separation,
so that it would truly be possible to build 'one Nigeria' of
which all recognized themselves to be citizens."   (All Hicks
1978:136)

TOTAL FEDERALISM   This term has the same meaning as
complete federalism.   Davis points to the nineteenth-century
methodology of arranging "unions or leagues of states in a
dichotomous federal scheme of perfect/imperfect, pure/impure, or
total/partial . . . " (Davis 1978:207)

TRADE UNION FEDERALISM   (1) Trade unions are normally associated on a federal basis--for example, the American Federation
of Labor, united in 1955 with the Congress of Industrial
Organizations, in the United States.   Cranston and Lakoff observe
that, "A trade-union federation may be either a group of unions
working together in a particular field (as mining, building,
etc.) or a central national organization open to all unions,
including those called federations." (Cranston and Lakoff
1969:53)   (2) In the 1930s, Mogi cited the British Trade Union
Congress, the Allgemeiner Deutscher Gewerkschaftsbund, the International Federation of Trade Unions, and the International Trans-
portworkers Federation as examples of nationally and inter-
nationally organized trade union fedrations. (Mogi 1931b:114)

TRADITIONAL FEDERALISM   (1) For Drucker what is traditional
about traditional federalism is that it places almost exclusive
emphasis on relationships between the federal government and the
states, relationships Drucker identifies as typifying "coexistence and competition."   More recent conceptualizations bring in
relationships of the federal government to other jurisdictions,

not only metropolitan governments but private organizations. (Drucker 1971:69) For critics upset with the slow pace of change, traditional federalism is something to decry. Thus former U.S. Senator Joseph Clark argued in 1961 that, "Our traditional concept of federalism" was "outmoded in the last century by the nationalization of our economy and in this century by the urbanization of our society." Traditional American federalism was, for Clark, "a case of political lag which urgently deserves our attention." (The Federal Government and the Cities, 1961:49) More recently "traditional federalism" has been identified as the view that Congress ought to "exercise great restraint in helping to solve problems previously regarded as the exclusive responsibility of the states." (ACIR, 1981a:35) The modern "traditional federalist" opposes "all but the most persuasive plan[s] for new federal initiatives in areas of traditional-state local concern. . . . " (ACIR, 1973:126, quoted in ibid.) (2) Davis identifies "two imperative requisites of 'traditional' federalism: the division of power, and its corollary, the independence of each member to conduct its affairs as it thinks best, without responsibility to anyone but its own electors." (Davis 1978:186) (3) Zeh predicts that federalism in the Federal Republic of Germany will undergo such vast changes in the future that it will be totally different from traditional federalism ("Hergebrachten Foderalismus," Zeh 1977:476) It is impossible either to prevent these changes or to undo them at a later time and return to traditional federalism. (4) From a broad comparative perspective, traditional federalism sometimes is equated with simply political federalism. Thus Djordjevic argues that, in Yugoslavia, "'traditional' federalism has been replaced . . . by a new . . . form" which "differs from the traditional political federalism," mostly due to the fact that "it recognizes the autonomy of ethnic groups and of functional units, such as economic enterprises and professional organizations." (Marc 1979:119 citing the work of Jovan Djordjevic) Djordjevic belives that "federalism must change from its 'traditional' form (as an association among co-equal territorial, i.e., political, communities) to a new . . . form constituted by . . . different types of territorial communities . . . and non-territorial, functional communities. . . . " (Schechter 1975:12, citing the view of Djordjevic)

TRANSNATIONAL FEDERALISM A federalism conception drawn from study of the thought of Pierre-Joseph Proudhon. "At the basis of Proudhonian society are the local communities, workshops and small factories which are autonomous and democratically self-managed. These federate in larger regions and units of production which in their turn form federalist nations and finally an all embracing transnational federation." (Kinsky 1979:153) Contemporary Proudhonians aim at "the construction of a federal Europe and the transformation of the U.N. into a world federation." (Ibid., p. 154)

TREATY-BASED FEDERALISM   (1) The argument was often made that when the thirteen American colonies broke away from Great Britain they were, at first, completely autonomous.   Then, by treaty, not by a Constitution, the states created the Articles of Confederation.   This was treaty-based federalism.   (See Stein 1979 and sources cited therein.) (2) More recently, the European Community, grounded solely in treaties, has been suggested for the (incipient) treaty-based federalism category. (Ibid., pp. 900-01.)   Stein finds "the extent to which judicial authorities in the member states have accepted the [European] Court's [treaty-based] jurisdictions and rulings . . . nothing short of remarkable," especially since its "opinions [have] called for important adjustments in national constitutional practice, including the introduction of judicial review of national legislation in . . . member states where it was unknown." (Ibid., p. 903.   Stein credits Covey T. Oliver with the most recent enunciation of the concept of treaty-based federalism.)

TREATY FEDERALISM   The expression treaty federalism has been applied to the corpus of law developed through treaty by the American federal government with the Indian tribes.   Cohen pointed out in 1942 that, although treaties were no longer being made, "The reciprocal obligations assumed by the Federal government and by the Indian tribes during a period of almost a hundred years [of pact making] constitute a chief source of present-day Indian law." (Cohen 1942:33)

TRIBAL FEDERALISM   (1) This expression of federalism denotes "federations or congeries of tribes converging into, but not fully amalgamated in, some new type of center." (Eisenstadt 1979:121)   A tribal federation is "a congregation of different 'tribal' units based largely on kinship and territorial units. . . ." (Ibid.)   Eisenstadt cites examples of tribal federalisms from the ancient Middle East, nomadic settlements in Asia, and also European expressions of tribal federalism.   (2) Fustel de Coulanges believes that the "sociological foundation of the ancient city" should be regarded as a type of tribal federalism. (Fustel view cited in Schechter 1975:5)   (3) Dennewitz also writes about tribal federalism.   By this expression he means groups such as the "historical peoples" of Russia and the Croatians who once were associated in the Austro-Hungarian Empire and who are now a key element in modern Yugoslavia. (Dennewitz 1947:24)   Centuries earlier tribal federalism could be discerned in the kingdom of Henry I of England.

TRILEVEL FEDERALISM   (1) This expression denotes tendencies toward the application of federalism within and beyond the national state.   Thus, in Europe, simultaneously there have been movements for federal structures in tradtionally unitary systems such as the United Kingdom, Belgium, and Italy, redistributing power between national and subnational regions, but also the delegation of significant functions to the supranational European

Community. (Stein 1979:900) Each trend has the effect of con-
straining national influence. (2) Trilevel federalism also may
be used synonymously with tripartite federalism.

TRIPARTITE FEDERALISM That view of the American federal
system which sees the localities as being on a par with the
states as concerns their relations to the national government.
The states are normally said to oppose the tripartite departure
from the traditional view that local governments should deal with
Washington primarily through their parent states. Tripartite
federalism is accepted, however, by the prestigious Advisory Commission on Intergovernmental Relations although the Commission is
not sanguine about its present condition or probable future.
"American federalism--the tripartite system involving shared and
separate powers among the federal, state, and local levels of
government"--in the Commission's view--"is in trouble. . . ."
(ACIR, 1980:1) This is because the federal government's influence on the other two parties "has become more pervasive, more
intrusive, more unmanageable, more ineffective, more costly, and,
above all, more unaccountable." (Ibid.) Especially as the
federal influence has become more pervasive and more intrusive
and local fiscal dependence on federal funds has increased, more
troubling questions have been raised about the viability of the
localities "as independent partners in the American tri-level
system of federalism." (Richter 1980:18) Richter suggests that
the localities may be "destined to come increasingly under the
influence of their two senior partners." (Ibid.) During the
Carter Administration, however, the states are reported for a
time to have felt that they were nothing more than "federal delivery agents" and, in that, not the equals of local
jurisdications. (Stanfield 1978:52-53) They had very little hope
at all of "reversing tripartite federalism." (Ibid.) Tripartite
federalism is sometimes referred to as trilevel federalism.

TRUE FEDERALISM (1) Grodzins's interpretation of American
federalism saw true federalism in the sharing of functions among
federal, state, and local governments. The national government
had insufficient power either to centralize their performance in
Washington or to specify the conditions under which they would be
carried out on a "decentralized" basis. (View of Grodzins reported in Elazar 1973:243) Neumann notes that, "In what is sometimes called a 'true' federation, the central and constitutent
authorities are in law independent, each within its own sphere."
He adds, however, that "even in the case of the United States
provision is made for the predominance of the central authority
in the event of conflict of powers. . . ." (Neumann 1951:597)
Daniel Elazar, the leading American federal theorist today, re-
grets that "in recent years, noncentralization or the true
principle of federalism has been confused with decentralization."
(Elazar 1973:241) (2) In the 1890s, Freeman "recognized [as] a
true and perfect Federal Commonwealth any collection of states in
which it is equally unlawful for the Central Power to interfere

with the purely internal legislation of the several members, and for the several members to enter into any diplomatic relations with other powers." (Freeman 1893:8) (3) Elazar is unwilling to classify multiple monarchies, legislative unions, empires, decentralized unitary systems, and unions of nonterritorial units as "true federations" because, although in each instance "the use of federal principles can have important consequences . . . the fact that such principles do not permeate them makes the distinction between them and true federations quite real." (Elazar 1972:19) (4) Montesquieu believed that "true federalism must be a league of small democratic republics." (Riley 1978:81) (5) Buber's "great ideal of socialism" was "a true federalism of the interhuman. . . ." (Susser 1979:112) This "true federalism," however, was "not a rigid, programmatic either-or," but "a living goal" which "must always 'satisfy a situation'"; this kind of federalism "cannot occur once and for all time: it must always be the moment's answer to the moment's question, and nothing more." (Ibid., citing and quoting Buber) (6) Mary Parker Follett saw true federalism from the ground up. She particularly stressed "[t]he community principle of the neighborhood group [which] she hope[d] to make the unit of political association." (Elliott 1928:433) (7) Davis, drawing from Larsen, identifies the Greek sympolities as "true federal states." (Davis 1978:13)

   TWIN-STREAM FEDERALISM This is a synonym for dual federalism. Davis believes that the label twin-stream federalism can be applied "to any state formation where 'power is divided' and practiced strictly in accordance with the separatist notions of 'twin-stream' or 'dual federalism.'" (Davis 1978:215)

   TWO-LEVEL FEDERALISM The more traditional view that the partners in the American federation are the national government and the states only. Marc contends that thinking about deviating from the two-level model began early. Indeed, "no sooner was the concept of two-level federalism worked out at Philadelphia, when thinking men such as Jefferson began speculating whether municipalities and whole regions should not also be given a constitutional status more or less like that enjoyed by the states." (Marc 1979:122-23)

   TWO-TIER FEDERALISM   This is one way of characterizing metropolitan federalism. Schoer identifies "a two level metropolitan governmental system" as a system with "a centralized regional level with the ability to deal with area wide problems through the use of economies of scale, technical professional competence, and the pooling of financial resources," but also with "a multifunctional neighborhood level with the ability to involve citizens and provide for more and better delivery of services." (Schoer 1974:84-85)   Schoer's second tier of neighborhoods rather than existing cities distinguishes this conceptualization from other discussions of metropolitian federalism. The federal government should, in his view, strongly prod American metropolitian areas to adopt this system.

UNCOOPERATIVE FEDERALISM   One of a number of views on a continuum related to the proper role of the federal government in the United States suggested by Shuman.   "Unco-operative federalism" favors "[f]ederal action only where required by the federal constitution," e.g., "[u]se of federal troops to defend against invasion; regulation of foreign relations; coining money." (Shuman 1968:12)

UNCREATIVE FEDERALISM   A critical interpretation of federal activism by the former Chief Judge of the New York Court of Appeals, Charles S. Desmond.   Judge Desmond acknowledged that the U.S. Supreme Court's decisions relating to human rights, equal protection, and the procedural safeguards "were noble, and its language and its judgments were bold assertions of freedom." But, he asked rhetorically, "does the end justify the means?   How much of our grand national Constitutional design do we lose when the Court gives itself to policy decisions and legislative-type decisions and when, by turning all sorts of questions into federal Constitutional issues, it takes on, in many fields, direct and detailed supervision of the state courts?   Is this 'creative federalism' or 'uncreative federalism'? (Desmond in Shuman 1968:93)

UNEASY FEDERALISM   The conflict between western American state water laws and actual and potential national water uses was identified in a 1980 law review article. (See Treleśe 1980:751-75.) The dissonance is characterized as a conditon of uneasy federalism.   It showed no signs of ending soon.

UNEQUAL FEDERALISM   A federal system in which one member enjoys excessive influence.   Young observed that, "The predominance of Prussia in the German federal system [was] the reason why democracy [had] periodically failed in Germany to the repeated disturbance of Europe." (Young 1941:19)   Anciently, an unequal federalism--a foedera inaequalia was an alliance (foedera) employed at times in both Greece and Rome in which "one member [of the alliance was], by virtue of some condition, placed in a superior position to others." (Davis 1978:38)   Thus the foedus aequum was an equal alliance, the foedus iniquum, an unequal alliance.   In the case of Rome, when the foedus iniquum prevailed, Rome played a hegemonic role. (Ibid., p. 9, citing the research of Sherwin-White in the Oxford Classical Dictionary, 1970:442)

UNFETTERED FEDERALISM   For Howard, "unfettered federalism" designates a situation in which the states are the dominant partners in the union.   This state of affairs is undesirable "when states and localities [are] unable to respond to national needs or . . . when state and local powers have been used to repressive or discriminatory ends." Thus, the "argument for unfettered federalism [is] as ill-considered as a case for limitless power in the central government." (All Howard in Hawkins 1982:235)

UNIQUE FEDERALISM   The regional councils set up under the Fishery Conservation and Management Act, passed by the U.S. Congress in 1976, are unique. They "are not modeled after any other authority; rather, they were shaped by the demands of compromise and necessity." (Rogalski 1980-81:164-65) Rogalski sees the regional fishery management councils as unique governmental bodies which, by national leave, now have the basic responsibility for shaping policy to manage fisheries, guided by practical, biological, and political standards, and subject to the review and rulemaking power of the U.S. Secretary of Commerce. This, in Rogalski's view, is an example of a commendable and unique federalism.

UNITARY FEDERALISM   (1) Some kind of mixture of federal and unitary elements in a political system. Davis speaks of confederal, devolutionary, unitary, and federal unitary forms of government, among many others. (Davis 1978:61) Unitary federalism could also refer to a system which exhibits federal forms but employs them unitarily. (2) "The more alarmed," Walker reports, "feel that a neo-unitary form of government has, in fact, emerged in the United States." (Walker 1978:112) But the federal/unitary "line of demarcation," the line "that distinguishes a federal system from a unitary structure," is unclear and, if the United States has not already trangressed this line, in Kirk's view, "no man can predict precisely when the nation may cross [it]." (Kirk in Goldwin 1974:51)   (3) Shifting from the United States to Europe, Livingston says, "The typical Continental conception of federalism . . . treats it as an alternative to complete unity and tends to consider that federalism is merely a form of decentralized unitary government." (Livingston in Earle 1968:97, reporting particularly the view of Kelsen 1946:316)   Michael Reagan feels that whether a system is "federal" or "unitary" really makes little difference, so long as it "is democratic . . . [and] the people and their organizations . . . have an opportunity to be heard, both through the vote and through parliamentary discussion." (M. Reagan 1972:159)   Friedrich, writing with specific reference to Yugoslavia, believes that "the unitary federal state . . . is [certainly] preferable to the centralized monolith of the extremes of totalitarianism." (Friedrich 1968:167)

UNIVERSAL FEDERALISM   Bakunin advocated "a universal federation of peoples--a global entity." Universal federalism, for Bakunin, "constituted the political framework of socialist anarchism." (King 1982:41) The universal federation would be built on the structure of unions beginning at the communal level and upwards.

UPSIDE DOWN CAKE FEDERALISM   Stavisky takes note of the fact that, "For years, [American] political scientists have amused each other with debates over 'layer cake' and 'marble cake' concepts of federalism." However, Stavisky feels that possibly "the most appropriate imagery for the system-in-transition is the 'upside down cake'--the inversion of power." (Stavisky 1981:701) Federal officials appear to have enormous power and can seemingly insist on conformity with all sorts of conditions as prerequisites if subnational governments are to receive centrally collected funds. However, the administration of programs is almost totally in state and local hands. Federal officials are virtually powerless to see that a program is successfully administered and that national objectives are accomplished.

URBAN-CENTERED FEDERALISM   This was Sharkansky's descriptor for American federalism in the early 1970s. "Increasingly it [was] the cities--and the biggest among them--that [were] attract[ing] the attention of reformers tinkering with the federal system." (Sharkansky 1973:1) Revenue sharing legislation in 1972, for example, provided that local governments, particularly those in metropolitan areas, would benefit most.

URBAN FEDERALISM   This term encompasses all possible kinds of contacts, but particularly direct contacts, between the federal government and local governments in the United States. Chapter 11 of Colman's 1975 study is entitled, "The Outlook for Urban Federalism." In essence, urban federalism is concerned with "the overall framework of the federal system and the place of cities and their suburbs in it, in relation to the state government on the one hand and Washington on the other." (Colman 1975:309)

UTOPIAN FEDERALISM   A characterization by Susser of the federalist thought of theologian Martin Buber. For Buber, Susser explains, federalism is "both a political and a metapolitical idea; the key to socio-political orderings, the foundation of personal integrity and responsibility, and, finally, bound up profoundly with the eschatological categories of redemption and direct theocracy." (Susser 1979:106) Buber's preoccupation, according to Susser, "the recurrent leitmotif of his writings, is the centrality of the 'interhuman,' the life 'between man and man,'" the "dimension between an I and a Thou." (Ibid.) "Only federalism," Susser interprets, "the building of the social body out of freely associating units, can preserve the social quality of association." (Ibid., p. 108.) The distinctiveness of Buber's utopian federalism "lies in his insistence that community derives not from the abstractions of social justice and public welfare but from the real relations existing 'between man and man.'" (Ibid., p. 114.) The expression utopian federalism was not used by Buber himself.

VERTICAL COOPERATIVE FEDERALISM   This term applies to patterns of working together between central and regional
authorities, as distinguished from interregional cooperation
(horizontal cooperative federalism). In Switzerland the federal
government and the cantons participate in a number of joint
activities, thus justifying discussions of "vertikalen
kooperativen Foderalismus." (Deuerlein 1972:295)

VERTICAL FEDERALISM   (1) One observed usage of vertical
federalism is to refer to relations between the American national
government and the states, in contrast with the horizontal
federalism of interstate relations. (Plano and Greenberg 1972:38)
(2) Neuberger applies this label to that kind of colonial
federalism in which territories were connected to the motherland
by means of a quasi-federal tie. (Neuberger in Elazar 1979a:171)
An example was the French Community in the Gaullist Fifth Republic.   (3) This expression is best used to refer to federal
systems in which power is shared among various ethnic, cultural,
and interest groups without regard to their territorial location.
(McWhinney 1966:41)   More commonly, federalism is horizontal,
amounting to the distribution of authority among "territorially
distinct and separate, and self-contained, units of the country."
(Ibid.)

VERTICAL JUDICIAL FEDERALISM   Identified by Porter and Tarr
as "the patterns of interaction between the highest [American]
state and Federal courts." (Porter and Tarr 1982, from the
abstract)

VIABLE FEDERALISM   A viable federalism is one which is fully operational and deserving of the label federal, in the view of
the observer.   (1) Occasionally, concern is expressed that there
will be so great a central shift of responsibilities, that the
adjective "viable" to describe American federalism will become
inappropriate. Thus Glendening and Reeves ask: "How many trans-
fers to higher governments can the system absorb and still remain
a viable federalism?" (Glendening and Reeves 1977:163)   Shapiro
writes of the need for a viable federalism in the management of
federal coastlands in the United States. Legitimately federal
arrangements presently exist; "the way to ensure a viable . . .
federalism in the management of such lands [in the future] is for
states to exercise, in cooperation with the federal government,
their full range of powers in a manner which will concurrently
serve state coastal management goals and recognize the unique
national interests associated with federal coastlands." (Shapiro
1979:1043) (2) Cohen argues that, for Canada, "the search for a
viable federalism," that is, the search for arrangements which
will permit his country to "survive as a federal system embracing
French Language Quebec and the other Provinces, and [to develop]
in the prcess a self-image at home that is acceptable politically
and psychologically, and an identity abroad that is identifiably
unique . . . is surely the Canadian question." (Cohen 1969:2-3)

VISIONARY FEDERALISM   Kruser observes that in all federal systems there appears to be a sentimental aspect. There is a vision of reconstructing a lost idyllic condition when there was no ruler, when only good will and cooperation among all counted for anything, when there was no command or obedience, no superiority or inferiority.   This idealistic view is labeled visionary federalism. ("Schwarmerischen Foderalismus," Vereinigung der Deutschen Staatsrechtslehrer, 1964:105)

WEAK FEDERALISM   Deuerlein notes that the French Revolution represented a pronounced movement of the nation-state toward centralization.   Even a weak federalism ("schwache Foderalismus") was reprehensible to the revolutionists and the term federalism was used most frequently in a reproachful context. (Deuerlein 1972:317)

WELFARE COOPERATIVE FEDERALISM   A specific policy (outcome)-oriented aspect of cooperative federalism. Welfare cooperative federalism was given judicial approval in the 1968 Supreme Court case of Smith v. King involving the Aid for Families with Dependent Children (AFDC) program. Chief Justice Warren cited the program as being "based on a scheme of cooperative federalism." (392 U.S. 309 quoted in Duchacek 1970:317)   The Court unanimously struck down an Alabama regulation terminating aid to children in fatherless homes where the mother was living with another man not her husband. In so doing, Duchacek comments, "The Supreme Court . . . approved the concept of welfare cooperative federalism." (Ibid.)

WESTERN FEDERALISM   Denoting federalism as practiced now or in the past in Europe and the Western Hemisphere. Western federalism is one of the current paradigms of federalism but there are many others. (Davis 1978:215)

WHIG-FEDERALISM   The blend of ideas from the old Federalist party and the new Whig party in early nineteenth-century America. This mixture was characterized by "an exuberantly nationalist spirit that sprang from the War of 1812." It sought national self-sufficiency as "the great ideal of America." To achieve this self-sufficiency "the Federal government [was looked to] for an adequate policy of internal improvements and national development." (Parrington II, 1927:240)

WORKABLE FEDERALISM   The expression workable federalism ("federalismo posible") was employed in a 1975 essay by Frias. Frias believes that with regard to most of the objects which might be affected by it, a workable federalism does not presently exist in Argentina. (Frias 1975:149ff.)

WORKING FEDERALISM   See operational federalism. Working federalism is referred to synonymously with operational federalism in Leach 1970:223, 234.

WORLD FEDERALISM   The notion of global union, particularly as a panacea against world war. (Trager in Franck 1968:ix)   In Kant's writings there is "the hope . . . for 'eternal peace' through a new kind of world federalism," which would amount to "an agreement of all states to observe lawfulness (if not law) out of 'sad experience' and developed reason. . . ." (Riley 1979b:60)   In Locksley Hall, Alfred Lord Tennyson looked to the time when "the war drum throbbed no longer and the battle flags were furled, In the Parliament of Man, The Federation of the World." (Quoted in Duchacek 1970:349)   A leading peace group, particularly in the immediate post-World War II years, was the United World Federalists.

BIBLIOGRAPHY

Adams, Henry. (ed.) Documents Relating to New-England Fed-
     eralism, 1800-1815. Boston: Little, Brown and Co.,
     1905.
Administrative Federalism. St. Lucia: Centre for Research
     on Federal Financial Relations, Australian National
     University, 1977.
Aiyar, S. P. Federalism and Social Change: A Study in
     Quasi-Federalism. New York: Asia Publishing House,
     1961.
Ake, Claude. A Theory of Political Integration. Homewood,
     Ill.: Dorsey Press, 1967.
Altshuler, Alan A. (ed.) The Politics of the Federal
     Bureaucracy. New York: Dodd, Mead & Co., 1968.
American Federalism in the 1980s: Changes and Consequences.
     Cambridge, Mass.: Roundtable on Governments, Lincoln
     Institute of Land Policy, 1981.
American Heritage Dictionary, 1971 ed.
Anderson, Thornton. (ed.) Jacobson's Development of Ameri-
     can Political Thought: A Documentary History. 2d ed.
     New York: Appleton-Century-Crofts, 1961.
Anderson, William. Federalism and Intergovernmental Re-
     lations: A Budget of Suggestions for Research.
     Chicago: Public Administration Service, 1946.
          . The Nation and the States, Rivals or Partners?
     Minneapolis: University of Minnesota Press, 1955.
Anon. The Republic of Republics: A Retrospect of Our
     Century of Federal Liberty. Philadelphia: William W.
     Warding, 1878.
Armand, Louis, and Darncourt, Michel. The European Chal-
     lenge. New York: Atheneum, 1970.
Aron, Robert. "A Suggested Study Scheme of Federalism."
     International Social Science Bulletin, IV (Spring,
     1952), 45-54.
Austin, John. The Province of Jurisprudence Determined.
     1st and 2d eds. London: J. Murray, 1832 and 1861-63.
Ayres, B. Drummond, Jr. "Panel on Federalism Focuses on
     Money." New York Times, June 24, 1981, p. B8.
          . "Reagan Plans to Push Proposal for 'New Federal-
     ism.'" International Herald Tribune, May 14, 1981, p.
     3.
          . "Reagan's Acts Renew, with Vigor, Nation's Debate
     about Federalism." New York Times, June 1, 1981, pp.
     A1f.
Babcock, Robert S. "Limitations to International Federal-

ism." Unpublished Ph.D. dissertation, Northwestern University, 1949.

Bailey, Stephen K. (ed.) American Politics and Government: Essays in Essentials. New York: Basic Books, 1965.

Baker, Earl M., et al. Federal Grants, the National Interest and State Response: A Review of Theory and Research. Philadelphia: Center for the Study of Federalism, Temple University, 1974.

"Balkanizing Canada: The Cost of Provincial Barriers." Business Week, September 15, 1980, pp. 52-54f.

Ballard, J. A. "Administrative Origins of Nigerian Federalism." African Affairs, LXX (October, 1971), 333-48.

Barker, Ernest. Social and Political Theory. Oxford: Clarendon Press, 1951.

Bartholomew, Paul C. Summaries of Leading Cases on the Constitution. 5th ed. Paterson, N.J.: Littlefield, Adams & Co., 1965.

Battle, Jackson B. "Transportation Controls under the Clean Air Act--An Experience in (Un)cooperative Federalism." Land & Water Law Review, XV (1980), 1-65.

Bayang, Martin E. "Local Interfaith Cooperation: The Federated Churches in New England." Unpublished Ph.D. dissertation, Boston University, 1974.

Beam, David R. "Forecasting the Future of Federalism." Intergovernmental Perspective, VI (Summer, 1980), 6-9.

Beard, Charles A. (ed.) The Enduring Federalist. Garden City, N.Y.: Doubleday, 1948.

Benjamin, J. "Le federalisme camerounais: l'influence des structures federales sur l'activitie economique ouest-camerounaise." Canadian Journal of African Studies, V (No. 3, 1971), 281-306.

Beaudoin, Gerald. "Nationalismes et federalism renouvele." Royal Society of Canada, Transactions, 4th ser., XVI (1978), 293-300.

Bebout, John E. "Space, Time and Jurisdiction and the 'New Federalism.'" National Civic Review, LXXI (November-December, 1982), 526-35.

Beck, Robert N. The Meaning of Americanism. New York: Philosophical Library, 1956.

Beer, Samuel H. "Federalism, Nationalism, and Democracy in America." American Political Science Review, LXXII (March, 1978), 9-21.

_____. "The Modernization of American Federalism." Publius, III (Fall, 1973), 49-95.

Belz, Herman. Emancipation and Equal Rights: Politics and Constitutionalism in the Civil War Era. New York: W. W. Norton & Co., 1978.

Benedict, Michael Les. "Preserving Federalism: Reconstruction and the Waite Court." Supreme Court Review (1978), 39-79.

Bennett, Walter H. American Theories of Federalism. University: University of Alabama Press, 1964.

Bercuson, David J. (ed.) Canada and the Burden of Unity. Toronto: Macmillan Co., 1977.

Berggren, Douglas. "The Use and Abuse of Metaphor, I." Review of Metaphysics, VI (December, 1962), 237-58.

Bishop, Jordan. "The New Federalism." Commonweal, CVII (December 5, 1980), 6.

Black, Edwin R. "Canadian Concepts of Federalism." Unpublished Ph.D. dissertation, Duke University, 1962.
_____. Divided Loyalties: Canadian Concepts of Federalism. Montreal: McGill-Queen's University Press, 1975.
_____, and Cairns, Alan C. "Different Perspectives on Canadian Federalism." Canadian Public Administration, IX (March, 1966), 27-44.

Black, Max. Models and Metaphors: Studies in Language and Philosophy. Ithaca, N.Y.: Cornell University Press, 1962.

Bliss, Howard. "A Process of Federalism: Belgium's Participation in the European Community." Unpublished Ph.D. dissertation, Cornell University, 1967.

Bloch, Frank S. "Cooperative Federalism and the Role of Litigation in the Development of AFDC Eligibility Policy." Wisconsin Law Review (1979), 1-53.

Bluntschli, J. K. The Theory of the State. Oxford: Clarendon Press, 1892.

Bolan, Richard S. "Planning and the New Federalism." Journal of the American Institute of Planners, XXXIX (July, 1973), 226-38.

Bone, Robert C. Action and Organization: An Introduction to Political Science. New York: Harper & Row, 1972.

Borden, Morton. The Federalism of James A. Bayard. New York: Columbia University Press, 1955.

Bos, Dieter A. "A Voting Paradox of Fiscal Federalism." Journal of Public Economics, XI (June, 1979), 369-82.

Boschken, Herman L. "Organization Theory and Federalism: Interorganizational Networks and the Political Economy of the Federalist." (unpublished article, 1979)

Bosselman, Fred P. "The Control of Surface Mining: An Exercise in Creative Federalism." Natural Resources

Journal, IX (April, 1969), 137-65.
Bouvier's Law Dictionary. Ed. Francis Rawle. Vol. I. 1867
ed.
Bowden, H. L. "Symposium on Federalism--In Search of Terms
of Coexistence." Journal of Public Law, XXII (No. 2,
1973), 389-482.
Brand, Jean, and Watts, Lowell H. Federalism Today.
Washington, D.C.: Graduate School Press, U.S. Department of Agriculture, 1969.
Break, George F. "Fiscal Federalism in the 1980s." Intergovernmental Perspective, VI (Summer, 1980), 10-14.
_____. "Fiscal Federalism in the United States:
The First Two Hundred Years, Evolution and Outlook."
(unpublished manuscript)
Breen, William J. "Mobilization and Cooperative Federal-
ism--The Connecticut State Council of Defense, 1917-
1919." Historian, XLII (November, 1979), 58-84.
Bresnick, David. "New Roles for State Officials in an Age
of Fiscal Federalism." State Government, LIII (Spring,
1980), 81-83.
Breton, Albert. "Le theorie [economique] du federalisme; un
apercu personnel de l'etat de la question, avec commen-
taires de George E. Drakos et Denis Bedard." Actualite
Economique, XLVII (October-December, 1971), 383-98.
Brie, Siegfried. Der Bundesstaat. Leipzig: W. Engelmann,
1874.
Brill, S. A. "Full Faith and Credit and Early American
Federalism." Journal of World History, XI (1969), 722-
54.
Brockhaus Enzyklopadie. Vol. VI. 1968 ed.
Brougham, Henry. Political Philosophy. Part I: Principles
of Government: Monarchical Government. London:
Charles Knight Co., 1844.
Broussard, James H. The Southern Federalists, 1800-1816.
Baton Rouge: Louisiana State University Press, 1978.
Brown, George D. "Beyond the New Federalism--Revenue Shar-
ing in Perspective." Harvard Journal of Legislation,
XV (December, 1977), 1-73.
Brugmans, Henri. L' idee europeene, 1918-1965. Bruges: De
Tempel, 1965.
_____. Panorama de la pensee federaliste. Paris: La Col-
ombe du Editions du Vieux Colombier, 1956.

_____, and Duclos, Pierre. Le federalisme contemporain.
Leyde: A. W. Sythoff, 1963.
Bryce, James. The American Commonwealth. Vol. I. Rev. ed.
New York: Macmillan Co., 1914.
Buber, Martin. Between Man and Man. New York: Macmillan
Co., 1965.
Burgess, Philip M. "Capacity Building and the Elements of
Public Management." Public Administration Review, XXXV
(si) (December, 1975), 705-16.
Burrows, B., and Denton, G. Devolution or Federalism?
Options for the United Kingdom. Atlantic Highlands,
N.J.: Humanities Press, 1981.
Burton, E. W. "Federation and Pseudo-Federalism." Law Quar-
terly Review, V (April, 1889), 170-78.
Butler, Nicholas M. Toward a Federal World. New York:
Carnegie Endowment for International Peace, 1939.
Calkins, Susannah, and Shannon, John. "The New Formula for
Fiscal Federalism: Austerity Equals Decentralization."
Intergovernmental Perspective, VIII (Winter, 1982),
23-29.
"Canada's Economic Federalism." Editorial. America, CXLIV
(January 17, 1981), 33.
Cappalli, Richard B. "Mandates Attached to Federal-Grants:
Sweet and Sour Federalism." Urban Lawyer, XIII
(Spring, 1981), 143-57.
Cappie-Wood, T. N. "Two Years of Cooperative Federalism--
Discussion." Public Administration (Sydney), XXXIV
(March, 1975), 94-97.
Carnathan, Ralph D. "Experiment in Regional Federalism:
Implementation of the Appalachian Regional Development
Act of 1965 in Georgia, North Carolina, and Tennessee."
Unpublished Ph.D. dissertation, University of Tennes-
see, 1973.
Carnell, Francis. The Politics of the New States. London:
Oxford University Press, 1961.
Carney, Frederick S. (trans.) The Politics of Johannes
Althusius. Boston: Beacon Press, 1964.
Castaños, S., and Sidjanski, Dusan. "Les criteres du
federalisme et le concept amphictyonique."
Federation, July-August, 1954, pp. 519-33.
Chacon, Vamireh. "Federalismo aparente e unitarismo
permanente." Revista brasileira de Estudos
Politicos, XLII (January, 1976), 107-26.
Chandler, Ralph C., and Plano, Jack C. The Public Adminis-
tration Dictionary. New York: John Wiley & Sons, 1982.
Chi, Keon Soo. "Creative Federalism: A Study of Inter-
governmental Relations under the Johnson Administra-
tion." Unpublished Ph.D. dissertation, Claremont

184

Graduate School, 1970.

Christenson, Reo M. Heresies Right and Left: Some
Political Assumptions Reexamined. New York:
Harper & Row, 1973.

"City-County Consolidations, Separations, and Federations."
American County, XXXV (November, 1970), 12-13ff.

Clark, Jane Perry. The Rise of a New Federalism. New
York: Columbia University Press, 1938.

Clark, Terry N. "Community Autonomy in the National
System--Federalism, Localism and Decentralization."
Social Science Information, XII (August, 1973),
101-28.

Coccia, Michael A. "New Federalism in Products Liability."
Forum, X (Spring, 1975), 1057-72.

Cohen, Felix S. Handbook of Federal Indian Law.
Washington, D.C.: U.S. Government Printing Office,
1942.

Cohen, Maxwell. "The Search for a Viable Federalism."
Manitoba Law School Journal, III (1969), 1-18.

Cohen, Morris. Reason and Nature: An Essay on the Meaning
of Scientific Method. New York: Harcourt, Brace and
Co., 1931.

Cole, Kenneth R., Jr. "On Nixonian New Federalism."
New York Times, November 6, 1973, p. 37.

Colman, William G. Cities, Suburbs, and States: Governing
and Financing Urban America. New York: Free Press,
1975.

_____. "Painful Adjustments--Long Overdue." National
Civic Review, LXXI (March, 1982), 126-35.

Committee for Economic Development. A Fiscal Program for
a Balanced Federalism. New York: By the Committee,
1972.

"Constitutional Law--Commerce Clause--The Reaffirmation of
State Sovereignty as a Fundamental Tenet of Consti-
tutional Federalism." Boston College Industrial &
Commercial Law Review, VIII (April, 1977), 736-82.

"Convocation on Federalism Gains Congressional Support."
Intergovernmental Perspective, VI (Fall, 1980), 5.

Corwin, Edward S. Constitutional Revolution Ltd.
Claremont, Calif.: Claremont Colleges, 1941.

_____. "The Passing of Dual Federalism." Virginia Law
Review, XXXVI (February, 1950), 1-24.

_____. The Twilight of the Supreme Court: A History of
Our Constitutional Theory. New Haven: Yale

University Press, 1934.

Cover, Robert M., and Aleinikoff, Alexander. "Dialectical Federalism: Habeas Corpus and the Court." Yale Law Journal, LXXXVI (April, 1977), 1035-1102.

Cox, Joseph W. Champion of Southern Federalism: Robert Goodloe Harper of South Carolina. Port Washington, N.Y.: Kennikat Press, 1972.

Craige, William A., and Hulbert, James R. (eds.) A Dictionary of American English on Historical Principles. Vol. II. Chicago: University of Chicago Press, 1940.

Cranston, Maurice, and Lakoff, Sanford A. A Glossary of Political Ideas. New York: Basic Books, 1969.

Cranston, Ross F. "From Co-operative to Coercive Federalism and Back?" Federal Law Review, X (June, 1979), 121-42.

Dachs, Herbert. "Über einige trends in modernen foderalismus." Zeitgeschichte, III (November, 1975), 56-64.

Dailey, Joanna. (ed.) Final Report--Annual Chief Justice Earl Warren Conference on Advocacy in the United States: The Courts--the Pendulum of Federalism. Washington, D.C.: Roscoe Pound-American Trial Lawyers Foundation, 1979.

Danielson, Michael N., et al. One Nation; So Many Governments. Lexington, Mass.: Lexington Books, 1977.

Dauer, Manning J. The Adams Federalists. Baltimore: Johns Hopkins University Press, 1953.

Davies, Arthur. "Migrants, Ethnics, Refugees and New Federalisms." Politics, XII (November, 1977), 167-74.

Davis, S. Rufus. "Cooperative Federalism in Retrospect." Historical Studies (Melbourne), V (November, 1952), 212-34.

_____. The Federal Principle: A Journey through Time in Quest of a Meaning. Berkeley: University of California Press, 1978.

De Blij, Harm. Systematic Political Geography. New York: John Wiley & Sons, 1967.

De Grazia, Alfred. Political Organization. Vol. II: The Elements of Political Science. Rev. ed. New York: Free Press, 1962.

DeGrove, John M. "State-Local Relations: The Challenge

of New Federalism." National Civic Review, LXXI (February, 1982), 75-83.

Delvoux, P. "Fondements philosophiques du federalisme chez Pierre-Joseph Proudhon." Archives de Philosophie du Droit, XXIV (1979), 307-28.

Dennewitz, Bodo. Der Föderalismus: Sein Wesen un Seine Geschichte. Hamburg: Drei Turme Verlag, 1947.

Desjardi, Alice, et al. "New Federalism: Approaches to Decentralizing Decisionmaking." American Society of International Law, Proceedings, LXVIII (April, 1974), 189-204.

Deuerlein, Ernst. Föderalismus: Die historischen und philosophischen Grundlagen des föderativen Prinzips. Munich: Paul List Verlag, 1972.

Deutsch, Karl, et al. Political Community and the North Atlantic Area: International Organization in the Light of Historical Experience. New York: Greenwood Press, 1969.

Dewey, John. German Philosophy and Politics. New York: G. P. Putnam's Sons, 1942.

Diamond, Martin. "The Ends of Federalism." Publius, III (Fall, 1973), 129-52.

Dictionnaire Encyclopedique Quillet, 1969 ed.

Dietze, Gottfried. The Federalist: A Classic on Federalism and Free Government. Baltimore: Johns Hopkins University Press, 1960.

Dikshit, Ramesh D. "Military Interpretations of Federal Constitutions: A Critique." Journal of Politics, XXXIII (February, 1971), 180-89.

Dillon, John F. The Law of Municipal Corporations. Vol. I. (2d ed.; New York: James Cockcroft & Co., 1873.

Dimock, Marshall E. Modern Politics and Administration: A Study of the Creative State. New York: American Book Co., 1937.

_____, and Dimock, Gladys O. American Government in Action. New York: Rinehart & Co., 1946.

Djordjevic, Jovan. "Remarks on the Yugoslav Model of Federalism." Publius, V (Spring, 1975), 77-88.

Doddy, Joanne L., and Etheredge, Larry C. "Federalism before the Court." Intergovernmental Perspective, II (Spring, 1976), 6-14.

Donahue, Michael. "Abstention Doctrine and Equitable Restraint: Old and New Perceptions of Federalism." Suffolk University Law Review, IX (Fall, 1974), 34-65.

Douglas, William O. Towards a Global Federalism. New York: New York University Press, 1970.

Drucker, Peter F. Men, Ideas & Politics. New York:
    Harper & Row, 1971.
Duchacek, Ivo D. Comparative Federalism: The Terri-
    torial Dimension of Politics. New York: Holt,
    Rinehart and Winston, 1970.
_____. "External and Internal Challenges to the Federal
    Bargain." Publius, V (Spring, 1975), 41-76.
Duncombe, Herbert S. County Government in America.
    Washington, D.C.: National Association of Counties
    Research Foundation, 1966.
Dunn, William. "Communal Federalism: Dialectics of
    Decentralization in Socialist Yugoslavia."
    Publius, V (Spring, 1975), 127-50.
Dunner, Joseph. (ed.) Dictionary of Political Science.
    New York: Philosophical Library, 1964.
Durenberger, David. "The Self-Government Balancing Act:
    A View from the Senate." National Municipal Review,
    LXXI (January, 1982), 23-27.
Dvorin, Eugene P., and Misner, Arthur J. Government
    in American Society. Reading, Mass.: Addison-
    Wesley Publishing Co., 1968.
Dwivedi, D. N. "A Critique of Indian Fiscal Federalism--A
    Comment." Public Finance, XXVI (No. 3, 1971), 497-501.
Dyck, Rand. "The Canada Assistance Plan--The Ultimate in
    Cooperative Federalism." Canadian Public Administra-
    tion, XIX (Winter, 1976), 587-602.
Dyer, Barbara. The Surface Mining Act in the West:
    A Challenge for Cooperative Federalism.
    Lexington, Ky.: Council of State Governments,
    1980.
Earle, Valerie. (ed.) Federalism: Infinite Variety in
    Theory and Practice. Itasca, Ill.: F. E. Peacock
    Publishers, 1968.
Egger, R. C. "Practical Federalism after National League
    of Cities--A Proposal." Georgetown Law Journal,
    LXIX (February, 1981), 773-801.
Ehrenberg, Victor. The Greek State. New York: Barnes &
    Noble, 1960.
Eisenstadt, S. N. (ed.) Political Sociology: A Reader.
    New York: Basic Books, 1971.
Elazar, Daniel J. "The Almost-Covenanted Polity." Paper
    prepared for "Federal Liberty as a Covenantal Theme in
    American Civil Society," a conference of the Workshop
    on Covenant and Politics, Center for the Study of
    Federalism, Temple University, Philadelphia, May 19-21,
    1982.

_____. American Federalism: A View from the
States. 1st ed. New York: Thomas Y. Crowell Co.,
1966.

_____. "American Federalism and Prefectorial
Administration." Publius, XI (Spring, 1981), 1-2.

_____. The American Partnership: Intergovernmental Co-
operation in the Nineteenth-Century United States.
Chicago: University of Chicago Press, 1962.

_____. "Authentic Federalism for America." National
Civic Review, LXII (October, 1973), 474-78.

_____. "Community Self-Government and the Crisis of
American Politics." Ethics, LXXXI (January, 1971),
91-106.

_____. Continuity and Change in American Federalism.
Philadelphia: Center for the Study of Federalism,
n.d.

_____. "Cursed by Bigness or Toward a Post-Technocratic
Federalism." Publius, III (Fall, 1973), 239-98.

_____. (ed.) Federalism and Political Integration.
Ramat Gan, Israel: Turtledove Publishing, 1979.

_____. "Federalism vs. Decentralization: The Drift from
Authenticity." Publius, VI (Fall, 1976), 9-19.

_____. "First Principles." Publius, III (Fall, 1973), 1-
10.

_____. "From the Editor of Publius: Federalism as Grand
Design." Publius, IX (Fall, 1979), 1-8.

_____. The Impact of Cooperative Financing Solutions upon
the States and Localities. Philadelphia: Center for
the Study of Federalism, Temple University, n.d.

_____. "Is Federalism Compatible with Prefectorial
Administration?" Publius, XI (Spring, 1981), 3-22.

_____. "National Systems, Cultural Systems, and Systems
Analysis." Publius, VII (Winter, 1977), 1-6.

_____. "New Federalism: Can the States be Trusted?"
Public Interest, Spring, 1974, pp. 89-102.

_____. The Outlook for Creative Federalism. Philadelphia:
Center for the Study of Federalism, Temple University,
n.d.

_____. "Prefects, Pragmatism and Practice: A Response to
the Respondents." Publius, XI (Spring, 1981), 55-58.

_____. The Principles and Practices of Federalism: A
Comparative Historical Approach. Philadelphia:
Center for the Study of Federalism, Temple University,
1972.

_____. "The Rebirth of Federalism: The Future Role of the States as Polities in the Federal System." Common-sense, IV (1981), 1-8.

_____. "The Resurgence of Federalism." State Government, XLIII (Summer, 1970), 166-73.

_____. "The Shaping of Intergovernmental Relations in the Twentieth Century." Annals of the American Academy of Political and Social Science, CCCLIX (May, 1965), 10-22.

_____, and Sharkansky, Ira. Alternative Federal Solutions to the Problem of the Administered Territories. Jerusalem: Institute for Federal Studies, 1978.

_____, et al. (eds.) Cooperation and Conflict: Readings in American Federalism. Itasca, Ill.: F. E. Peacock Publishers, 1969.

Elliott, W. Y. The Pragmatic Revolt in Politics. New York: Macmillan Co., 1928.

Else-Mitchell, R. "The Rise and Demise of Coercive Federalism." Australian Journal of Public Administration, XXXVI (June, 1977), 109-21.

"Emerging Concepts of Federalism: Limitations on the Spending Power and National Health Planning." Washington & Lee Law Review, XXXIV (Fall, 1977), 1133-58.

Emerson, Rupert. State and Sovereignty in Modern Germany. New Haven: Oxford University Press, 1928.

Engelman, Frederick C., and Schwartz, Mildred A. "Perceptions of Austrian Federalism." Publius, XI (Winter, 1981), 81-93.

Ermacora, Felix. Osterreichischer Föderalismus: vom patriomonialen zum kooperativen Bundesstaat. Vienna: W. Braumuller, 1976.

Esterbauer, Fried. "Föderalistische Modelle für Israel und Palastina." Staat, XVII (No. 4, 1978), 591-99.

Etheredge, Lloyd S. "Optimal Federalism: A Model of Psychological Dependence." Policy Sciences, VIII (June, 1977), 161-71.

Eulau, Heinz. "Polarity in Representational Federalism: A Neglected Theme of Political Theory." Publius, III (Fall, 1973), 153-71.

Evans, Ross. "Reagan Federalism in Practice: State, Local Officials Assess Void Left by Budget Cuts; Ask Program Swap, Tax Turnback." Congressional Quarterly Weekly Report, XXXIX (October 24, 1981), 2047-51.

Fairweather, Gordon L. "Canada--Faltering Exemplar of Federalism." Journal of Canadian Studies, XII (July, 1977), 126-27.

The Federal Government and the Cities. Washington, D.C.: School of Government, Business, and International Affairs, George Washington University, 1961.

The Federal Harmony: in Three Parts compiled for the Use of Schools and Singing Societies. Boston: John Norman, 1793.

Federalism. Edinburgh: Edinburgh University Center of Canadian Studies, 1975.

Federalism. Missoula: Bureau of Government Research, University of Montana, 1976.

Ferrara, Ralph C., and Steinberg, Marc I. "A Reappraisal of Santa-Fe: Rule 10B-5 and the New Federalism." University of Pennsylvania Law Review, CXXIX (December, 1980), 263-301.

Ferry, W. H. "The Case for a New Federalism." Saturday Review, June 15, 1968, pp. 14-17.

"Fiscal Restraint or Fiscal Paralysis," National Civic Review, LXVIII (July, 1979), 341-61.

Fiszman, Joseph R. (ed.) The American Political Arena: Selected Readings. Boston: Little, Brown and Co., 1966.

Flagg, Ronald S. "Stone v. Powell and the New Federalism: A Challenge to Congress." Harvard Journal on Legislation, XIV (December, 1976), 152-71.

Föderalismus als Partnerschaft. Frankfurt: Peter Lang, 1977.

Foley, Joseph P. (ed.) The Jeffersonian Cyclopedia. New York: Funk & Wagnalls Co., 1900.

Follett, Mary Parker. The New State: Group Organization the Solution of Popular Government. New York: Longmans, Green and Co., 1918.

Fordham, Jefferson B. "Some Observations upon Uneasy American Federalism." North Carolina Law Review, LVIII (January, 1980), 289-318.

Forsyth, Murray. "Towards a Global Federalism. By William O. Douglas. New York University Press, 1968; University of London Press, 1970." Review. International Affairs, XLIV (October, 1970), 766.

Franck, Thomas M. (ed.) Why Federations Fail: An Inquiry into the Requisites for Successful Federalism. New York: New York University Press, 1968.

Freeman, Edward A. History of Federal Government in Greece
and Italy. Ed. J. B. Bury. 1st and 2d eds. London:
Macmillan and Co., 1863 and 1893.
_____. _____. Freeport, N.Y.: Books for Libraries, 1972.
_____(reprint)
Freeman, Harrop A. "Dynamic Federalism and the Concept of
Preemption." De Paul Law Review, XXI (Spring, 1972),
630-48.
Frenkel, Max. "Kooperative und andere Föderalisme."
Schweizer Monatshefte, LIV (January, 1975), 725-36.
Frias, Pedro J. "El federalismo posible." Boletin de la
Facultad de Derecho y Ciencias Sociales (Cordoba),
XXXIX (January-July, 1975), 149-83.
_____. "Nuevo federalismo o postfederalismo?" Revista de
la Facultad de Derecho de Mexico, XXVI (July-December,
1976), 213-18.
Friedrich, Carl J. "Corporate Federalism and Linguistic
Politics." Indian Journal of Political Science, VI
(January-June, 1972), 1-12.
_____. (ed.) The Philosophy of Kant. New York: Modern
Library, 1949.
_____. Trends of Federalism in Theory and Practice.
New York: Frederick A. Praeger, 1968.
Frochling, Helmut. Der Bundesrat in der Koordinierungs-
praxis von Bund und Landern: zur Rolle d. Bundes-
rates im kooperativen Föderalismus. Freiburg:
Universitatsverlag Becksmann, 1972.
Funston, Richard Y. "The Traynor Court and Criminal
Defendants' Rights: A Case Study in Judicial
Federalism." Unpublished Ph.D. dissertation, University
of California, Los Angeles, 1970.
Furman, Gerald. "Grants-in-Aid: State or Federal Output?
Some Preliminary Notes." Conference for Federal
Studies Notebook, II (1974), 10-20.
Fustel de Coulanges, Numas D. The Ancient City: A Study
on the Religion, Laws, and Institutions of Greece and
Rome. Trans. Willard Small. Garden City, N.Y.:
Doubleday, 1956.
Fyock, Jack W., and Long, John J. "The New Federalism: A
Challenge to State Legislative Responsibility." State
Government, L (Spring, 1977), 77-82.
Galt, Anthony H., and Smith, Larry J. Models and the Study
of Social Change. Cambridge, Mass.: Schenckman
Publishing Co., 1976.

Gangulee, N. The Making of Federal India. London:
    James Nisbet and Co., 1936.
Gardiner, John A. (ed.) Public Law and Public Policy. New
    York: Praeger Publishers, 1977.
Garner, James W. Introduction to Political Science:
    A Treatise on the Origin, Nature, Functions,
    and Organization of the State. New York:
    American Book Co., 1910.
Garson, G. David. "Federalism: From Religious to
    Bureaucratic Ideal." Paper presented at the annual
    meeting of the American Political Science Association,
    San Francisco, September 2-5, 1975.
Gawthrop, Louis C. Bureaucratic Behavior in the Executive
    Branch. New York: Free Press, 1969.
Gelfand, M. David. "The Burger Court and the New
    Federalism: Preliminary Reflections on the Roles of
    Local Governmental Actors in the Political Dramas of
    the 1980s." Boston College Law Review, XXI (May,
    1980), 763-850.
Germann, Raimund E. "Vollsugföderalismus in der Schweiz als
    Forschungsobjekt." Verwaltung, IX (No. 2, 1976),
    223-41.
Geyer, Alan. "World Federalism Reconsidered." Worldview,
    XVII (November, 1974), 35-38.
Giovannini, Adalberto. Untersuchungen über die Nature und
    die Anfange der bundesstaatlichen Sympolitie in
    Griechenland. Gottingen: Vandenhoeck & Ruprecht,
    1971.
Glendening, Parris N., and Reeves, Mavis Mann.
    Pragmatic Federalism: An Intergovernmental
    View of American Government. Pacific Palisades,
    Calif.: Palisades Publishers, 1977.
Goldberg, Delphis C. "Intergovernmental Relations: From
    the Legislative Perspective." Annals of the American
    Academy of Political and Social Science, CDXVI
    (November, 1974), 52-66.
Goldwin, Robert A. (ed.) A Nation of States: Essays
    on the American Federal System. 1st and 2d eds.
    Chicago: Rand McNally College Publishing Co.,
    1963 and 1974.
Gooch, R. K. Regionalism in France. New York:
    Century Co., 1931.
Goodloe, Daniel R. Federalism Unmasked . . . Washington,
    D.C.: Buell & Blanchard, 1860.

Gordon, Harold J., and Nancy M. (eds.) The Austrian
    Empire: Abortive Federation? Lexington, Mass.:
    D.C. Heath, 1974.
Gordon, Milton M. "Models of Pluralism: The New American
    Dilemma." Annals of the American Academy of Political
    and Social Science, CDLIV (March, 1981), 178-88.
Govea, Rodger M., and Wolohojian, George C. The Good
    Federalism Game: Participant's Manual for a Simulation
    of Intergovernmental Relations. New York: Learning
    Resources in International Studies, 1975.
Grant, Daniel R., and Nixon, H. C. State and Local
    Government in America. 4th ed. Boston: Allyn and
    Bacon, 1982.
Graves, Thomas J. "IGR and the Executive Branch: The New
    Federalism." Annals of the American Academy of
    Political and Social Science, CDXVI (November, 1974),
    40-51.
Graves, W. Brooke. American Intergovernmental Relations:
    Their Origins, Historical Development, and Current
    Status. New York: Charles Scribner's Sons, 1964.
Grawert, Rolf. Verwaltungsabkommen zwischen Bund und Land-
    ern in der Bundesrepublik Deutschland. Berlin:
    Duncker & Humblot, 1967.
Gray, George. "The New Federalism." Report of the
    Thirteenth Annual Meeting of the Pennsylvania Bar
    Association (1907), pp. 411-51.
Green, Roy E. "Reactions and Recommendations: Local Views
    Toward Tailoring the Grants System for Small Cities."
    Paper presented at the annual Southeastern
    Regional Conference of the American Society for Public
    Administration, Montgomery, Ala., October 9-12, 1979.
Greenwood, F. Murray. "David Mills and Co-ordinate
    Federalism, 1867-1903." University of Western Ontario
    Law Review, XVI (December, 1977), 93-112.
Gribbs, Roman S. "Symposium--New Federalism and Cities--New
    Federalism is Here to Stay." Journal of Urban Law,
    LII (August, 1974), 55-60.
Grimes, Alan Pendleton. American Political Thought. Rev.
    ed. New York: Holt, Rinehart and Winston, Inc.,
    1960.
Gripp, Richard C. "The Theory of Recent American
    Federalism, 1932-1952." Unpublished Ph.D.
    dissertation, University of Southern California, 1954.
Grodzins, Morton. The American System: A New View of

Government in the United States. Ed. Daniel J.
Elazar. Chicago: Rand McNally & Co., 1966.
Gulick, Luther H. The Metropolitan Problem and American
Ideas. New York: Alfred A. Knopf, 1962.
Hall, Robert H. "The Rocky Path of Federalism--Our Dual
System of Courts." Mercer Law Review, XXIII (Summer,
1972), 711-22.
Hall, Timothy A., et al. "Western States and National
Energy Policy: The New States' Rights." American
Behavioral Scientist, XXII (November-December, 1978),
191-212.
Hammond, B. E. Outlines of Comparative Politics.
London: Rivingtons, 1903.
Hanus, Jerome J., and Marfin, Gary C. "State Dependency and
Cooperative Federalism." State Government, LIII
(Autumn, 1980), 174-77.
Harriss, C. Lowell, et al. Federal-State-Local Fiscal
Relationships. Princeton, N.J.: Tax Institute of
America, 1968.
Hart, Henry C. "The Dawn of a Community-Defining
Federalism." Annals of the American Academy of
Political and Social Science, CCCLIX (May, 1965),
147-56.
Hawkins, Gordon. (ed.) Concepts of Federalism.
Toronto: Canadian Institute on Public Affairs,
1965.
Hawkins, Robert B., Jr. (ed.) American Federalism: A New
Partnership for the Republic. San Francisco: Insti-
tute for Contemporary Studies, 1982.
Hay, Peter. Federalism and Supranational Organizations:
Patterns for New Legal Structures. Urbana:
University of Illinois Press, 1966.
Heald, David. Making Devolution Work. London: Fabian
Society, 1976.
Heberle, Klaus H. "Modern Judicial Theories of Federalism:
An Examination of the Opinions of Justices Black and
Frankfurter." Unpublished Ph.D. dissertation,
University of Chicago, 1963.
Heller, Walter W. "Federalism and the State-Local Fiscal
Crisis." Wall Street Journal, January 22, 1982, p. 30.
_____. New Dimensions of Political Economy. Cambridge,
Mass.: Harvard University Press, 1966.
Hellerstein, Jerome R. "Current Issues in Fiscal Federal-
ism: Federal Grants-in-Aid." University of Florida

Law Review, XX (Spring, 1968), 505-27.
Helliwell, John F. The Distribution of Energy Revenues
    within Canada: Functional or Factional Federalism?
    Vancouver, B.C.: Program in Natural Resource
    Economics, University of British Columbia, 1980.
Henle, Paul. (ed.) Language, Thought, & Culture. Ann
    Arbor: University of Michigan Press, 1958.
Henry, Nicholas. Public Administration and Public
    Affairs. Englewood Cliffs, N.J.: Prentice-Hall,
    1975.
Heraud, G. "Anti-etatisme: le federalisme integral."
    Archives de Philosophie du Droit, XXI (1976), 167-80.
Hesse, Mary B. Models and Analogies in Science. Notre
    Dame, Ind.: University of Notre Dame Press, 1966.
Heubel, Franz. "Föderalismus als Modell für Staat und
    Gesellschaft von Morgen." Politische Studien,
    XXIII (No. 203, 1972), 227-36.
Hicks, U. K. Federalism--Failure and Success: A Compara-
    tive Study. New York: Oxford University Press,
    1978.
Higgs, Henry. (ed.) Palgrave's Dictionary of Political
    Economy. Vol. II. New York: Augustus M. Kelley,
    1963.
Hitchner, Dell G., and Harbold, William H. Modern
    Government: A Survey of Political Science. 2d
    ed. New York: Dodd, Mead & Co., 1965.
    _____, and Levine, Carol. Comparative Gov-
    ernment and Politics. New York: Dodd, Mead & Co.,
    1968.
Hodges, Bruce W., et al. (eds.) Federalism in Canada: The
    Early Years. Waterloo, Ont.: Wilfrid Laurier Univer-
    sity Press, 1978.
Hoetjes, B. J. S. "Federaties en federalisme: Een raamwerk
    voor theorie en onderzoek." Res publica, XX (No. 4,
    1978), 561-84.
Holcombe, Arthur N. Our More Perfect Union. Cambridge,
    Mass.: Harvard University Press, 1950.
Holloway, William V. Intergovernmental Relations in the
    United States. New York: MSS Information Corpor-
    ation, 1972.
Howard, George E. Comparative Federal Institutions: An
    Analytic Reference Syllabus. Lincoln: Department of
    Political Science and Sociology, University of
    Nebraska, 1907.
Hudson, William E. "The New Federalism Paradox." Policy
    Studies Journal, VIII (Summer, 1980), 900-05.
Hueglin, Thomas. "Johannes Althusius: Medieval

Constitutionalist or Modern Federalist?" <u>Publius</u>, IX (Fall, 1979), 9-41.

Hughes, Christopher. <u>Confederacies</u>. Leicester: University Press, 1963.

Inagaki, M. "Chiho-teki Rempo no Mondai." <u>Sekai Kokka</u>, VIII (January, 1954), 10-15.

Inman, Robert P., et al. <u>Financing the New Federalism: Revenue Sharing, Conditional Grants, and Taxation</u>. Baltimore: Johns Hopkins University Press, 1975.

Inns, Graham J. "Public Services and Cooperative Federalism." <u>Public Administration</u> (Sydney), XXXIV (March, 1975), 19-38.

"Intergovernmental Focus." <u>Intergovernmental Perspective</u>, VII (Spring, 1981), 4-7.

International Political Science Association. <u>New Trends in the Theory and Practice of Federalism</u>. Paris: By the Association, 1964.

Jacobson, J. Mark. (ed.) <u>The Development of American Political Thought</u>. New York: D. Appleton Century Co., 1932.

Jaensch, Dean. (ed.) <u>The Politics of "New Federalism"</u>. Adelaide: Australian Political Studies Association, 1977.

Jaffary, Karl D. "Correctional Federalism." <u>Canadian Journal of Criminology and Corrections</u>, VII (1965), 362-76.

James, Judson L. "Block Grants, Grant Consolidation, and the New Federal Assistance Packet: Some Issues and New Relationships." Paper presented at the annual meeting of the American Society for Public Administration, Chicago, April 1-4, 1975.

Jankovic, Branimir M. "Kolonjalni Federalizam." <u>Pregled</u>, V (May, 1953), 353-58.

Jena, Bok B. "Equilibrium Model and Federal Polity: A Conceptual Exercise." <u>Indian Journal of Political Science</u>, XXXVIII (October-December, 1977), 444-50.

Jenkin, Thomas P. "Recent Theories and Problems of Federalism." (unpublished article)

Johansen, R. B. "New Federalism--Toward a Principled Interpretation of the State Constitution." <u>Stanford Law Review</u>, XXIX (January, 1977), 297-321.

Johnson, Lyndon B. <u>My Hope for America</u>. New York: Random

House, 1964.

Johnston, Richard E., and Thompson, John I. "The Burger Court and Federalism: A Revolution in 1976?" Western Political Quarterly, XXXIII (June, 1980), 197-216.

Kadushin, Max. Organic Thinking: A Study in Rabbinic Thought. New York: Jewish Theological Seminary of America, 1938.

Kane, Daniel A. "Comprehensive Health Planning: A Study in Creative Federalism." American Journal of Public Health, LIX (September, 1969), 1706-12.

Kanouse, Randele. "Achieving Federalism in the Regulation of Coastal Energy Facility Siting." Ecology Law Quarterly, VIII (1980), 533-81.

Karnig, Albert K., et al. "New Federalism and Retrenchment: Challenges, Options, Actions." National Civic Review, LXXI (November-December, 1982), 493-99f.

Karve, D. C. Federations: A Study in Comparative Politics. London: Oxford University Press, 1932.

Kasperson, Roger E., and Minghi, Julian V. (eds.) The Structure of Political Geography. Chicago: Aldine Publishing Co., 1969.

Katz, Ellis, and Schuster, Benjamin F. (eds.) Dialogue on Federal Theory. Philadelphia: Center for the Study of Federalism, Temple University, 1979.

_____. The Practice of American Federalism. Philadelphia: Center for the Study of Federalism, Temple University, 1978.

Kazemier, B. H., and Vuysje, D. (eds.) The Concept and the Role of the Model in Mathematics and Natural and Social Sciences. Dordrecht, Holland: D. Reidel Publishing Co., 1961.

Kearney, Richard C., and Garey, Robert B. "American Federalism and the Management of Radioactive Wastes." Public Administration Review, XLII (January-February, 1982), 14-24.

Keller, Bill. "State, Local Lobbying Groups Suffer Withdrawal Pangs under Reagan's Federalism." Congressional Quarterly Weekly Report, XXXIX (October 31, 1981), 2108-12.

Kelly, Alfred H., and Harbison, Winfred A. The American Constitution: Its Origins and Development. 4th and 5th eds. New York: W. W. Norton & Co., 1970 and 1976.

Kelsen, Hans. General Theory of Law and State. Trans. Wedberg. Cambridge, Mass.: Harvard University Press, 1946.

Kemp, Udo. "Cooperation in the Federal State--A Study on
     Cooperative Federalism in Federal Republic of Germany.
     By Gunter Kisker. Tubingen: J. C. B. Mohr, 1971."
     Review. Modern Law & Society, VII (No. 1, 1974),
     26-27.
Kempf, Hubert, and Toinet, Marie-France. "La fin du
     federalisme aux Etats-Unis?" Revue Francaise de
     Science Politique, XXX (August, 1980), 735-75.
Kenyon, Cecelia M. (ed.) The Antifederalists. Indiana-
     polis: Bobbs-Merrill, 1966.
Kettl, Donald F. "The 4th Face of Federalism." Public
     Administration Review, XLI (May-June, 1981), 366-71.
     . Managing Community Development in the New
     Federalism. New York: Praeger Publishers, 1980.
     . "Regulating the Cities." Publius, XI (Spring,
     1981), 111-25.
Kilpatrick, James J. "New Federalism or Old Despotism?"
     Pacific Business, LXI (May-June, 1971), 28-30ff.
King, Preston. Federalism and Federation. Baltimore:
     Johns Hopkins University Press, 1982.
Kinsky, Ferdinand. "Personalism and Federalism." Publius,
     IX (Fall, 1979), 131-56.
Kirschbaum, Stanislav. "Nationalisme et federalisme en
     theorie communiste: Le cas de la Tchecoslovaquie."
     Etudes Internationales, VI (March, 1975), 3-29.
Kisker, Gunter. Kooperation im Bundesstaat: eine
     Untersuchung zum kooperativen Föderalismus in der
     Bundesrepublik Deutschland. Tubingen: J. D. B.
     Mohr, 1971.
Kornberg, Allan, et al. "Federalism and Fragmentation:
     Political Support in Canada." Journal of Politics,
     XLI (August, 1979), 889-906.
Koury, A. Frank. "Section 1983 and Civil Comity: Two for
     the Federalism Seesaw." Loyola Law Review, XXV (Fall,
     1979), 659-712.
Kunze, Renate. Kooperative Föderalismus in der Bundes-
     republik; zur Staatspraxis der Koordinierung von Bund
     und Landern. Stuttgart: G. Fischer, 1968.
Lamb, Charles M. "'New Federalism'
     and Civil Rights." University of Toledo Law Review,
     IX (Summer, 1978), 816-45.
Lamontagne, Maurice. "Federalisme ou association d'etats
     independants." Etudes Internationales, VIII (June,
     1977), 208-30.

Landau, Martin. "Federalism, Redundancy and System
    Reliability." Publius, III (Fall, 1973), 173-96.
_____. "On the Use of Metaphor in Political Analysis."
    Social Research, XXVIII (Autumn, 1961), 331-53.
Lang, Kaspar. Die Philosophie des Föderalismus. Zurich:
    Schulhess Polyographischer Verlag, 1971.
Larsen, J. A. O. "Federation for Peace in Ancient Greece."
    Classical Philology, XXXIX (July, 1944), 145-61.
Lawrence, David. "Creative or Destructive Federalism?"
    U.S. News & World Report, April 11, 1966, p. 108.
Lawson, Jean, and Stenberg, Carl W. "'Rebalanced
    Federalism': The States' Role and Response."
    Intergovernmental Perspective, VIII (Winter, 1982),
    30-34f.
Leach, Richard H. American Federalism. New York: W. W.
    Norton & Co., 1970.
_____. "Divided Loyalties: Canadian Concepts of
    Federalism. By Edwin R. Black. Montreal:
    McGill-Queen's University Press, 1975." Review.
    Publius, VII (Spring, 1977), 127-28.
_____. "Federalism: A Battery of Questions." Publius, III
    (Fall, 1973), 11-47.
_____. (ed.) Intergovernmental Relations in the 1980s.
    New York: Marcel Dekker, 1983.
_____. "Prelude to New Federalism." Paper presented at the
    annual meeting of the American Society for Public
    Administration, Chicago, April 1-4, 1975.
Lederman, Laszlo. Federation Internationale: Idees
    d'hier--Possibilites de demain. Neuchatel, Switz.:
    Editions de la Baconniere, 1950.
Lederman, W. R. "Unity and Diversity in Canadian
    Federalism." Canadian Bar Review, LIII (September,
    1975), 597-620.
Leger, Jean-Marc. "Cooperative Federalism or the New Face
    of Centralization." Canadian Forum, XLIII (October,
    1963), 155-56.
Lehning, Arthur. "Michael Bakounine: theorie et pratique
    du federalisme anti-etatique en 1870-71."
    International Review of Social History, XVII (Nos. 1-2,
    1972), 455-73.
Lemon, Anthony. "Federalism and Plural Societies: A Cri-
    tique with Special Reference to South Africa."
    Plural Socities, XI (Summer, 1980), 3-24.
Lenz, C. O. "Modelle zur Weiterentwicklung des föderativen

Systems." Zeitschrift für Politik, XVII (June, 1970),
138-47.
Lerner, Max. America as a Civilization: Life and Thought
in the United States Today. New York: Simon and
Schuster, 1957.
Leroy, Maxime. La ville francaise; institutions et libertes
locales. Paris: M. Riviere, 1927.
Levin, I. D., and Vajl, I. M. (eds.) Sovremennyj burzuaznyj
federalizm. Moscow: Nauka, 1978.
Levitan, Sar A. "Manpower Programs and 'New Federalism.'"
Conference Board Record, VII (April, 1970), 51-56.
Lewis, John D. "The Genossenschaft Theory of Otto van
Gierke in Relation to Federalism." Unpublished Ph.D.
disseration, University of Wisconsin, 1934.
Lewontin, R. C. "Models, Mathematics and Metaphors."
Synthese, XV (1963), 222-44.
Lieber, Francis. On Civil Liberty and Self-Government. 2
vols. Philadelphia: Lippincott, Grambo and Co., 1853.
Lieber, Harvey. Federalism and Clean Waters. Lexington,
Mass.: D. C. Heath and Co., 1975.
Lieberman, Carl. "George Washington and the Development of
American Federalism." Social Science, LI (Winter,
1976), 3-10.
Light, Alfred B. "Drawing the Wagons in a Circle:
Sectionalism and Energy Politics." Publius, VIII
(Winter, 1978), 21-37.
Lindblom, Charles E. The Intelligence of Democracy. New
York: Free Press, 1965.
Lithwick, N. H., and Paquet, Gilles. (eds.) Urban Studies:
A Canadian Perspective. Toronto: Methuen, 1968.
_____, and Winer, Stanley L. "Faltering Federalism and the
French Canadians." Journal of Canadian Studies, XII
(July, 1977), 44-52.
Livermore, Shaw. The Twilight of Federalism. Princeton,
N.J.: Princeton University Press, 1962.
Livingston, William S. Federalism and Constitutional
Change. Oxford: Clarendon Press, 1956.
_____. "A Note on the Nature of Federalism." Political
Science Quarterly, LXVII (March, 1952), 81-95.
Loeb, Louis S., and Berman, Daniel M. American Politics:
Crisis and Challenge. New York: Macmillan Co., 1975.
Logan, Robert K. "Federation with a Difference." Canada
and the World, XLIV (December, 1978), 22-23.
Loucks, Edward A. "The New Federalism and the Suburbs."

Growth & Change, IX (October, 1978), 2-7.
Lovell, Catherine. "Mandating: Operationalizing Domination." _Publius_, XI (Spring, 1981), 59-78.
Low, Alfred D. _Lenin on the Question of Nationality._ New York: Bookman Associates, 1958.
Lower, A. R. M., et al. _Evolving Canadian Federalism._ Durham, N.C.: Duke University Press, 1958.
Lowi, Theodore J. _The End of Liberalism: Ideology, Policy, and the Crisis of Public Authority._ New York: W. W. Norton & Co., 1969.
_____, and Stone, Alana. (eds.) _Nationalizing Government._ Beverly Hills, Calif.: Sage Publications, 1978.
Lyall, Francis. "Of Metaphors and Analogies: Legal Language and Covenant Theology." _Scottish Journal of Theology_, XXXII (No. 1, 1979), 1-19.
Lyon, Noel. "Anti-Inflation Act Reference: Two Models of Canadian Federalism." _Ottawa Law Review_, IX (Fall, 1977), 176-82.
Lysyk, K. M. _Reshaping Canadian Federalism._ Toronto: Ukranian Professional & Business Club of Toronto, 1979.
Maass, Arthur A. (ed.) _Area and Power._ Glencoe, Ill.: Free Press, 1959.
MacDonald, H. Malcolm, et al. (eds.) _Outside Readings in American Government._ New York: Thomas Y. Crowell Co., 1949.
MacKinnon, Victor S. _Comparative Federalism: A Study in Judicial Interpretation._ The Hague: M. Nijhoff, 1954.
McCloskey, Robert G. (ed.) _Essays in Constitutional Law._ New York: Alfred A. Knopf, 1962.
McClure, Charles E., Jr. "Revenue Sharing: Alternative to Rational Fiscal Federalism?" _Public Policy_, XIX (Fall, 1971), 567-93.
McDougal, Luther L., III. "Contemporary Authoritative Conceptions of Federalism and Exclusionary Land Use Planning." _Boston College Law Review_, XXI (January, 1980), 301-44.
McLaughlin, Andrew C., and Hart, Albert Bushnell. _Cyclopedia of American Government._ Vol. I. New York: D. Appleton and Co., 1914.
McLean, Joseph E. _Politics is What You Make It._ New York: Public Affairs Committee, 1952.
Macmahon, Arthur W. _Administering Federalism in a Democracy._ New York: Oxford University Press, 1972.

_____. (ed.) Federalism, Mature and Emergent. Garden
City, N.Y.: Doubleday & Co., 1955.
McWhinney, Edward. "'Classical' Federalism and
Supra-National Integration or Treaty-Based Association:
The European Community Movement as a Case-Study."
American Society of International Law, Proceedings,
LVII (April, 1963), 241-49.
_____. Comparative Federalism: States'
Rights and National Power. 2d ed. Toronto:
University of Toronto Press, 1965.
_____. "Constitutional Particularism and the New
Particularistic Federalism." Challenges (1979), 38-56.
_____. Federal Constitution-Making for a Multi-
National World. Leyden: A. W. Sythoff, 1966.
_____, and Pescatore, Pierre (with the assistance of
Raymond Baeyens). Federalism and Supreme Courts
and the Integration of Legal Systems. Bruselles:
UGA, 1973.
Madden, Richard. "New Federalism Failed at Home." Decatur
(Ala.) Daily, August 9, 1974, p. 4.
Maier, Harold G. "Cooperative Federalism in International
Trade--Its Constitutional Parameters." Mercer Law
Review, XXVII (Winter, 1976), 391-417.
Mallory, J. R. "Canadian Federalism in Transition."
Political Quarterly, XLVIII (April-June, 1977), 149-63.
Marando, Vincent L., and Thomas, Robert D. The Forgotten
Governments: County Commissioners as Policy Makers.
Gainesville: University Presses of Florida, 1977.
Marc, Alexandre. Dialectique de Dechainement: Fondements
philosophiques du federalisme. Paris: La Colombe,
1961.
_____. Federalism Old and New. Adap. fr. Fr. by
Vukan Kuic. Philadelphia: Center for the Study of
Federalism, Temple University, 1979.
Martin, Charles E. An Introduction to the Study of the
American Constitution. New York: Oxford University
Press, 1926.
Martin, Ged. "Empire Federalism and Imperial Parliamentary
Union, 1820-1870." Historical Journal, XVI (March,
1973), 65-92.
Martin, R. B., Jr. "Renewed Government: A Real New
Federalism." Vital Speeches, XL (April 1, 1974),
369-72.
Martin, Roscoe C. The Cities and the Federal System. New

York: Atherton Press, 1965.

Matheson, Scott M. "Sovereign States--Sovereign Nation."
National Civic Review, LXXI (November-December, 1982),
506-09.

Mathews, Mitford M. (ed.) A Dictionary of Americanisms on
Historical Principles. Chicago: University of
Chicago Press, 1951.

Mathews, R. L. (ed.) Federalism in Australia and the Federal Republic of Germany: A Comparative Study.
Canberra: Australian National University Press, 1980.

Maxwell, Judith, and Pestieau, Caroline. Economic Realities
and Contemporary Confederation. Montreal: Howe
Research Institute, 1980.

Maxwell, William A. "The Canadian Constitutional Conference
(1968-1971): A Study of Conflicting Perceptions of
Federalism." Unpublished Ph.D. dissertation,
Georgetown University, 1975.

Mayfield, James J. (ed.) A Scrap Book on Constitutional
Government. Atlanta: Foote & Davies Co., 1925.

Mayton, William T. "Ersatz Federalism under the
Anti-Injunction Statute." Columbia Law Review, LXXVIII
(March, 1978), 330-70.

Mazruli, Ali A. A World Federation of Cultures: An African
Perspective. New York: Free Press, 1976.

Mazzeo, Joseph A. Renaissance and Seventeenth-Century
Studies. New York: Columbia University Press, 1964.

Medley, G. W. The Fiscal Federation of the Empire. London:
Cobden Club, 1892.

Meekison, J. Peter. (ed.) Canadian Federalism: Myth or
Reality? Toronto: Methuen, 1968.

Merriam, Charles E., and Robert E. The American Government:
Democracy in Action. Boston: Ginn and Co., 1954.

Merriam, Robert E. "Federalism Realigned." National Civic
Review, LXXI (March, 1982), 123-25.

Mertins, Herman, Jr. "The 'New Federalism' and Federal
Transportation Policy." Public Administration Review,
XXXIII (May-June, 1973), 243-52.

Michael, Richard A. "New Federalism and the Burger Court's
Deference to the States in Federal Habeas Corpus
Proceedings." Iowa Law Review, LIV (January, 1979),
233-73.

Miller, Arthur S. "The Constitutional Law of the 'Security
State.'" Stanford Law Review, X (July, 1958), 620-71.

Miller, Eugene F. "Metaphor and Political Knowledge."

American Political Science Review, LXXIII (March, 1979), 155-70.

Miller, Kenneth E., and Samuels, Norman. (eds.) Power and the People: Readings in American Politics. Pacific Palisades, Calif.: Goodyear Publishing Co., 1973.

Mitrany, David. A Working Peace System. Chicago: Quadrangle Books, 1966.

Mogi, Sobei. The Problem of Federalism: A Study in the History of Political Theory. Vols. I and II. New York: Macmillan Co., 1931.

Monaghan, Henry P. "The Burger Court and Our Federalism." Law & Contemporary Problems, XLIII (Summer, 1980), 39-50.

Morris, David, and Hess, Karl. Neighborhood Power: The New Localism. Boston: Beacon Press, 1975.

Mosk, Stanley. "Contemporary Federalism." Pacific Law Journal, IX (July, 1978), 711-21.

Mouskhelry, Michel. Confederation or Federation? Paris: European Youth Campaign, 1952.

Mueller, Dennis C. "Fiscal Federalism in a Constitutional Democracy." Public Policy, XIX (Fall, 1971), 567-93.

"Municipal Bankruptcy, the 10th Amendment, and the New Federalism." Harvard Law Review, LXXXIX (June, 1976), 1871-1905.

Musgrave, Richard A. Essays in Fiscal Federalism. Washington, D.C.: Brookings Institution, 1965.

_____. "Theories of Fiscal Federalism." Public Finance, XIV (No. 4, 1969), 521-32.

Mushkin, Selma J., and Cotton, John F. Functional Federalism: Grants-in-Aid and PPB Systems. Washington, D.C.: State-Local Finances Project, George Washington University, 1968.

Muskie, Edmund S. "The Challenge of Creative Federalism." Saturday Review, June 25, 1966, pp. 12-14.

Meyers Enzyklopadisches Lexikon. Vol. XIV. 1975 ed.

Naftalin, Arthur. "Not without Aid--It Still Holds." National Civic Review, LXXI (March, 1982), 135-40.

_____, and Naftalin, Frances. "Minnesota Government in the Future Society." Journal of Minnesota Academy of Science, XL (1974), 36-42.

Nathan, Richard P. "The New Federalism versus the Emerging New Structuralism." Publius, V (Summer, 1975), 111-29.

Nelson, Ralph. "The Federal Idea in French Political Thought." Publius, V (Summer, 1975), 7-62.

Neumann, Robert G. European and Comparative Government.
    New York: McGraw-Hill Book Co., 1951.
"New Federalism." Florence (Ala.) Times, February 21, 1982,
    p. 5.
"New Federalism or Feudalism?" Time, February 8, 1982, pp.
    19-20.
The New Federalism: Possibilities and Problems in Re-
    structuring American Government. Washington, D.C.:
    Woodrow Wilson International Center for Scholars,
    1973.
"The New, New Federalism [of Jerry Brown]." Editorial.
    Wall Street Journal, January 10, 1979, p. 20.
Newton, Robert D. "Administrative Federalism." Public
    Administration Review, XXXVIII (May-June, 1978),
    252-55.
Nicgorski, Walter. "The New Federalism and Direct Popular
    Election." Review of Politics, XXXIV (January, 1972),
    3-15.
Nichols, Roy F. Blueprints for Leviathan: American Style.
    New York: Atheneum, 1963.
Nicoll, Donald E. Creative Federalism. Washington, D.C.:
    Graduate School Press, U.S. Department of Agriculture,
    1967.
Nisbet, Robert. Sociology as an Art Form. New York:
    Oxford University Press, 1976.
Nolan, Martin. "Walter Heller's Federalist Papers."
    Reporter, June 1, 1967, pp. 14-17.
Nyman, Olle. Der westdeutsche Föderalismus: Studien zum
    bonner Grundgesetz. Stockholm: Almqvist & Wiksell,
    1960.
Oakerson, Ronald J. "Reciprocity, Consumerism, and
    Collective Action: A Response to 'Is Federalism
    Compatible with Prefectorial Administration'?"
    Publius, XI (Spring, 1981), 47-53.
Oberle, James P. "Consociational Democracy and the Canadian
    Political System." Unpublished Ph.D. dissertation,
    University of Maryland, 1976.
Oates, Wallace E. Fiscal Federalism. New York: Harcourt,
    Brace, Jovanovich, 1972.
    . The Political Economy of Fiscal Federalism.
    Lexington, Mass.: D. C. Heath and Co., 1977.
Onuf, Peter. "Toward Federalism: Virginia, Congress and
    the Western Lands." William & Mary Quarterly, s3
    (July, 1977), 353-74.

Ostrom, Vincent. "Can Federalism Make a Difference?"
Publius, III (Fall, 1973), 197-237.
_____. "The Contemporary Debate Over
Centralization and Decentralization." Publius, VI
(Fall, 1976), 21-32.
_____. "Dewey and Federalism: So Near and Yet So Far."
Publius, IX (Fall, 1979), 87-101.
_____. The Intellectual Crisis in American Public
Administration. University: University of Alabama
Press, 1973.
_____. "Operational Federalism: Organization for the Pro-
vision of Public Services in the American Federal
System." Public Choice, VI (Spring, 1969), 1-17.
"The Overloaded System." National Civic Review, LXIX (June,
1980), 301-06ff.
Oxford Classical Dictionary. 1949 and 1970 eds.
Oxford English Dictionary. 1933 ed.
Oxford Universal Dictionary. 1955 ed.
Parkin, George R. Imperial Federation: The Problem of Na-
tional Unity. London: Macmillan and Co., 1892.
Parrington, Vernon L. Main Currents in American Thought.
Vols. I (The Colonial Mind, 1620-1800) and II (The
Romantic Revolution, 1800-1860). New York: Harcourt,
Brace & World, Inc., 1927.
Pasler, Rudolph J., and Margaret C. The New Jersey
Federalists. Rutherford, N.J.: Fairleigh Dickinson
University Press, 1974.
Patterson, James T. The New Deal and the States:
Federalism in Transition. Princeton, N.J.: Princeton
University Press, 1969.
Paul-Boncour, Joseph. Le federalism economique; etude sur
les rapports de l'individu et des groupements pro-
fessionels. Paris: F. Alcan, 1900.
Peachment, A. New Federalism in Australia. Sydney:
Australiasian Political Studies Association, 1977.
Pedrosa, Bernardette. "Perspectiva do Federalismo Brasi-
leiro." Revista Brasileira de Estudos Politicos,
LII (January, 1981), 105-28.
Peirce, Neal R. "A 'Federalist' Spin: Watch Reagan's New
Advisory Groups for Radical Reversal of National
Policies." Nation's Cities Weekly, IV (May 25, 1981),
3.
_____. "In Interview, President Offers Scant Hope for
States." Birmingham News, November 29, 1981, p. 3F.
_____. "New Panels to Move Quickly to Help Reagan 'Unbend'
the Federal System." National Journal, XIII (May 2,
1981), pp. 785-88.

_____. "'Pinwheel Federalism': Funding without Coordination." Nation's Cities Weekly, II (December 10, 1979), 5.

_____. "Reagan's Federalist Thinking." Journal of Commerce, CCCXLVIII (May 6, 1981), 4.

_____. "The State of American Federalism." National Civic Review, LXIX (January, 1980), 5-9.

_____. "There's More Than Meets Eye in Reagan's Federalism." Birmingham News, January 28, 1982, p. 7A.

_____, and Hamilton, Jay. "'Flypaper Federalism'--States, Cities Want to Shed Rules that Accompany Aid." National Journal, XIII (September 12, 1981), 1636-39.

Penchans, R., and Axelson, E. "Old Values, New Federalism, and Program Evaluation." Medical Care, XII (November, 1974), 893-905.

Pentland, Charles. International Theory and European Integration. New York: Free Press, 1973.

Pike, Frederick B., and Stritch, Thomas. (eds.) The New Corporatism: Social-Political Structures in the Iberian World. Notre Dame, Ind.: Notre Dame Press, 1974.

Plano, Jack C., and Greenberg, Milton. The American Political Dictionary. 3d ed. Hinsdale, Ill.: Dryden Press, 1972.

Plischke, Elmer J. (ed.) Systems of Integrating the International Community. Princeton, N.J.: D. Van Nostrand & Co., 1964.

Political and Administrative Federalism. Canberra: Centre for Research on Federal Financial Relations, Australian National University, 1976.

Polk, Ann E. "The North Carolina Federalists, 1787-1789." Unpublished M.A. thesis, Emory University, 1965.

Pollock, James K. (ed.) Readings in American Government. New York: Henry Holt and Co., 1927.

Popham, John. "Making Federalism Work." Chattanooga Times, August 15, 1981, p. A9.

Porter, Mary C., and Tarr, G. Alan. "Judicial Federalism and the Alabama Supreme Court." A paper presented at the annual meeting of the American Political Science Association, Denver, Sept. 2-5, 1982.

Porter, Roger B. "John Stuart Mill and Federalism." Publius, VII (Spring, 1977), 101-24.

Posey, Rollin Bennett. American Government. 6th ed. Totowa, N.J.: Littlefield, Adams & Co., 1965.

Pouliot, Robert. "Why Can't Federalism Evolve?"
Financial Post, LXX (December 4, 1976), 7.
Pranger, Robert J. "The Decline of the American National
Government." Publius, III (Fall, 1973), 97-127.
Prentiss, Harvey P. Timothy Pickering as the Leader of New
England Federalism. New York: Da Capo Press, 1972.
Price, Don K. Government and Science: Their Dynamic Rela-
tion in American Democracy. New York: New York
University Press, 1954.
Pyziur, Eugene. The Doctrine of Anarchism of Michael A.
Bakunin. Milwaukee: Marquette University Press, 1955.
Raines, Howell. "Reagan and States' Rights." New York
Times, March 4, 1981, p. A1.
Rankin, Robert S. The Impact of Civil Rights upon Twenti-
eth-Century Federalism. Urbana: Department of
Political Science, University of Illinois, 1963.
Ranney, Austin. The Governing of Men. Rev. ed. New York:
Holt, Rinehart and Winston, 1966.
Ranney, David C. Planning and Politics in the Metropolis.
Columbus, Ohio: Charles E. Merrill Publishing Co.,
1969.
Rawlyk, George A., et al. Regionalism in Canada:
Flexible Federalism or Fractured Nation? Scar-
borough, Ont.: Prentice-Hall of Canada, 1979.
Raymond, Walter J. Dictionary of Politics. 6th ed.
Lawrenceville, Va.: Brunswick Publishing Co., 1978.
Rayside, David M. "Federalism and the Party System--
Provincial and Federal Liberals in the Province of
Quebec." Canadian Journal of Political Science,
XI (September, 1978), 499-528.
Reagan, Michael D. The New Federalism. 1st ed. New
York: Oxford University Press, 1972.
"Reagan's First Task: Sell His New Program on Local Level."
Birmingham News, January 28, 1982, p. 7B.
Reeves, Mavis Mann, and Glendening, Parris N. "Areal
Federalism and Public Opinion." Publius, VI
(Spring, 1976), 135-67.
Reinhold, Richard L. "National Standards for No-Fault
Insurance Act--Good Intentions and Bad Federalism."
Buffalo Law Review, XXV (Winter, 1976), 575-606.
Renzulli, Libero M., Jr. "Maryland Federalism, 1787-1819."
Unpublished Ph.D. disseration, University of Virginia,
1962.
"Reperes pour en federalisme revolutionnaire." Europe en

Formation, Nos. 190-92, January-March, 1976, pp.
    25-213.
"Restructuring Urban Government: The Two Tier Federation
    and the Role of the Federal Government." St. Louis
    Law Journal, XIX (Fall, 1974), 78-99.
Richter, Albert J. "Strengthening Local Government: A Call
    for Restructuring." Intergovernmental Perspective, VI
    (Fall, 1980), 13-19.
Ricoeur, Paul. The Rule of Metaphor: Multi-Disciplinary
    Studies of the Creation of Meaning in Language. Tr.
    Robert Czerny. Toronto: University of Toronto Press,
    1977.
Riker, William. Federalism: Origin, Operation, Signifi-
    cance. Boston: Little, Brown and Co., 1964.
Riley, Patrick. "Federalism in Kant's Political
    Philosophy." Paper presented at the annual meeting of
    the American Political Science Association, Washington,
    D.C., August 31-September 3, 1979.
_____. _____. Publius, IX (Fall, 1979), 43-64.
_____. "Martin Diamond's View of The Federalist." Publius
    VIII (Summer, 1978), 71-101.
_____. "Rousseau as a Theorist of National and
    International Federalism." Publius, III (Spring,
    1973), 5-17.
_____. "Three 17th Century German Theorists of Federalism:
    Althusius, Hugo and Leibniz." Publius, VI (Summer,
    1976), 7-41.
Risjord, Norman K. "The Virginia Federalists." Journal of
    Southern History, XXXIII (No. 4, 1967), 486-517.
Robins, Leonard. "The Plot That Succeeded: The New
    Federalism as Policy Realignment." Presidential
    Studies Quarterly, X (Winter, 1980), 99-106.
Roche, John P. (ed.) Origins of American Political Thought.
    New York: Harper Torchbooks, 1967.
Rockefeller, Nelson A. The Future of Federalism. Cam-
    bridge, Mass.: Harvard University Press, 1962.
Rodee, Carlton C., et al. Introduction to Poilitical Sci-
    ence. 2d ed. New York: McGraw-Hill Book Co., 1967.
Rodriquez, Celso. "Cantonismo: A Regional Harbinger of
    Peronism in Argentina." Americas, XXXIV (October,
    1977), 170-201.
Roemfeld, Lutz. Integral Föderalismus: Modell für Europe.
    Munich: Ernst Vogel, 1978.
Rogalski, William R. "The Unique Federalism of the Regional

Councils under the Fishery Conservation and Management
Act of 1976." Boston College Environmental Affairs
Law Review, IX (1980-81), 163-203.
Rogers, Henry W. "The Constitution and the New Federalism."
North American Review, CLXXXVIII (September, 1908),
321-35.
Rolletta, Vincent M. "A Quality-Quantity Factor in Dynamic
Federalism." Journal of Higher Education, XL (January,
1969), 53-58.
Rosenbaum, William A., et al. Analyzing American Politics.
Belmont, Calif.: Wadsworth Publishing Co., 1974.
Rosenfarb, Joseph. Freedom and the Administrative State.
New York: Harper & Bros., 1948.
Roth, Hans-George. "Landerpartikularismus oder kooperativer
Bildungsfoderalismus?" Politik und Zeitgeschichte
(Austria), Nos. 1-2, January 3, 1976, pp. 3-17.
Rothchild, Donald S. Toward Unity in Africa: A Study of
Federalism in British Africa. Washington, D.C.:
Public Affairs Press, 1960.
Rothman, Rozanne. "The Ambiguity of American Federal
Theory." Publius, VIII (Summer, 1978), 103-22.
Rougemont, Denis de. "Toward a New Definitiion of
Federalism." Atlantic Community Quarterly, VIII (No.
2, 1970), 224-33.
"Ryan's Road to a Renewed Federalism: Excerpts from A New
Canadian Federation." Report Magazine, III (March,
1980), 35-38.
Safire, William. "Mechanics of New Federalism." Montgomery
Advertiser-Alabama Journal, November 25, 1973, p. 4A.
_____. "The New Federalism is Bolder." Birmingham Post-
Herald, January 29, 1982, p. A5.
Saladin, Peter. "Lebendiger Foderalismus." Zeitschrift für
Schweizerisches Recht, XCVII (No. 1, 1978), 407-34.
Sanford, Terry. Storm Over the States. New York: McGraw-
Hill Book Co., 1967.
Sapir, J. David, and Crocker, J. Christopher. (eds.)
The Social Use of Metaphor: Essays on the Anthro-
pology of Rhetoric. Philadelphia: University of
Pennsylvania Press, 1977.
Savage, Robert L. "Federal Grants and the Pluralistic
Universe of American States." Paper presented at the
annual meeting of the American Political Science
Association, San Francisco, September 2-5, 1975.
Sawer, Geoffrey. "Cooperative Federalism in Australia."

Checkpoint, VIII (July, 1971), 3-8.
____. Modern Federalism. London: C. A. Watts & Co., 1969.

Schaefer, Walter V. Courts and the Commonplaces of Federalism. Urbana: Institute of Government and Public Affairs, University of Illinois, 1959.

Schechter, Stephen L. "The Concorde and Port Noise Complaints: The Commerce and Supremacy Clauses Enter the Supersonic Age." Publius, VIII (Winter, 1978), 135-58.

____. "Federalism and Community in Historical Perspective." Publius, V (Spring, 1975), 1-14.

____. "On the Compatibility of Federalism and Intergovernmental Management." Publius, XI (Spring, 1981) 127-41.

Schiller, A. Arthur. The Formation of Federal Indonesia, 1945-1949. The Hague: W. van Hoeve, 1955.

Schlauch, Paul J. "Tripartite Federalism--The Emerging Role of Local Government as a Regulator of Extractive Industries." Rocky Mountain Mineral Law Institute, XX (1965), 359-97.

Schlesinger, Rudolf. Federalism in Central and Eastern Europe. New York: Oxford University Press, 1945.

Schmandt, Henry J., and Steinbicker, Paul G. Fundamentals of Government. Milwaukee: Bruce Publishing Co., 1954.

Schnapper, Dominique. "Centralisme et federalisme culturels: les emigres italiens en France et aux Etat-unis." Annales, XXIX (September-October, 1974), 1141-59.

Schneider, Herbert W. A History of American Philosophy. 2d ed. New York: Columbia University Press, 1963.

Schnore, Leo F., and Fagin, Henry. (eds.) Urban Research and Policy Planning. Beverly Hills, Calif.: Sage Publications, 1967.

Schoenbaum, Thomas J. "Federalism in the Coastal Zone: Three Models of State Jurisdiction and Control." North Carolina Law Review, LVII (February, 1979), 231-60.

Schoer, Gary. "Restructuring Urban Government: The Two Tier Federation and the Role of the Federal Government." St. Louis Law Journal, XIX (Fall, 1974), 78-99.

Schram, Sanford F. "Politics, Professionalism, and the Changing Federalism." Social Service Review, LV

(March, 1981), 78-92.

Schroth, John Andrew. "Dual Federalism in Constitutional Law." Unpublished Ph.D. dissertation, Princeton University, 1941.

Scott, F. R. "Canadian Federalism: The Legal Perspective." Alberta Law Review, V (1967), 263-73.

Seabury, Samuel. The New Federalism: An Inquiry into the Means by Which Social Power May be So Distributed between State and People as to Insure Prosperity and Progress. New York: E. P. Dutton and Co., 1950.

Seidman, Harold. Politics, Position, and Power: The Dynamics of Federal Organization. 2d ed. New York: Oxford University Press, 1975.

Shapiro, Michael E. "Coastal Zone Management and Excluded Federal Lands--Viability of Continued Federalism in the Management of Federal Coastlands." Ecology Law Quarterly, VII (1979), 1011-43.

Sharkansky, Ira. "Urban-Centered Federalism in the United States." Paper presented at the conference on the "Politics of Intergovernmental Relations in Federal Systems: Urban Perspectives," Center for the Study of Federalism, Temple University, August 26-28, 1973.

Sharma, B. M., and Choudhry, L. P. Federal Polity. Bombay: Asia Publishing House, 1967.

Shaw, Albert. Political Problems of American Development. New York: Columbia University Press, 1907.

Shibles, Warren. (ed.) Essays on Metaphor. Whitewater, Wisc.: Language Press, 1972.
_____. Metaphor: An Annotated Bibliography and History. White Water, Wisc.: Language Press, 1971.

Shuman, Samuel I. (comp.) The Future of Federalism. Detroit: Wayne State University Press, 1968.

Sidgwick, Henry. The Elements of Politics. London: Macmillan and Co., 1919.

Sidjanski, Dusan. Federalism amphictyonique: Elements de system et tendance internationale. Lausanne: Librarie de l'Universite, F. Rouge & Cie., 1956.

Siegrist, Ulrich K. Die schweizerische Verfassungsordnung als Grundlage und Schranke des interkantonalen kooperativen Foderalismus. Vols. I and II. Zurich: Schulthess, 1976-78.

Silvert, Frieda. "The New Federalism and the New Corporatism." American Society of International Law, Proceedings, LXVIII (April, 1974), 198-204.

Simandjuntak, B. Malayan Federalism 1945-1963. London:
     Oxford University Press, 1969.
Simeon, Richard. "Inter-governmental Relations and the
     Challenges to Canadian Federalism." Canadian Public
     Administration, XXIII (Spring, 1980), 14-32.
Simon, Yves. "A Note on Proudhon's Federalism." Publius,
     III (Spring, 1973), 19-30. (Tr. Vukan Kuic)
Simpson, Lewis P. (ed.) The Federalist Literary Mind:
     Selections from the Monthly Analogy, and Boston Review,
     1803-1811, including documents relating to the Boston
     Athenaeum. Baton Rouge: Louisiana State University
     Press, 1962.
Sinclair, T. A. History of Greek Political Thought.
     Cleveland: World Publishing Co., 1968.
Sinkha, S. D. "Growth of Federal Ideas and Institutions in
     India Since 1919." Unpublished Ph.D. dissertation,
     Lucknow University, 1957.
Smallwood, Frank. (ed.) The New Federalism. Hanover,
     N.H.: Public Affairs Center, Dartmouth College, 1967.
Smiley, Donald V. "The Canadian Federation and the
     Challenge of Quebec Independence." Publius, VIII
     (Winter, 1978), 199-224.
     . "Public Administration and Canadian
     Federalism." Canadian Public Administration, VII
     (September, 1964), 371-88.
     . "Structural Problems of Canadian Federalism."
     Canadian Public Administration, XIV (No. 3, 1971),
     326-43.
Smith, Edward Conrad, and Zurcher, Arnold John. Dictionary
     of American Politics. New York: Barnes & Noble,
     1955.
Smith, Herbert Arthur. Federalism in North America: A
     Comparative Study of Institutions in the United States
     and Canada. Boston: Chipman Law Publishing Co., 1923.
Sneed, Joseph A., and Waldhorn, Steven A. (eds.)
     Restructuring the Federal System: Approaches to
     Accountability in Postcategorical Programs. New York:
     Crane, Russak & Co., 1975.
Spadijer, Balsa. "Razvoj yugoslovenskog samoupravnog
     federalizma: ustavni amandmani." Socijalizam, XV
     (January, 1972), 27-41.
Spain, August O. "Champion of Southern Federalism: Robert
     Goodloe Harper of South Carolina. By Joseph W. Cox.
     Port Washington, N.Y.: Kennikat Press, 1972." Review.

Social Science Quarterly, LIV (March, 1974), 888-89.

Sparrow, Glen W. "Sacramento County, California, Experiments with Metro-Federalism." Paper presented at the annual National Conference on Government of the National Municipal League, San Diego, November 19, 1974.

"Special Tribute to Hans Kohn." Orbis, X (Winter, 1967), 1006-43.

Sperber, Hans, and Trittschuh, Travis. American Political Terms: An Historical Dictionary. Detroit: Wayne State University Press, 1962.

Stalin, Joseph. Marxism and the National Question: Selected Writings and Speeches. New York: International Publishers, 1942.

The Standard Library Cyclopedia of Political, Constitutional, Statistical and Forensic Knowledge . . .. Vol. II. 1860 ed.

Stanfield, Rochelle M. "The Development of Carter's Urban Policy: One Small Step for Federalism." Publius, VIII (Winter, 1978), 39-53.

_____. "Ready for 'New Federalism' Phase II? Turning Tax Sources Back to the States." National Journal, XIII (August 22, 1981), 1492-97.

Stark, Frank M. "Federalism in Cameroon: The Shadow and the Reality." Canadian Journal of African Studies, X (No. 3, 1976), 423-42.

Starr, Graeme. "America's 'Federalism without Washington': Australia's Missing Link?" Australian Quarterly, XLVIII (September, 1976), 62-72.

_____. "Federalism as a Political Issue: Australia's Two New Federalisms." Publius, VII (Winter, 1977), 7-26.

Stavisky, Leonard. "State Legislatures and the New Federalism." Public Administration Review, XLI (November/December, 1981), 701-10.

Stedman, Murray S., Jr. (ed.) Modernizing American Government. Englewood Cliffs, N.J.: Prentice-Hall, 1968.

Stein, Eric. "Treaty-Based Federalism, A.D. 1979: A Gloss on Covey T. Oliver at the Hague Academy." University of Pennsylvania Law Review, CXXVI (April, 1979), 897-908.

Stein, Michael B. "Federal Political Systems and Federal Societies." World Politics, XX (July, 1968), 721-47.

_____. "Quebec and Canada: The Changing Equilibrium

between 'Federal Society' and 'Federal Political System.'" Journal of Canadian Studies, XII (July, 1977), 113-17.

Stenberg, Carl W., III. "Tripartite Federalism: The Impact of New York State 'Buying Into' the Federal-Aid Airport Program." Unpublished Ph.D. dissertation, State University of New York at Albany, 1970.

Stettner, Rupert. "Neues Leben fur Föderalismus? Gedanken zu den Empfehlungen der Enquete-Kommision Verfassungsreform fur eine Neuregelung der Gesetzgegungskompetenzen von Bund und Landern." Zeitschrifte fur Politik, XXIV (June, 1977), 152-62.

Stevens, R. Michael. "Asymmetrical Federalism: The Federal Principle and the Survival of the Small Republic." Publius, VII (Fall, 1977), 177-203.

Stevenson, T. H. Politics and Government. Totowa, N.J.: Littlefield, Adams & Co., 1973.

Stever, James A. "Modern Federalism: A Sociology of Knowledge Analysis." Unpublished Ph.D. dissertation, Purdue University, 1974.

Stewart, Maxwell S. "Nixon's New Federalism--Is It the Answer?" Current History, LXI (November, 1971), 279-83.

Stewart, William H. "Metaphors, Models, and the Development of Federal Theory." Publius, XIV (Spring, 1982), 5-24.

Stokes, Anson Phelps. Church and State in the United States. Vol. I. New York: Harper & Bros., 1950.

Stokes, M. D. "How to Reform Australian Federalism." University of Tasmania Law Review, VI (1980), 277-93.

Stone, Donald C. "Intergovernmental Policy and Program Management." (programmed instruction in intergovernmental relations originally issued in 1977)

Story, Joseph. Commentaries on the Constitution of the United States. Vol. I. Boston: Hilliard, Gray, and Co., 1833.

Sundquist, James L. "In Defense of Pragmatism: A Response to 'Is Federalism Compatible with Prefectorial Administration?'" Publius, XI (Spring, 1981), 31-37.

_____. Making Federalism Work: A Study of Program

Coordination at the Community Level. Washington,
    D.C.: Brookings Institution, 1969.
Susser, Bernard. "The Anarcho-Federalism of Martin Buber."
    Publius, IX (Fall, 1979), 103-15.
Swan, George S. "Newfoundland Offshore Claims--Interface of
    Constitutional Federalism and International Law."
    McGill Law Journal, XXII (Winter, 1976), 541-73.
    . "Remembering Maine: Offshore Federalism in the
    United States and Canada." California Western
    International Law Journal, VI (Spring, 1976), 296-322.
"Symposium: The New Federalism and the Cities." Journal
    of Urban Law, LII (August, 1974), 55-113.
Tansill, Charles C. (ed.) Documents Illustrative of the
    Formation of the Union of the American States.
    Washington, D.C.: U.S. Government Printing Office,
    1927.
Tapp, E. J. "New Zealand and Australian Federation."
    Historical Studies (Melbourne), V (November 1952),
    244-57.
Tarlton, Charles D. "Symmetry and Asymmetry as Elements of
    Federalism: A Theoretical Speculation." Journal of
    Politics, XXVII (November, 1965), 861-74.
Taylor, Hannis. The Origin and Growth of the American
    Constitution. Boston: Houghton, Mifflin Co., 1911.
Tewiata, T. C. "Soviet Theory of Federalism." Indian
    Journal of Political Science, XXXVI (April-June, 1975),
    177-91.
"Text of Nixon's Address to the Nation . . . " New York
    Times, August 9, 1969, p. 10c.
"Text of President's Message to Nation . . . " New York
    Times, January 27, 1982, p. A16.
Thatcher, Max B. "The Political Island of Quebec: A Study
    in Federalism." Unpublished Ph.D. dissertation,
    Northwestern University, 1953.
"There's More Than Meets Eye in Reagan Federalism."
    Birmingham News, January 28, 1982, p. 7A.
Thiam, Doudou. Le federalisme africain: Ses principes et
    sex regles. Paris: Presence Africaine, 1972.
Thieme, Werner. Föderalismus im Wandel. Cologne: Heyman,
    1970.
Thomas, William V. "Reagan's 'New Federalism.'" Editorial
    Research Reports, April 3, 1981, pp. 251-68.
Tilford, R. B., and Preece, R. J. C.
    Federal Germany: Political and Social Order.

London: Wolff, 1969.

Todres, Elaine M. "Adaptive Federalism: Taxation Policy in
Canada." Unpublished Ph.D. dissertation, University of
Pittsburgh, 1977.

Tonnies, Ferdinand. Community and Society. East Lansing:
Michigan State University Press, 1957.

Trelease, Frank J. "Uneasy Federalism--State Water Laws and
National Water Uses." Washington Law Review, LV
(November, 1980), 751-75.

Trendelenburg, Adolf. Naturrecht auf dem Grunde der Ethik.
2 vols. Leipzig: Z. Hirzel, 1868.

Tribe, Laurence H. "Unraveling National League of Cities:
The New Federalism and Affirmative Rights to Essential
Government Services." Harvard Law Review, XC (April,
1977), 1065-1104.

Trippett, Frank. "States' Rights and Other Myths." Time,
February 9, 1981, pp. 97-98.

Trudeau, Pierre Elliott. Federalism and the French
Canadians. New York: St. Martin's Press, 1968.

Trujillo, Gumesindo. Introducion al federalismo espanol;
ideologia y formulas constitutionales. Madrid:
Edicusa, 1967.

Ullner, Rudolf. Die Idee des Foderalismus in Jahrzent der
Einigungskriege dargestellt under besonder
Berucksichtigung des Modells der amerikanischen
Verfassung fur das deutsche politische Denken. Lubeck:
Matthiesen, 1965.

U.S. Advisory Commission on Intergovernmental Relations.
American Federalism: Into the Third Century--Its
Agenda. Washington, D.C.: By the Commission, 1974.

_____. Federalism in 1974: The Tension of Interdependence.
Washington, D.C.: By the Commission, 1975.

_____. Financing Schools and Property Tax Relief: A State
Responsibility. Washington, D.C.: By the Commission,
1973.

_____. In Brief: The Federal Role in the Federal
System--The Dynamics of Growth. Washington, D.C.: By
the Commission, 1980.

_____. In Brief: State and Local Roles in the Federal
System. Washington, D.C.: By the Commission, 1981.

_____. The Condition of Contemporary Federalism:

Conflicting Theories and Collapsing Constraints.
Washington, D.C.: By the Commission, 1981.
. The Federal Role in the Federal System: The
Dynamics of Growth--An Agenda for American Federalism:
Restoring Confidence and Competence. Washington, D.C.:
By the Commission, 1981.
. The Future of Federalism in the 1980s: Reports and
Papers from the Conference on the Future of Federalism.
Washington, D.C.: By the Commission, 1981.
. Studies in Comparative Federalism: Canada,
Australia, and West Germany. (3 separate
reports) Washington, D.C.: By the Commission,
1981.
. Summary and Concluding Observations. Washington,
D.C.: By the Commission, 1976.
. Trends in Fiscal Federalism, 1954-1974. Washington,
D.C.: By the Commission, 1975.
. Congress. House. Committee on Government Operations.
New Federalism (Organizational and Procedural
Arrangements for Federal Grant Administration).
Hearings before the Intergovernmental Relations
Subcommittee of the Committee on Government Operations,
House of Representations, 93d Cong., 2d Sess., 1974.
. Congress. House. Congressional Record. 93d Cong.,
1st session., 1973, H10645-46.
. Congress. Senate. Committee on Governmental Affairs.
Intergovernmental Relations in the 1980s. Hearings
before the Subcommittee on Intergovernmental Relations,
Senate, 97th Cong., 1st Sess., 1981.
. Congress. Senate. Committee on Government
Operations. A New Federalism. Hearings before the
Subcommittee on Intergovernmental Relations of the
Committee on Government Operations, Senate, on the
Impact of the President's Proposals for a New
Federalism in the Relationships between the Federal
Government and State and Local Governments, 93d Cong.,
1st sess., 1973, Parts I and II.
. Congress. Senate. Federal-State Relations by the
Council of State Governments: Report of the Commission
on Organization of the Executive Branch of the Govern-
ment, 81st Cong., 1st sess., 1949.
. President. Office of Management and Budget.
Responsive Federalism: A Report to the President on
the Federal Assistance Review Project, 1973.
. President. Public Papers of the Presidents, Lyndon
B. Johnson, 1963-64. Remarks at the University of
Michigan, May 22,1964.
. President's Commission on National Goals. Goals for

Americans: The Report of the President's Commission
    on National Goals and Chapters Submitted for the
    Consideration of the Commission. Englewood Cliffs,
    N.J.: Prentice-Hall, 1960 and 1965.
Uribe, Jorge R., et al. Federalismo moderno. Medellin,
    Colombia: Editorial Bedout, 1974.
Vanhorn, Carl E. "Evaluating the New Federalism: National
    Goals and Local Implementation." Public Administration
    Review, XXXIX (January, 1979), 17-22.
Venkatarangaiya, Mamidipudi. Some Theories of Federalism.
    Poona: University of Poona, 1971.
Veroffentlichungen der Vereinigung der Deutschen Staats-
    rechtslehrer. Vols. XIX and XXI. 1961 and 1964 eds.
Vile, M. J. C. "Federal Theory and New Federalism."
    Politics, XII (November, 1977), 1-14.
    . The Structure of American Federalism. London:
    Oxford University Press, 1961.
Viteri, Miguel H. For a Federated Latin America. New York:
    Exposition Press, 1965.
Von Mohrenschildt, D. "Schnapov: Exponent of Regionalism
    and the Federal School in Russian History." Russian
    Review, XXXVII (October, 1978), 387-404.
Wagstaff, Henry McG. Federalism in North Carolina. Chapel
    Hill, N.C.: James Sprunt Historical Publications,
    University of North Carolina, 1910.
Walker, David B. "Dysfunctional Federalism--The Congress
    and Intergovernmental Relations." State Government,
    LIV (No. 2, 1981), 53-57.
    . "Federal Aid Administrators and the
    Federal System." Intergovernmental Perspective,
    III (Fall, 1977), 10-17.
    . "How Fares Federalism in the Mid-Seventies?"
    Annals of the American Academy of Political and Social
    Science, XDXVI (November, 1974), 17-31.
    . "Intergovernmental Relations and Dysfunctional
    Federalism." National Civic Review, LXX (February,
    1981), 68-76f.
    . "A New Intergovernmental System in 1977." Publius,
    VIII (Winter, 1978), 101-16.
    . Toward a Functioning Federalism. Cambridge, Mass.:
    Winthrop Publishers, 1981.
Wallace, Elisabeth. "The West Indies: Improbable
    Federation?" Canadian Journal of Economics and
    Political Science, XXVII (1961), 444-59.

Walston, Roderick. "Reborn Federalism in Western Water
    Law--New Melonese Dam Decision." Hastings Law Journal,
    XXX (July, 1979), 1645-82.
Warner, David C. "Fiscal Federalism in Health Care."
    Publius, V (Fall, 1975), 79-100.
Warner, Richard R. "The Concept of Creative Federalism in
    the Johnson Administration." Unpublished Ph.D.
    dissertation, American University, 1970.
Watts, R. L. New Federations: Experiments in the
    Commonwealth. Oxford: Clarendon Press, 1966.
    _____. "Recent Trends in Federal Economic Policy and
    Finance in the Commonwealth." Paper presented at the
    Sixth World Congress of the International Political
    Science Association, 1964.
Wauwe, Ludo van. Federalisme, utopie ou possibilite?
    Paris: Librarie generale de droit de jurisprudence,
    1971.
Ways, Max. "'Creative Federalism' and the Great Society."
    Fortune, January, 1966, pp. 120-23ff.
Webster's New Collegiate Dictionary, 1977 ed.
Webster's New International Dictionary. 3d ed.
Weiler, Conrad J. "Metropolitan Federation Reconsidered."
    Urban Affairs Quarterly, VI (June, 1971), 411-20.
Weinberg, Louise. "The New Judicial Federalism." Stanford
    Law Review, XXIX (July, 1977), 1191-1244.
    _____. "A New Judicial Federalism." Daedalus, CVII
    (Winter, 1978), 129-41.
Weissert, Carol S. "ACIR and the Intergovernmental System:
    A 20-Year Review." Intergovernmental Perspective, VI
    (Winter, 1980), 14-23.
    _____. "1981: A Threshold Year for Federalism."
    Intergovernmental Perspective, VIII (Winter, 1982), 4.
Welch, Claude E., Jr. Dream of Unity: Pan-Africanism and
    Political Unification in West Africa. Ithaca, N.Y.:
    Cornell University Press, 1966.
Westmacott, Martin. "The National Transportation Act and
    Western Canada: A Case Study in Cooperative
    Federalism." Canadian Public Administration, XVI
    (Fall, 1973), 444-67.
"What Kind of Federalism?" Social Service Review, XLII
    (June, 1973), 278-85.
Wheare, K. C. Federal Government. 1st, 2d, 3d, and 4th
    eds. New York: Oxford University Press, 1946, 1951,
    1953, and 1964.

_____. _____. Westport, Conn.: Greenwood Press, 1980.
(reprint)
Wheaton, William L. C. "The New Federalism." Paper
presented at the annual conference of the American
Institute of Planners, Atlanta, October 24, 1973.
Wheeler, Gerald R. "New Federalism and the Cities--A Double
Cross." Social Work, XIX (November, 1974), 659-64.
_____. "Welfare and Revenue Sharing: The Politics of New
Federalism." Public Welfare, XXXV (Spring, 1977),
38-42.
White, Leonard D. The States and the Nation. Baton Rouge:
Louisiana State University Press, 1953.
Whitlam, Edward A. "New Federalism." Australian Quarterly,
XLIII (September, 1971), 6-17.
Wiggins, Charles B. "Federalism Balancing and the Burger
Court: California's Nuclear Law as a Preemption Case
Study." University of California at Davis Law Review,
XIII (Winter, 1980), 1-87.
Wildavsky, Aaron. (ed.) American Federalism in Perspective.
Boston: Little, Brown and Co., 1967.
_____. "Bare Bones: The Federal Skeleton in the Closet of
American Government." (unpublished manuscript)
_____. "The 1980s; Monopoly or Competition?" Inter-
governmental Perspective, VI (Summer, 1980), 15-18.
Wilson, Francis Graham. The American Political Mind. New
York: McGraw-Hill Book Co., 1949.
Williamson, Richard S. "Reagan Federalism: Restoring the
Balance." (unpublished article, 1981)
Wilson, Leonard U. "White House Conference Urges a More
Balanced Federalism." State Government, V (Winter,
1978), 11-16.
Wiltshire, Kenneth. "New Federalisms--The State
Perspective." Politics, XII (November, 1977), 76-85.
Winkle, John W., III. "Dimensions of Judicial Federalism."
Annals of the American Academy of Political and Social
Science, CDXVI (November, 1974), 67-76.
_____. "Interjudicial Relations." Paper presented at the
annual meeting of the Southern Political Science
Association, Atlanta, November 6-8, 1980.
Winks, Robin W. Failed Federations. Nottingham:
University of Nottingham, n.d.
Wofford, Harris, Jr. It's Up to Us: Federal World
Government in Our Time. New York: Harcourt, Brace and
Co., 1946.

Wood, M. "The New Federalisms of Whitlam and Fraser and
     Their Impact on Local Government." Politics, XII (Nov-
     ember, 1977), 104-15.
World Book Dictionary. 1977 ed.
Worrall, Denis J. "Nigerian Federalism: Its Genesis and
     Development." Unpublished Ph.D. dissertation, Cornell
     University, 1965.
Wright, Benjamin Fletcher, Jr. (ed.) A Source Book on
     American Political Theory. New York: Macmillan Co.,
     1929.
Wright, Deil S. "Intergovernmental Relations: An
     Analytical Overview." Annals of the American Academy
     of Political and Social Science, CDXVI (November,
     1974), 1-16.
     . Understanding Intergovernmental Relations: Public
     Policy and Participants' Perspectives in Local,
     State, and National Governments. 1st ed. North
     Scituate, Mass.: Duxbury Press, 1978.
Wynner, Edith. World Federal Government in Maximum Terms.
     Afton, N.Y.: Fedonat Press, 1954.
     , and Lloyd, Georgia. Searchlight on Peace Plans.
     New York: E. P. Dutton, 1944.
Yarbrough, Tinsley E., et al. Politics 72: Trends in
     Federalism. Greenville, N.C.: Department of Political
     Science, East Carolina University, 1972.
Young, George. Federalism and Freedom or Plan the Peace to
     Win the War. London: Oxford University Press, 1941.
Zashin, Elliot, and Chapman, Phillip C. "The Uses of
     Metaphor and Analogy: Toward a Renewal of Political
     Language." Journal of Politics, XXXVI (May, 1974),
     290-326.
Zeh, Wolfgang. "Spatföderalismus: Vereinigungs-oder
     Differenzierungs-foderalismus? Zur Arbeit der Enquete-
     Kommission an ihrem schweieriegsten Objekt."
     Zeitschrift fur Parlamentsfragen, VIII (December,
     1977), 475-90.
Zenkl, Peter. T. G. Masaryk and the Idea of European and
     World Federation. Trans. Vlasta Vraz. Chicago:
     Czechoslovak National Council of America, 1955.
Zimmerman, Joseph F. The Federated City: Community
     Control in Large Cities. New York: St. Martin's
     Press, 1972.
Zylstra, Bernard. From Pluralism to Collectivism: The
     Development of Harold Laski's Political Thought.
     Assen, The Netherlands: Van Gorcum & Co., 1968.

NAME INDEX

Adams, John 129
Aiyar, S. P. 150
Albertini, Mario 89
Alexander 74
Aleinikoff, Alexander 63
Althusius, Johannes 30, 46, 49, 75, 93, 128, 141, 164
Altshuler, Alan A. 77
Anderson, Martin 162
Anderson, Thornton 88, 104, 110, 111, 148
Anderson, William 34, 84, 129
Armand, Louis 66
Aron, Robert 136
Ashley, Thomas 123
Ayres, B. Drummond, Jr 123, 124, 156
Azikwi, Nnamdi 95

Bailey, Stephen K. 42, 80
Baker, Earl M 11, 55.
Bakunin, Mikhail 32, 34, 173
Barker, Ernest 115, 140, 149, 161, 165
Bartholomew, Paul C. 144
Baumgartner, J. 120
Bayang, Martin E. 41
Beam, George F. 50
Bebout, John E. 154
Beck, Robert N. 144
Beer, Samuel H. 10, 48, 51-52, 99, 117, 145, 162, 165-66
Belz, Herman 116, 162
Bennett, Walter H. 68
Berggren, Douglas 11
Berle, Adolpf A., Jr. 69, 72, 74, 119, 139
Bercuson, David J. 110
Berman, Daniel M. 104
Beyerle, Konrad 145
Biaggi, Mario 83
Bismarck, Otto von 36
Black, Edwin R. 39, 55, 67-68, 117
Bloch, Richard S. 54
Bluntschli, J.K. 93, 94, 152

Bodin, Jean 71
Bond, Julian 125
Bone, Robert C. 113
Bonsiepe, Gui 4
Boschken, Herman L. 131
Bouvier, John 114
Break, George F. 80, 82
Breen, William J. 54
Brie, Siegfried 92
Brougham, Henry 93, 94, 146
Brugmans, Henri 50, 95-96, 99, 163, 164
Bryce, James 66
Buber, Martin 31, 34, 37, 141, 171, 174
Buganda, Edward 40
Burger, Warren E. 43, 58, 163
Burgess, John W. 126
Burgess, Philip M. 155
Burris, William 70

Calhoun, John C. 37-38, 88, 110
Calkins, Susannah 65, 81, 125
Calvin, John 48, 62
Campbell, Alan K. 97
Cappalli, Richard B. 164
Careless, Anthony 163
Carey, George 90
Carey, Hugh 125-126
Carnell, Francis 150
Carney, Frederick S. 46, 48, 49, 62, 83-84, 93, 128, 164
Carter, Jimmy 37, 170
Casey, Joan A. 108
Cavanaugh, Jerome 60
Cerny, Karl H. 46, 48, 55, 104, 140
Chacon, Vamireth 33
Chapman, Philip 2, 8, 9, 12
Christenson, Reo M. 67
Clark, Jane Perry 51-52, 119
Clark, Joseph S. 115-16, 168
Clinton, George 104
Cohen, Felix 169
Cohen, Maxwell 175

Cohen, Morris 8
Colman, William G. 39, 64, 95, 121, 127, 129, 130, 137, 152,
    158, 174
Conlan, Timothy 54, 66-67, 86-87
Corwin, Edward S. 46, 52, 65, 66, 67, 81, 88, 100-01, 102,
    116, 161
Cover, Robert M. 63
Cranston, Maurice 43, 47, 55-56, 69, 120, 167
Crocker, J. Christopher 7, 10

Dailey, Joanna 43, 44, 163
Davis, S. Rufus 5, 29, 30, 57, 61, 71, 86, 87, 89, 101, 128,
    135, 136, 141, 149, 156, 158, 159, 167, 168, 171, 172, 173
De Blij, Harm 46-47, 94, 115, 158
De Grazia, Alfred 158
DeGrove, John M. 81
Dennewitz, Bodo 43, 63-64, 68, 72, 89, 99, 134-35, 152,
    157, 169
Desmond, Charles 40, 172
De Tocqueville, Alexis 45, 92
Deuerlein, Ernst 29, 36, 40, 41, 49, 59, 64, 70, 74, 75, 86,
    89, 90, 92, 102, 106, 117, 129, 141, 147, 160
Dewey, John 98-99
Diamond, Martin 42, 61, 87, 113, 139, 159-60
Dikshit, Ramesh D. 111, 112
Dillon, John F. 106, 149
Dimock, Marshall E. 51, 76, 84
Disraeli, Benjamin 93-94
Djordjevic, Jovan 32, 114, 130-31, 134, 139, 140, 147,
    160, 168
Douglas, William O. 87
Drancourt, Michel 76
Drucker, Peter F. 119-20, 167-68
Duchacek, Ivo D. 30, 34, 35, 40, 70, 73, 79, 85, 92, 98, 99,
    105, 108, 114, 115, 128, 130, 140, 146, 150, 152, 159,
    176, 177
Duclos, Pierre 95-96, 98, 99
Duncombe, Herbert S. 97-98
Dunn, William 11-12, 44, 127
Dunner, Joseph 36, 41, 64
Dupre, J. Stefan 163

Durenberger, David 54
Dvorin, Eugene P. 31, 53
Dyck, Rand 55

Earle, Valerie 2, 46, 48, 55, 66, 70, 75, 76, 83, 90, 104,
    140, 150, 156, 162
Eisenhower, Dwight D. 47, 119
Eisenstadt, S. N. 169
Elazar, Daniel J. 10, 33, 34, 35-36, 42-43, 45, 46, 47, 49,
    52, 53-54, 56, 57, 59, 60-61, 62, 65, 79, 81, 88, 89, 96,
    107, 109, 112-13, 114, 122, 125, 127-28, 134, 135, 138,
    142, 143-44, 147, 148, 149, 150, 153, 157, 166-67, 171,
    175
Elliott, W. Y. 42, 118, 119, 171
Engelmann, Frederick C. 147
Esterbauer, Fried 49
Etheredge, Lloyd S. 131-32
Eulau, Heinz 10, 139-40, 155

Fagin, Henry 102
Feeley, Malcolm M. 60
Fernandez, James W. 7
Ferry, W. H. 119
Foley, Joseph P. 148
Follett, Mary Parker 118, 171
Ford, Gerald R. 122
Ford, Henry 142
Forsyth, Murray 87
Franck, Thomas M. 32, 40, 59, 75, 92, 110, 111, 134, 143,
    150, 153-54, 177
Franz, Constantin 39-40, 147
Fraser, Malcolm 120
Freeman, Edward 47, 68, 92, 102, 113, 135, 149, 152, 157,
    170-71
Frenkel, Max 31, 39, 70, 73, 120, 165
Frias, Pedro J. 176
Friedrich, Carl J. 46, 48, 49, 56, 62, 74, 83-84, 88, 93,
    99, 128, 145, 160, 164, 173
Furman, Gerald 162
Fustel de Coulanges, Numas D. 157, 169

Gallant, Edgar 55
Galt, Anthony H. 2, 9, 11
Gangulee, N. 70
Gardiner, John A. 60
Garey, Robert B. 50
Garner, James W. 92, 93
Garson, G. David 37, 154
Gawthrop, Louis C. 131
Germann, Raimund E. 73
Gilbert, Charles E. 51, 119, 126, 144, 148, 153
Gitelman, Zvi 44-45
Glendening, Parris N. 53, 64, 72, 83, 90, 100, 106-07, 143,
    144, 175
Goldwater, Barry M. 117
Goldwin, Robert A. 51, 173
Gooch, R. K. 68, 97
Gordon, Harold J. 29
Gordon, Nancy M. 29
Govea, Rodger M. 87
Grant, Daniel R. 115, 134
Graves, W. Brooke 103, 108, 111
Grawert, Rolf 77
Green, Roy E. 159
Greenberg, Milton 90, 175
Greilsammer, Ilan 89, 107
Grodzins, Morton 3, 31, 52, 54, 98, 103, 108, 170
Gulick, Luther 107, 111

Haldane, Lord 152
Hall, Robert H. 40, 106
Hamilton, Alexander 9, 82, 92, 116, 126, 148, 161
Hammond, B. E. 77
Harbison, Winfred A. 76, 161
Harbold, William Henry 72
Harrington, James 10
Hart, Alfred B. 73
Hart, Henry C. 45
Hawkins, Gordon 105
Hawkins, Robert B., Jr 36, 107, 109, 125, 156, 173.
Hay, Peter 76, 83, 87, 96, 98, 99, 105, 134, 138
Hegel, G. F. 157

Hellerstein, Jerome R. 82
Helliwell, John F. 74
Henry I 169
Henry, Nicholas 30, 33, 59, 80
Heraud, Guy 63, 101, 156
Hess, Karl 118
Hesse, Mary 7, 9, 10, 12
Hicks, U. K. 42, 55, 76, 81, 95, 107, 108, 112, 141-42, 167
Higgs, Henry 44
Hitchner, Dell G. 72, 150
Hobbes, Thomas 11
Howard, A. E. Dick 172-73
Hudson, William E. 123
Hueglin, Thomas 30
Hurd, John C. 78

Jacobson, J. Mark 37-38
Jaffary, Karl D. 56
Jay, John 148
Jefferson, Thomas 65, 99f., 148, 161, 171
Jenkin, Thomas P. 139
Jennings, W. Ivor 105-06
Johnson, Lyndon 45, 58, 59, 82, 84, 85, 122, 143, 146, 161
Jones, Charles O. 40

Kadushin, Max 5-6, 7, 8
Kant, Immanuel 30, 56-57, 65, 83, 98, 102, 110, 133, 177
Kantor, Harry 76
Karnig, Albert K. 95
Kasperson, Roger E. 33
Katz, Ellis 2, 35, 57, 159
Kazmier, B. H. 8-9
Kearney, Richard C. 50
Kelly, Alfred H. 66, 161
Kelsen, Hans 101-02, 104, 173
Kennedy, John F. 64
Kenyon, Cecelia M. 118
Kettl, Donald F. 154
King, Preston 34, 72, 103, 134, 173
Kinsky, Ferdinand 136-37, 147, 168
Kirk, Russell 173

Koury, A. Frank 41, 133
Kruser, Herbert 176
Kreisky, Bruno 147
Kropotkin, Peter 103
Kuic, Vukan 39, 57, 136

Labilliere, F. P. 43
Lakoff, Sanford A. 47,69, 167
Landau, Martin 1, 5, 11, 91, 96, 105, 116, 136
Larsen, J. A. O. 171
Laski, Harold 75, 85, 128
Lawrence, David 63
Lawson, Jean 47, 153
Leach, Richard H. 39, 45, 55, 58, 68, 80, 88-89, 101, 108,
    117, 119, 120, 129, 131, 161, 176
Leger, Jean-Marc 55
Lenin, V. I. 44, 104-05
Lerner, Max 80, 81, 119
Leroy, Maxime 97
Levin, I. D. 36-37, 150
Lieber, Frances 126, 135
Lieber, Harvey 106
Light, Alfred B. 38
Lindblom, Charles E. 131
Lithwick, N. H. 75
Livingston, William S. 10, 75, 96, 128, 160, 162, 166, 173
Locke, John 10
Loeb, Louis S. 104
Logan, Robert K. 78
Low, Alfred D. 104, 105
Lowi, Theodore J. 59

Maass, Arthur A. 166
MacDonald, H. Malcolm 129
Macmahon, Arthur W. 9, 69, 70, 72, 74, 102, 109, 119, 139,
    147
Madden, Richard 122-23
Madison, James 65, 92, 107, 148
Maier, Harold G. 54
Mallory, J. R. 99, 166
Manley, Norman 94

Marando, Vincent L. 112
Marc, Alexandre 2, 10, 69, 71, 73, 90, 96-97, 101, 117, 131, 136, 139-40, 156, 160, 168, 171
Marshall, John 100, 109, 116, 156, 161
Martin, Charles E. 93
Martin, Ged 71, 74
Martin, Roscoe 30-31, 42, 73, 80, 99-100, 104, 145, 149
Mason, Alpheus T. 66, 156
Matheson, Scott M. 33, 137, 156
Mayfield, James J. 66
Mayton, William T. 71-72
Mazzeo, Joseph A. 7
McCloskey, Robert G. 100, 101, 116, 161
McLaughlin, Andrew C. 73
McLean, Joseph E. 103, 108
McWhinney, Edward 6, 10, 37, 40, 41, 56, 67, 76, 90-91, 92, 99, 106, 109, 113, 129-30, 138, 145-46, 175
Medley, G. W. 80
Meekison, J. Peter 55, 100
Meese, Edwin 162
Merkl, Peter H. 73
Merriam, Charles E. 62
Merriam, Robert E. 62, 153
Meyer, Philip 133, 144
Mill, John Stuart 86, 92, 114
Miller, Arthur S. 69, 139
Miller, Eugene 7
Minghi, Julian V. 33
Misner, Arthur J. 31, 53
Mitrany, David 143
Mogi, Sobei 30, 32, 43, 71, 93-94, 101-02, 104, 113, 133, 135, 140, 167
Montesquieu, Baron de 10, 33, 62, 83, 110, 114, 149, 159-60, 171
Moore, W. C. 156
Morley, John 32
Morris, David 118
Mueller, Dennis C. 82
Musgrave, Richard A. 82

Naftalin, Arthur 125

Napoleon 64
Nathan, Richard P. 121, 145
Nelson, Ralph 45, 48, 136
Neuberger, Benyamin 144, 157, 175
Neumann, Franz 5, 102, 170
Nichols, Roy F. 61
Nisbet, Robert 1
Nixon, H. C. 115, 134
Nixon, Richard 39, 51, 56, 115, 120ff., 134, 142, 143, 154,
   155

Oates, Wallace E. 48, 82
Obote, Milton 40
Oliver, Covey T. 111, 169
Olson, David J. 133, 144
Ostrom, Vincent 9, 10, 99, 127

Parrington, Vernon L. 86, 88, 95, 110, 126, 135, 176
Paterson, William 148
Peirce, Neil R. 82, 86, 94, 122, 138, 153, 156
Pentland, Charles 35, 68, 76, 78, 96, 144-45, 160-61, 165
Pescatore, Pierre 41, 76, 145
Peter II 33
Plano, Jack C. 90, 175
Polybius 88
Porter, Mary C. 45, 91, 175
Porter, Roger B. 86, 90
Posey, Rollin Bennett 118
Pranger, Robert J. 87
Price, Don K. 77
Procrustes 145
Proteus 147
Proudhon, Pierre-Joseph 30, 31, 32, 69, 75, 77, 115, 140,
   147, 161, 165, 168
Publius 148
Pufendorf, Samuel 136
Pyziur, Eugene 34

Raines, Howell 162
Randolph, Edmond 110-11
Ranney, Austin 62, 64

Ranney, David C. 102
Rawlyk, George A. 82
Raymond, Walter J. 57, 61-62, 85
Reagan, Michael D. 6, 50, 51, 64, 82-83, 84, 106, 120-21,
    127, 130, 136, 144, 173
Reagan, Ronald 34, 58, 81, 83, 94, 109, 123ff., 126-27,
    140, 151-52, 153, 154, 156, 162, 163
Reeves, Mavis Mann 53, 64, 72, 83, 90, 100, 107, 143, 144,
    175
Richter, Albert J. 170
Ricoeur, Paul 6, 11
Riker, William 39, 62, 64, 110, 111-12, 135-36
Riley, Patrick 30, 33, 47, 56-57, 65, 83, 98, 102, 110,
    113, 114, 128, 133, 149, 171, 177
Roche, John P. 118
Rockefeller, John D. 142
Rockefeller, Nelson A. 57-58, 141, 142
Rodee, Carlton C. 69
Rogalski, William R. 173
Roosevelt, Franklin D. 51, 67
Rosenbaum, William A. 70
Rosenfarb, Joseph 63, 84
Rosenfeld, S. Stephen 43, 44, 163
Roth, Hans-George 51
Roth, William V. 113
Rothman, Rozanne 91, 109
Rousseau, Jean Jacques 62

Safire, William 123, 126-27
St. Pierre, Abbe de 98
Saladin, Peter 35, 63, 107
Sanford, Terry 137
Sapir, J. David 7, 10
Sawer, Geoffrey 54, 94-95, 97, 132
Schechter, Stephen L. 32, 45, 59, 99, 107, 133, 140, 144,
    146-47, 156-57, 165, 168, 169
Scheiber, Harry N. 39, 53
Schiller, A. Arthur 141
Schlesinger, Rudolf 97
Schmandt, Henry J. 87
Schneider, Herbert W. 44, 78, 129

Schnore, Leo F. 102
Schoer, Gary 171
Schuster, Benjamin R. 2, 35, 57, 159
Schwartz, Mildred A. 147
Seabury, Samuel 50, 72
Servan-Scheiber, Jean-Jacques 48
Seydel, Max 145
Shannon, John 65, 81, 125
Shapiro, Michael E. 50, 175
Sharkansky, Ira 49, 174
Sharma, B. M. 40, 62, 140, 152
Shaw, Albert 45, 76
Sherwin-White, A. N. 172
Shibles, Warren 3, 7, 11
Shuman, Samuel I. 32, 40, 58, 117, 172
Sidgwick, Henry 142, 151, 154
Siegrist, Ulrich K. 90, 97
Simandjuntak, B. 44
Sinclair, T. A. 99
Smallwood, Frank 39, 53
Smiley, Donald V. 153
Smith, Goldwin 32
Sneed, Joseph A. 81
Sommer, Theo 102
Spadijer, Balsa 157
Spanier, John W. 70
Spinelli, Altiero 89
Stalin, Joseph 132
Stanfield, Rochelle M. 38, 170
Starr, Graeme 120
Stavisky, Leonard 174
Stedman, Murray S., Jr. 51, 119, 126, 144, 148, 153
Stein, Michael B. 111, 169-70
Steinbicker, Paul G. 87
Stenberg, Carl W., III 48, 153
Stevens, R. Michael 34
Stevenson, T. H. 64-65, 147, 152, 158
Stewart, William H. 91
Stockman, David 162
Stone, Donald C. 38
Story, Joseph 47-48, 148

Streit, Clarence K. 106
Sugg, H. A. I. 37, 150
Sundquist, James 10, 115
Suppes, Patrick 9
Susser, Bernard 31, 34, 36-37, 117, 171, 174
Swann, George S. 129

Taney, Roger B. 100-101, 156
Tansill, Charles C. 110, 148
Tarlton, Charles D. 10, 33, 160-61, 164-65
Tarr, Alan G. 45, 91, 175
Taylor, Hannis 47, 88, 103-04
Tennyson, Alfred Lord 177
Teune, Henry 2, 70, 75, 83, 150
Thomas, William V. 112
Thucydides 88
Todres, Elaine M. 29
Tonnies, Friedrich 117
Trager, Frank N. 56, 60, 178
Trelease, Frank J. 172
Trudeau, Pierre Elliott 72, 154-55
Truman, Harry S. 47
Tupper, Charles 74

Vajl, I. M. 36-37
Vile, Maurice 56, 67, 87, 138
Vuysje, D. 9

Waldhorn, Steven A. 81
Walker, David 32, 35, 37, 48-49, 51, 52, 53, 58-59, 67, 69,
    82-84, 86, 100, 101, 108, 116, 120, 122, 131, 133, 137,
    138, 149, 159, 161, 162, 173
Wallace, Elisabeth 94
Warner, Richard R. 82
Warren, Earl 165, 176
Washington, George 67
Watt, James 103
Watts, Ronald L. 5, 76-77, 78, 148-49, 150-51
Wauwe, Ludo van 61, 88
Ways, Max 56, 58
Webster, Daniel 116
Weidenbaum, Murray L. 140-41

Weinberg, Louise 126
Weissert, Carol S. 124, 138
Welch, Claude E., Jr. 78
Wescher, Louis F. 166
Wheare, K. C. 55, 113, 149-50
Whitlam, Gough 120
Whitman, Walt 138
Wildavsky, Aaron 5, 36, 46, 83, 123, 157-58, 163, 164
Williamson, Richard S. 103, 151, 156
Wilson, Francis G. 42
Wilson, Woodrow 96
Winer, Stanley L. 75
Winkle, John W., III 101, 133
Wolohojian, George G. 87
Wood, Robert 99-100
Woolsey, Theodore 126
Wright, Benjamin F., Jr. 48, 148
Wright, Deil S. 1, 3, 8, 21, 32, 39, 41, 46, 47, 50, 58, 69,
   79, 82, 83, 85, 103, 115, 127, 137, 139, 146, 161
Wright, J. Skelly 58
Wynner, Edith 106

Yarbrough, Tinsley E. 37, 39, 50, 89, 98, 108, 119, 136,
   150, 163-64, 166
Ylvisaker, Paul 99-100
Young, George 84, 132, 172

Zashin, Elliot 2, 8, 9, 12
Zeh, Wolfgang 62, 64, 68, 103, 168
Zylstra, Bernard 85, 128

GEOGRAPHICAL INDEX

Achaea 29, 88, 103-04, 135
Africa 32, 40, 134, 144, 157
Alabama 176
Alberta 74
Austria 29, 30, 56, 112, 114, 132, 147, 152, 169
Australia 36, 43, 54, 55-56, 70, 76, 86, 102, 114, 120,
  134, 152
Argentina 148, 176
Asia 169

Bangladesh 107, 158
Bavaria 135
Belgium 61, 88, 169
Brazil 33, 70, 79, 130, 148, 158
Burma 140, 158

Cameroun 70, 150
Canada 29, 36, 37, 39, 41, 55, 56, 62, 66-67, 72, 74,
  75, 77, 78, 82, 93, 99, 100, 102, 111, 115, 117, 129,
  134, 140, 149-50, 152, 153, 154-55, 163, 166
Caribbean Islands 142
Caucasus 132
Central Africa 94, 142
Curacao 33
Cyprus 56, 145-46
Czechoslovakia 140, 147, 158

Dahomey 144
Dominica 112

East Africa 59, 75, 92, 111, 142, 143, 153-54
England 44, 93, 94, 95, 134, 169
Europe 41, 48, 67, 76, 78, 83, 88, 89, 90, 95-96, 99, 105,
  111, 113, 147, 160, 168, 169, 172, 173, 176
France 31, 33, 34, 69, 73, 85, 92, 96, 98, 105, 134, 144,
  146, 157, 175, 176

Germany 29, 36, 39, 40-41, 46, 48, 49, 51, 55, 59, 62, 63,
  64, 68, 70, 73, 74, 76, 79, 81, 85, 86, 89, 90, 92, 93,
  94, 101-02, 103, 104, 106, 111, 114, 126, 129, 134, 140,
  141, 147, 148, 152, 155, 167, 168, 172

Ghana 134
Great Britain 32, 43, 44, 66, 70, 71, 74, 80, 90, 91, 92,
    93-94, 98, 107, 108, 115, 129, 149, 166, 167, 169
Greece 29, 30, 42, 45, 74, 83, 99, 139, 157, 158, 159,
    165, 171, 172
Guinea 134, 144
Holy Roman Empire 72, 74, 93, 149

India 47, 70, 77, 106, 107, 108, 115, 140, 142, 150, 166
Indonesia 141
Ireland 91, 93, 94, 95
Israel 36, 46, 49, 57, 167
Italy 89, 169
Ivory Coast 144

Jamaica 94

Kentucky 161
Kenya 39, 110, 111, 141

Latin America 114
Libya 150
London 41, 115

Malawi 75
Malaya 150, 166
Malaysia 59, 142
Mauritania 144
Miami 41, 111, 115, 134
Middle East 169

Netherlands 33, 147, 157
New England 41, 167
New York 104, 172
Niger 144
Nigeria 42, 47, 77, 95, 142, 166, 167
Nyasaland 59, 75, 111, 150, 166

Pakistan 77, 107, 158, 166
Palestine 49
Prussia 68
Puerto Rico 33

Quebec 56, 75, 153, 154-55

Rhodesia 59, 75, 111, 150, 166
Rome 45, 71, 149, 152, 156-57, 172

St. Lucia 112
St. Vincent 112
Scotland 93, 94
Senegal 144
Singapore 142
South 90
South Africa 90, 134
Soviet Union 37, 62, 65, 83, 102, 104-05, 110, 112, 115,
  140, 150, 158, 160
Spain 93, 94
Sparta 33, 62, 98
Sudan 144
Switzerland 31, 36, 39, 47, 65, 70, 73, 86, 89, 92, 96, 102,
  106, 120, 140, 144, 147, 152, 157, 165, 175

Tanganyika 40, 110
Tanzania 142
Turkey 113

Uganda 70, 142, 150
United Arab Emirates 79, 113
United Kingdom 169
United States (see subdivision, classification
  of concepts, or name index)
Upper Volta 144

Venezuela 147, 148
Vienna 147
Virginia 161

West Africa 134
Western Hemisphere 176
West Indies 59, 75, 94, 140, 166

Yugoslavia 32, 44, 74, 114, 127, 130, 140, 148, 157, 158,
  160, 168, 169, 173

Zaire 158

LIST OF CASES

Abelman v. Booth, 21 How. 506 (1859) 66

Attorney General for the Commonweath of Australia v.
   Colonial Sugar Refining Co., Ltd., 17 C.L.R. 144
   (1914) 152

Brown v. Board of Education, 347 U.S. 483 (1954) 90

Cohens v. Virginia, 19 U.S. 264 (1821) 100

Erie Railroad Co. v. Tompkins, 304 U.S. 64 (1938) 44

Fay v. Noia, 372 U.S. 391 (1963) 63

King v. Smith, 392 U.S. 309 (1968) 176

Reynolds v. Sims, 377 U.S. 533 (1964) 106

Rizzo v. Goode, 423 U.S. 6 (1976) 126

South Australia v. Commonwealth, 65 C.L.R. 373 (1942) 43

U.S. v. Cruikshank, 92 U.S. 542 (1876) 66

Younger v. Harris, 401 U.S. 37 (1971) 44, 126, 133